W9-BOL-509

Mummies
and Death
in Egypt

Mummies and Death in Egypt

Françoise Dunand

Roger Lichtenberg

FRANKLIN SQ. PUBLIC LIBRARY
19 LINCOLN ROAD
FRANKLIN SQUARE, N.Y. 11010

Foreword by Jean Yoyotte

Translated from the French by David Lorton

Cornell University Press

Ithaca and London

English translation copyright © 2006 by Cornell University
Press
French edition, *Les momies et la mort en Égypte,* copyright ©
Editions Errance, 1998 (Paris)

All rights reserved. Except for brief quotations in a review,
this book, or parts thereof, must not be reproduced in any
form without permission in writing from the publisher. For
information, address Cornell University Press, Sage House,
512 East State Street, Ithaca, New York 14850.

First published 2006 by Cornell University Press

Printed in the United States of America

Library of Congress Cataloging-in-Publication Data

Dunand, Françoise.
    [Momies et la mort en Egypte. English]
    Mummies and death in Egypt / Françoise Dunand and
Roger Lichtenberg ; foreword by Jean Yoyotte ; translated
from the French by David Lorton.
        p. cm.
    Includes bibliographical references and index.
    ISBN-13: 978-0-8014-4472-2 (cloth : alk. paper)
    ISBN-10: 0-8014-4472-1 (cloth : alk. paper)
    1. Mummies—Egypt.   I. Lichtenberg, Roger.   II. Title.
DT62.M7D8513 2006
393'.30932—dc22
                                            2006019346

Cornell University Press strives to use environmentally
responsible suppliers and materials to the fullest extent
possible in the publishing of its books. Such materials include
vegetable-based, low-VOC inks and acid-free papers that are
recycled, totally chlorine-free, or partly composed of nonwood
fibers. For further information, visit our website at
www.cornellpress.cornell.edu.

Cloth printing   10 9 8 7 6 5 4 3 2 1

Contents

Foreword

Some peoples bury their dead in the ground so that they may "return to dust." Some keep only the skull or the bones in some sort of reliquary. Still others reduce the body to ashes, which they either keep or disperse. And there are peoples who destroy the mortal coil by abandoning it to predatory birds. Few, however, like the Egyptians, have wanted, and knew how, to preserve what we call the remains as a basic condition for survival after death. Mummification was an object of astonishment in and of itself for foreign contemporaries, both Greeks and others, and a source of admiration and even seduction in the face of a practice that, along with other mysterious forms of magic, was believed to secure a happy eternity for each and every individual.

From this singular practice of the former Infidels, Arabized and Islamicized Egyptians drew only, when all is said and done, a source of profit, adding to the treasures of gold and silver that their embalmed ancestors had taken to the tomb: *mumia,* that is, mummy reduced to powder, which as recently as the seventeenth century was used as a panacea in Egypt and exported as far away as the pharmacies of France. Rarer was the export of whole bodies at the demand of westerners interested in antiquities—an undertaking that was not without risk, for the vengeful deceased was believed capable of bringing a storm down on the ship that carried it.

The unusual, disquieting appearance that the blackened cadavers present, and which the arts of fantasy continue to exploit to this day, did not prevent learned "mummyology" from making a beginning among antiquarians, as they were called in those days. Serious unwrapping sessions sometimes occurred in France and England in the eighteenth century. Travelers who had gone to explore the catacombs of the "Plain of the Mummies" (that is, the necropolis of Saqqara) would collect mummies, along with canopic jars, funerary statuettes, amulets, and wooden coffins, all of them evidence of the beliefs and the rituals that accompanied the act of embalming. We note that coffins shaped like the cadavers they contained were at that time also called "mummies," a homonymy that unconsciously brought together the common meaning of the container and the content.

Paradoxically, the properly scientific study of mummies did not occur with the transition to the nineteenth century, even though the decipherment of the hieroglyphs and a growing knowledge of the languages of ancient Egypt, the accumulation of vast collections of objets d'art and texts, and the beginning of controlled excavations and epigraphic missions were all leading to an ever-better knowledge and understanding of the myths and rituals of this nation so fond of embalming. Interest in the bodies themselves was aroused in 1881 by the discovery of those of the pharaohs. The fact-oriented attitude of historians tempted them to learn just who these illustrious personalities had physically been. The possibility of medically studying these remains from the past ever better, with methods that were less and less destructive of the objects of study, was furnished by the development of observational and analytical technologies. At the same time, issues of historical research were being refined: demography, nutritional history, the history of health issues, and the history of the ancient techniques themselves.

Today, a good century after the first X-rays of mummies, Egyptology has the benefit of all the methods and means at the disposal of forensic medicine. The "mummy stories" we tell have changed their tone, but they have enjoyed much success, with fantastic scientific and technological results resolving the mysteries of the ancient land of the pharaohs. Still, historians do not always find what they are looking for. To be sure, certain biographical details concerning given individuals, either known or anonymous, are revealed or corroborated. And by the same token, variations in the procedures for treating the bodies of the deceased are discovered or confirmed, and some mummies turn out to be makeshift messes, both picturesque and amusing to describe.

Over time, on behalf of their dead, the Egyptians developed a complex array of equipment in which each individual made an investment according to his resources, and which enabled him to survive forever: not only to avoid the dangers of both this world and the next but to enjoy the advantages of our human condition and acquire the superhuman power of divine beings. Mummification was only one element in this array. During the funeral, magical formulas were recited, and these and others were copied onto a Book of the Dead that lay in the tomb along with the deceased. A selection of figurines and ritual implements, along with a panoply of amulets and utilitarian objects from this life, accompanied the body. Once placed in the tomb, the individual could simultaneously move about in the realm where the dead were and also share in the course of the sun as it set and was reborn daily. The mobile "soul," the *ba*, soared up toward the daylight and then returned to animate its home base, the embalmed corpse in its coffin. The *ka*, the other "soul" and the immaterial double of the material body, consumed the food and drink the survivors brought to the funerary chapel, at the same time perpetuating, by speaking it out loud, the name of the person, which they could read on a stela. This whole system—which implies a far more complex anthropological representation of a living, thinking being than our own—was believed to

confer the potential capacities of a god on the deceased. The classical form of a sarcophagus—a mummy with the mask and the heavy wig that were proper to images of deities—served as the hieroglyphic symbol for the idea of superior dignity (the Egyptian word was *sah*).

Every deceased person was Osiris, the murdered and revivified god, and, like the sun and the moon, the Nile and the vegetation, he passed away and returned. Once upon a time, King Osiris, killed by Seth, had been reconstituted and resuscitated in the next life by his sister-wife Isis, an expert in magic spells, with the help of Thoth, lord of knowledge and writing, and that of Anubis, the prototype of embalmers. Used correctly, the mythic model opened a wonderfully optimistic perspective on the ultimate destiny of mortals, a more enviable future than that described by Ulysses or than the sinister *sheol* of the ancient Hebrews.

Having done his research, Herodotus was happy to report, correctly enough, what he had heard about mummification procedures. He had even learned from his informants that the most expensive coffins represented "the one whose name I think it would be a sacrilege to pronounce" (*Histories,* 2.85.90), but otherwise, he did not comment on this singular practice, or upon its mythological presuppositions. Ever the tourist, Herodotus derived his information from other Greeks, and some of them were surely beneficiaries of Osirian rituals and doctrine. Dating to the sixth and fifth centuries, stelae carved with images in pharaonic style and hieroglyphic inscriptions that ended with words in a foreign language give us a glimpse of how families of military colonists (Aramaean, Greek, Carian) whom the sovereigns of Egypt had settled in Memphis had begun to adopt the funerary religion of the land. Certain stelae depict Anubis caring for an Osiris of immigrant origin, while others depict him in *prothesis* (that is, dressed in the finery of a living person). But nearly all these stelae depict the foreign Osiris presenting himself before the Egyptian god Osiris, who is often accompanied by Isis and other Egyptian deities. This evidence leaves us to believe that the hope of an Osirian survival and the practice of mummification had spread among these immigrants, even those who preferred to retain their ancestral customs during life. For all concerned, the success of these beliefs and practices would be considerable. When the geographer Strabo visited Alexandria around 27/26 B.C.E., he noted that in the suburb called Necropolis, there were "welcoming places suited to the mummification of the dead." With its population consisting mostly of Greek colonists, Alexandria was the center of the letters, sciences, arts, and customs of the Hellenic world. And yet, three centuries after its founding, many of the city's inhabitants had recourse to the assistance of Anubis and Isis. As for the populations of Hellenic origins who had been settled throughout the land by the Ptolemies, the successors of Alexander the Great, they retained their Greek language, status, and education, but they quickly adopted the deities and the religion of the natives of the villages where they settled.

Under Roman domination, nearly everyone in Egypt became an Osiris and assumed the form of a mummy. An exception, though, was the fact that instead of the traditional divine mask, some of these mummies had a molded or painted portrait of themselves, with their hair and their headdress in Graeco-Roman style.

The history traced by Françoise Dunand and Roger Lichtenberg is based squarely on that of the culture of ancient Egypt. These scholars are fully qualified to study this history via both the history of mummies and the technological results of the study of mummies encountered in the field. A papyrologist well versed in the Greek texts that tell of the daily life of people in Egypt, as well as in Egyptian and Graeco-Egyptian art, Françoise Dunand has devoted herself principally to the religious life of Egypt between the fourth century B.C.E. and the fourth century of our own era. These are the centuries from which the greatest number of embalmed bodies have come down to us. Dr. Roger Lichtenberg, a radiologist, is one of those relatively few who have understood to what extent the medical study of mummies, so rich in technological results and information for historians, can be brought to bear on homogeneous populations. Together, they have worked in the field, and together, reaching back to the distant time of origins, they have enriched the information that these embalmed Egyptians can offer to Egyptology.

JEAN YOYOTTE
Professor Emeritus, Collège de France

Translator's Note

In this book, the following conventions have been followed in the citations from ancient texts:

Parentheses ( ) enclose words or brief explanations that have been added for clarity.

Square brackets [ ] enclose words that have been restored in a lacuna.

Ellipses . . . indicate that a word or words in the original text have been omitted in the citation.

English-speaking Egyptologists have no single set of conventions for the rendering of ancient Egyptian and modern Arabic personal and place names. Most of the names mentioned in this book occur in a standard reference work, John Baines and Jaromir Malek, *Cultural Atlas of Ancient Egypt* (New York: Checkmark Books, 2000), and the renderings here follow those in that volume. The principal exception is the omission of the typographical sign for *ayin;* this consonant does not exist in English, and it was felt that its inclusion would serve only as a distraction to the reader.

D. L.

Mummies
and Death
in Egypt

Introduction

Mummy: inevitably, the term evokes Egypt. And yet mummies are not exclusive to that land, for other peoples have made use of mummification to preserve a dead body. What these peoples generally had in common was that they lived in dry climates in which it was undoubtedly possible to observe the spontaneous preservation of interred bodies when they came to light again thanks to the depredations caused by grave robbers and animals.

From Mexico to Tierra del Fuego, Amerindians "produced" mummies in the thousands. Around 6000 B.C.E., the Chinchorros of the northern coast of Chile developed rather complex methods of defleshing and eviscerating human remains, and then re-creating the shape of the body and placing a mask on the face. Much later, the inhabitants of the Atacama Desert of Chile desiccated their dead via the combined action of cold and dry air. The mummies of these regions were wrapped, always in a fetal position, in large pieces of cloth, or sometimes in animal skins, in such a way that they constituted a sort of package or bundle, the *fardo*. The same practice existed in Peru, where mummies (in fact, funerary packets) have been found, not only in desert environments but also in wet ones (Chachapoya mummies). The richly bejeweled royal Inca mummies (fourteenth to sixteenth centuries C.E.) were the object of a veritable cult, and they were carried in procession on the occasion of religious festivals. In the tombs of the chiefs, archaeologists have found rich funerary furnishings, thus explaining, as in Egypt, the pillaging to which they fell victim. While some of these mummies must have benefited from treatment, most of them, which have conserved only their skin and bones, are to be considered "spontaneous" mummies. The same is true of the mummies of children, found on certain summits of the Andes, who were in fact sacrificial victims and whose frozen bodies were in perfect condition.

In the Canary Islands, on the isle of Tenerife, a large number of mummies were discovered in a volcanic grotto at the end of the eighteenth century: the Guache mummies. They had been treated according to a procedure perhaps similar to that of the Egyptians. Few have survived to us, for they were used, like Egyptian mummies, for medicinal purposes. Most of our information regarding the Guache mummies was handed down by the fifteenth-century Spanish conquerors.

At the end of the first millennium C.E., in the Altai region of Siberia, the dead were treated by evisceration and excerebration and then transformed into mannequins of a sort. They were packed with straw before being deposited in the funerary chambers of the *kurgan*s (burial mounds).

While it is clear that these cultures deliberately sought to preserve bodies, in other contexts, mummies have been found that had not been the object of intentional treatment. Sometimes, it was the salinity of the soil that contributed to their preservation, as in the case of the mummies of the Tarim Valley of central Asia. In northern Europe, the "bog mummies" found in Denmark and England, which have been dated from the end of the Iron Age (sixth century B.C.E.) to the Roman era, were preserved by their immersion in acidic waters with low oxygen content. This was the case with the Grauballe Man, who was doubtless a person condemned to death or the victim of a murder. Others, who had been strangled or had their throats cut, were perhaps sacrificial victims, for the Germans were practitioners of this custom.

The man discovered more recently in the glacier of Similaun, on the Austro-Italian border, was preserved accidentally by the cold for more than 5,300 years. In the same way, bodies of Inuit Eskimos have been discovered in a cliffside in Greenland, well preserved by the low temperature.

The mummies of Egypt, however, are a special case. They are evidence of a civilization's lost desire for eternity and of its deliberate will to deny death. Mummification was the indispensable condition for a survival envisaged as the happy pursuit of life as it had been enjoyed in this world. This custom is valuable to us because it placed at our disposal an object of study that is unique in the world: the thousands of bodies available to scientists enable an ever-more precise understanding of the population of ancient Egyptian. Moreover, thanks to these mummies, this vanished people and their civilization seem extraordinarily present and close to us.

Part One

*Mummification:
From This Life
to the Next Life*

1 From Prehistory to the First Two Dynasties

The first human settlements in the Nile valley probably date back to the Early Paleolithic (Acheulian); archaeological traces dating to about 300,000 B.C.E. have been found. Indications of human habitation become much more evident in the Middle Paleolithic, around 90,000 B.C.E., and especially in the Late Paleolithic, between 40,000 and 15,000 B.C.E.[1] The earliest human remains are represented by the two skeletons found at Nazlet Khatar in Middle Egypt (the site is dated to between 32,000 and 29,000 B.C.E.). Human groups that must have come from the area of the Sahara were undoubtedly no longer able to sustain their populations through a nomadic lifestyle, so they settled on terraces towering above the Nile. They were doubtless still in part nomadic, though certain sites evidence a beginning of sedentarism. These populations left us a rich harvest of stone tools.

Progressively, human groups settled in the valley. Traces of their settlements, characterized by a high-quality tool kit, have been found in Egypt, in particular at Gebel el-Silsila and (from a slightly later date) at Helwan.[2] One of the earliest cemeteries found in the valley, north of Wadi Halfa in present-day Sudan, dates to this period.

From 7000 B.C.E. on, sedentarism increased, and the population made the transition from a lifestyle of seminomadic hunting to one based largely on agriculture and on the livestock raising made possible by the domestication of several species of animal. But this transition was a slow one, and for a long period of time, already sedentary populations coexisted with others that retained their hunting and gathering practices.

The Neolithic civilization of the Faiyum, which dates to around 5000 B.C.E., left traces of the cultivation of grains and the remains of domestic animals, basket weaving, linen cloth, and also a beautiful stone tool kit. The Badarian culture of Middle Egypt might date to the same period, or just a little later.[3]

Progressively (between about 4000 and 3200), the Naqada culture, named after one of its principal sites in Upper Egypt, spread through the valley. It is agreed that the populations that developed this culture originated in desert regions located on either side of the valley at the latitude of the First Cataract. Large settlements have been identified at Gebelein and Hierakonpolis in the south, and at Heliopolis and Maadi in the north. There are perceptible affinities, especially in the northern sites, between this culture and those of the neighboring Near East. It is to this civilization of farmers and herders, who employed various artisanal techniques, especially pottery, that we owe the first somewhat elaborate burials.

In the Neolithic Period, at the beginning of the fifth millennium, tombs were simple oval pits, or rectangular pits with rounded corners, dug shallowly into the ground. One or more bodies were deposited in them, in contracted position, wrapped in skins or basketwork, head oriented south and facing west. Such is the appearance of the tombs of Merimda Beni Salama in the delta. A little later, at el-Omari

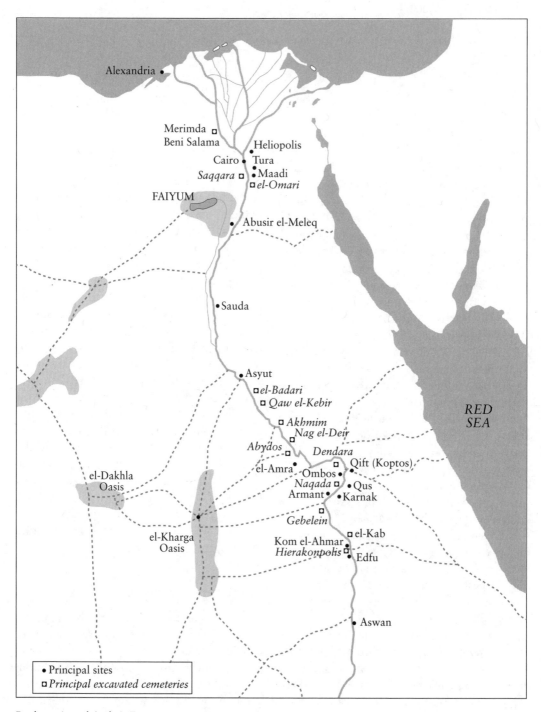

Alexandria •

Merimda □
Beni Salama
Heliopolis
•
Cairo • Tura
Saqqara □ • Maadi
□*el-Omari*

FAIYUM

Abusir el-Meleq
•

Sauda
•

Asyut
•
□*el-Badari*
□ *Qaw el-Kebir*

□ *Akhmim*
Nag el-Deir
□
Abydos
□ *Dendara*
el-Amra □ Qift (Koptos) □
Ombos •
el-Dakhla *Naqada* □ • Qus
Oasis Armant • • Karnak

□
Gebelein

el-Kharga □ el-Kab
Oasis Kom el-Ahmar
Hierakonpolis □ • Edfu

Aswan
•

RED
SEA

• Principal sites
□ *Principal excavated cemeteries*

Predynastic and Archaic Egypt

near Helwan, the burials were of the same type, but certain deceased persons wore necklaces of shells or belts of steatite beads. It was especially at Badari in Middle Egypt, from 4500 B.C.E., that the grave goods increased in number.[4] Objects were placed around the body: pottery, sharpened pieces of flint (arrowheads), pieces of jewelry or toilet articles (needles, ivory or wooden combs, cosmetic palettes). We also find glazed steatite beads of a brilliant blue obtained from minerals of copper, malachite, or azurite. In certain tombs, we begin to find statuettes of stone, ivory, or terra cotta; they depict women who, though highly stylized, often have exaggerated sexual organs.[5] The pits are sometimes rectangular and the burials sometimes multiple. Tombs of animals, themselves also wrapped in skins, occur among the human tombs. From this time on, the tombs testify to a social differentiation, from one cemetery to another but also within individual cemeteries. The richest tombs are the most disturbed, and the pillaging must have occurred early, shortly after burial.[6]

A little later, at the time of the Naqada I (or Amratian, after the site of el-Amra) culture, beginning around 3800 B.C.E., the same sort of equipment is found in the tombs, but with new types of ceramics, numerous objects of bone or ivory, and many examples of high-quality palettes, in the form of highly stylized animals, whose function might have been magico-religious. In a tomb at the necropolis of Gebelein (middle of the fourth millennium), there was found a fragment of cloth with painted decoration that must have been used to wrap a deceased person; on it, there are representations of dancers, men hunting hippopotami, boats with men plying oars, and so forth.[7] Another tomb contained a wooden bed foot in the form of the split hoof of an animal. There were numerous human figurines, both male and female. Objects of beaten copper (jewels, spear points) made their appearance.

A good example of a cemetery of the Naqada era is that of Adaima in Upper Egypt, on the west bank of the Nile across from el-Kab.[8] Excavations conducted by B. Midant-Reynes and her team for over a decade revealed the existence of two cemeteries dating respectively to 3700–3300 and 3300–3000 B.C.E., the latter being essentially a cemetery for children. These were not rich tombs, but they contained ceramics, wooden coffins, mats, and so forth. One notable feature is the way the bodies were handled: skulls were removed and skeletons were rearranged, reminding us of practices associated with reburial. Cuts on the cervical vertebrae, which occur in some cases, could testify to human sacrifice.

From the middle of the fourth millennium on, the tombs were larger, more carefully prepared, and often richly equipped, characteristics that certainly reflect greater prosperity and, at the same time, a beginning of social differentiation.[9] The rectangular form predominated, and brick was used to line the internal walls. Ceramics were abundant, often decorated with representations of stylized animals and boats. Terra cotta figurines represented women with upraised arms; these might have been connected with fertility or with rebirth after death. From this period on, these tombs contained beautiful pieces that were certainly not objects of daily use, but rather were intended to signal the importance of their owner: for example, a hard stone vase in the form of a frog and a flint knife with an ivory handle carved with animals, both now in the British Museum,[10] or the knife from Gebel el-Arak in the Louvre.[11] These high-quality items are veritable "artworks" that were surely never used. At the end of the fourth millennium, we begin to find jewels of gold, silver, and fine stone, whose presence once again reflects the social status of their owner, and which also bear witness to an already extensive trade activity (lapis and obsidian were imported products). In these tombs, the bodies, in fetal position, were generally wrapped in a mat or a piece of cloth, and they were oriented in various directions. There was a growing use of coffins made of wicker, clay, or wood.

At Hierakonpolis, tomb 100, dating to about 3300 B.C.E., is particularly interesting. Rectangular and rather large (about 20 by 10 feet), and its walls and floor of brick, it preserved, along with numerous objects, painted

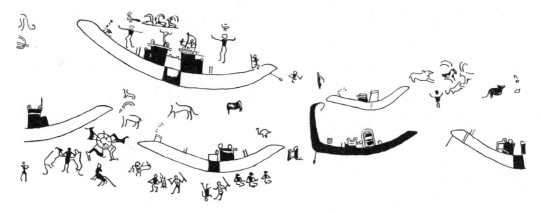

Fig. 1. Paintings from tomb 100 at Hierakonpolis. Predynastic Period (3500–3200 B.C.E.). After J. E. Quibell and F. W. Green.

murals, executed on yellow-painted stucco, representing six boats, wild animals, and men fighting with one another or battling with animals: lions, ibex, oryx (figure 1). Here we see a universe of hunting and warfare that recalls the depictions on vases and decorated palettes.[12]

From the predynastic era on, ceramics and luxury items were produced specifically to be placed in tombs: there are major differences in quality between vases found in tombs and those stemming from settlements. Moreover, the diversity of the funerary equipment indicates an ever-growing social differentiation. Objects of a magico-religious sort appear only in the wealthiest tombs. Jars filled with ash and carbonized bones, which could be interpreted as a sacrificial offering rite, have sometimes been found at the edge of a pit.[13] We can only hypothesize regarding the funerary beliefs of

the people of this period. Still, the boat motif, so widespread on fourth-millennium ceramics and also found in the decoration of the tomb at Hierakonpolis, could have had a religious significance, referring to a voyage of the deceased in the next world.

In these tombs, when the bodies were in direct contact with the desert sand, they were sometimes remarkably well preserved. "Ginger," in the British Museum, is the most striking example: the corpse, in contracted position, has a nearly normal volume, lending it an astonishingly lifelike appearance (figure 2). The hair and nails are preserved, and the skin has a light reddish-brown color. This spontaneous mummy can be dated to about 3200 B.C.E.[14]

Few examples of this type of "natural mummy" have come down to us, however. Their rudimentary protection easily explains this fact; desert animals must often have dug

Fig. 2. Spontaneous mummy called "Ginger." C. 3200 B.C.E. © Copyright the Trustees of The British Museum.

up and damaged such corpses. But the chance reappearance of such well-preserved human remains could have given the Egyptians, once they got past the terror such spectacles must have inspired, the idea of a survival of the individual after death.[15]

Predynastic burials found by W. M. F. Petrie at Naqada reveal an unusual custom.[16] The bodies seem to have been dismembered, and sometimes the skull was missing. In certain cases, the bones were arranged according to categories: long bones, vertebrae, and so forth. This evidence can be interpreted as proof of secondary burials. The bodies could first have been buried until they completely decomposed, and then they were exhumed and the skeletons reburied after having been cleaned and disarticulated. The expression "gather the bones," which we encounter rather later in the Pyramid Texts, would perhaps be an allusion to this practice.[17] According to another hypothesis, though, this type of burial could be interpreted as the putting back in order of burials plundered by thieves. In fact, scholars think that tomb robbery began quite early in the Nile valley. Still, in one case reported by Petrie (tomb T5 at Naqada), the bones seem to display traces of bite marks, which some have interpreted as proof of ritual cannibalism. The evidence in fact continues to pose problems, though investigation of the cemetery at Adaima has revealed the existence of various kinds of manipulation of corpses.

FUNERARY PRACTICES DURING THE EARLIEST DYNASTIES

Tombs and Their Furnishings

There thus seem to have been different types of funerary practices at the end of the fourth millennium: dismemberment of corpses, their "rearrangement," and reburial. Eventually, however, the rule was to place wholly preserved bodies in a definitive resting place. The desire to keep the bodies of the deceased safe from depredations, and perhaps also the desire to prevent them from reappearing, in fact led to the development of methods of burial more

apt to protect them. At the end of the predynastic era, bodies were more and more often placed in wooden or terra cotta coffins, and there was a widespread custom of covering the pit with pieces of wood or with branches. Inside the tomb, a compartment was reserved for deposits of offerings, a practice that appeared in the Naqada era. From the beginning of the third millennium on, these were often no longer just pits; rather, parts of them were constructed, including on the one hand a substructure lined with bricks and on the other a superstructure ranging from a simple wooden cover to a structure of unbaked brick, which soon assumed the form of a *mastaba*. This last type of tomb, so called after an Arabic word meaning "bench," assumed an elongated, rectangular form, with walls presenting a more or less marked slope. Mastabas would become especially common in the Old Kingdom.

Beginning with Dynasty 1, "rich" tombs were built entirely of brick and could be of considerable size, such as the royal tombs of Saqqara and Abydos (figure 3). Thus, the tomb thought to be that of King Wadj at Saqqara

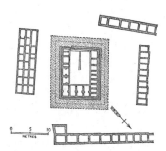

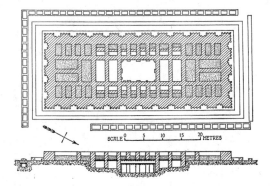

Fig. 3. Plan of the tomb of King Wadj at Abydos (top). Plan and section of King Wadj at Saqqara (bottom). Dynasty 1. After W. B. Emery, 1961.

measured about 165 by 50 feet and presented the appearance of an enormous brick massif with "place façade" walls. A staircase blocked by a stone portcullis led to the burial chamber, which was dug rather deep. This chamber was surrounded by a number of rooms, veritable "magazines" intended to contain the funerary equipment, in particular the stone and ceramic vessels that have usually been found in great quantity in tombs of this type.[18] In one of the Dynasty 2 (c. 2780–2653 B.C.E.) royal burials at Saqqara, the excavators found a whole funerary repast near the sarcophagus. It included bread, fish, fowl, pieces of beef, fruits, cakes, and wine.[19]

The royal burials were surrounded by those of nobles, artisans, and servants. The tombs of the nobles followed, in principle, the same plan as those of the kings, but on a smaller scale, of course. They generally included a funerary chamber flanked on each side by two storerooms. Mastaba 1532 at Nag el-Deir is a good example of this type of tomb.[20]

The tombs of servants generally consisted of an oblong pit with a wooden ceiling covered by a superstructure of sand mixed with loose stones, above which was a convex brick roof. At Abydos, small tombs were placed around the mastabas of pharaohs (Aha, Den, Semerkhet, Qaa); some of the persons buried in them might have been intentionally killed, arguing for a continuation of the practice of human sacrifice.[21] We also find this practice at Saqqara, in the tombs of servants surrounding the mastaba of Queen Merneith. Objects, often of a professional nature, were deposited next to the coffin. Thus, the tombs of Merneith's servants contained tools of copper and flint, paint jars, miniature boats, and butcher's knives, all undoubtedly reflecting the activities of the occupants.[22]

A necropolis of this type at Saqqara, consisting of 231 tombs, was investigated by Rizkallah Macramallah in 1939. Most were from the era of simple pits covered with reeds. The walls of some were lined with bricks, and those of others with *muna* (unfired clay mixed with straw). The bodies were in contracted position, head to the north and facing east. This necropolis, which could be dated to King Den (Dynasty 1, 2950–2780 B.C.E.), furnished a relatively large number of ivory, flint, and ceramic objects.[23]

The tombs of the poorest were simple oval holes dug in the sand and summarily covered with branches or wickerwork, above which was a tumulus consisting of the sand dug from the hole. Even in these poor tombs, we find some pots or implements deposited around the body.

The Bodies and Their Wrappings

In the tombs of kings and nobles, the bodies were carefully bandaged and placed in wooden sarcophagi. With few exceptions, these bodies have not been preserved (or were destroyed); nevertheless, examples dating to Dynasty 2 have been found at Saqqara. The linen bandages around them had been impregnated with resin, which, as it hardened, preserved the shape of the body; special attention seems to have been paid to the face and the genitals.[24] The earliest example of this treatment is the forearm found by Petrie in the tomb of King Djer at Abydos (Dynasty 1, figure 4). In fact, nothing is left of it but the bones, some linen, and four bracelets made of lapis lazuli, turquoise, and amethyst held together by elements of gold.[25] Certain sarcophagi leave us to think that the bodies were buried in extended position, though the contracted position remained more frequent.

Poor burials, since they were less likely to be plundered, have preserved a rather large number of bodies, arranged in contracted position and lying on their left side (figures 5 and 6).

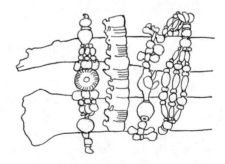

Fig. 4. Forearm of King Djer, still wearing its bracelets. Dynasty 1. After a photograph kept at the Petrie Museum, University College, London.

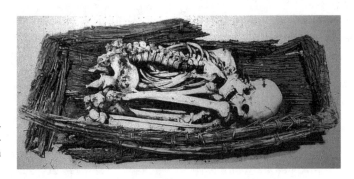

Fig. 5. Skeleton in contracted position in a basket. Dynasty 1. © Copyright the Trustees of The British Museum.

SCALE |———0———| METRE

Fig. 6. Tomb of an artisan or servant. Plan (top) and section (bottom). Beginning of Dynasty 1. After W. B. Emery, 1961.

None of the bodies buried in this type of tomb was found in the form of a natural mummy, like some of those from the prehistoric era; there were only skeletons.[26]

Thus, in this period, the desire to protect the body from the beasts of the deserts or from robbers led to elaborate, sometimes complex structures, whose common feature was the absence of contact with the desiccating sand; this absence of contact permitted decomposition to occur. Protected from the canines of the desert, the bodies were delivered over to flesh-eating worms! It is clear that in this period, the Egyptians did not understand the preservative nature of sand in contact with a dead body. Perhaps this is understandable in a land where life is an incessant battle against sand: how could such a daily nuisance be considered an ally?

The Problem of Mummification

At a very early date, the existence of natural, spontaneous mummies dried out by contact with the sand must have suggested to Egyptians that it was possible for a body to be preserved. Such preservation was of course a problem in a land with a hot climate. This problem already presented itself to hunters and fishers, who understood that in order to preserve their catches, they had to gut and then salt or dry them. This same approach would be followed in the mummification process.

This technique was developed rather slowly, at the price of much trial and error and with unequal results. The principal difficulty was undoubtedly the attempt to practice abdominal evisceration, which, above and beyond the technical problem, entailed violating a taboo regarding the bodies of close relatives.[27] A proof that this taboo existed is to be found in the account of Diodorus Siculus, according to whom the *paraschistes*, the man who made the abdominal incision, "flees at a run, while those present pursue him hurling stones."[28]

We now know that the essential components of mummification (a term whose Egyptian equivalent remains unknown) were:

    abdominal evisceration
    a natron "bath"
    excerebration
    application of unguents and resin
    bandaging

This list, which is not exhaustive, has no strict chronological character, for the date when certain procedures were first implemented has not been conclusively established. Even when they were already known, certain steps could be omitted, according to the quality of the mummification process that was chosen. This fact explains, among other things, the diversity in the state of preservation of bodies, without our being able to take into consideration, of course, the considerable influence of external factors, including pillaging, that occurred after the mummy was placed in its tomb.

These components of the mummification process were progressively devised and put into use over the course of millennia, reaching their apogee in the New Kingdom. This process took nearly two thousand years.

2 The Old Kingdom

The Old Kingdom shows all the signs of a powerful and centralized state. Its system of governance was an absolute monarchy whose essence was divine. The king was the center around which everything revolved, and for this reason, the most prestigious monuments were reserved for him. While no traces remain of the royal palaces of this period, the gigantic pyramids of Giza, constructed under Dynasty 4 (2561–2450), are stunning proof of the power of the monarchs. As for funerary beliefs and practices, our information stems essentially from the royal tombs. While the tombs of the members of the royal entourage are less prestigious, they are nevertheless also rich in information.

PROGRESS IN THE TECHNIQUE OF MUMMIFICATION

Down to the end of Dynasty 3 (2635–2561), the desire to preserve the dead body, though evident, did not lead to conclusive results. The only procedure used consisted of wrapping the deceased in resin-impregnated linen; for us, the result is hollow molds of the bodies thus treated. Aside from some fragments of a body, including a still-bandaged foot, found in the pyramid of Djoser, which we cannot be certain is from the king's mummy, no royal body from this period has survived to us.[1]

At the beginning of Dynasty 4, a major step was taken. Queen Hetepheres, wife of Snofru and mother of Cheops, was definitely subjected to abdominal evisceration. In fact, in 1925, G. A. Reisner[2] discovered part of the funerary equipment of the queen in a small chamber at the bottom of a shaft near the pyramid of Cheops. The equipment included an alabaster box with four compartments that contained the remains of her viscera, wrapped in linen cloths and still immersed in a natron solution. This discovery made it possible to affirm that from that time on, the Egyptians recognized the importance of removing the viscera, a procedure that assured the effectiveness of the desiccation process by avoiding the decay of the body. This practice was probably reserved for kings and important personages. Only one complete royal mummy from the Old Kingdom has been preserved to us, that of the young and obscure pharaoh Merenre-Nemtyemzaf of Dynasty 6, which was found in his pyramid at Saqqara.[3] While the royal tombs have been thoroughly plundered throughout the course of history, some remains of the skeletons of Snofru, Djedkare Izezi, Wenis, and perhaps Teti have been found in their respective pyramids, and they bear more or less clear traces of mummification.

A good example of mummification in this period is that of the prince Renefer (c. 2550), whose remains were found by W. M. F. Petrie in his mastaba at Maidum.[4] The body was wrapped in linen impregnated with resin, forming a sort of mold. The face was "re-created" as though by an impression. The internal abdominal organs had been removed, wrapped in pieces of cloth, and placed in a niche dug into one of the walls of the burial chamber. This mummy, which had been kept in London, was unfortunately destroyed in a bombing raid during World War II. Such niches have been found in other, contemporary tombs in the necropolis of Maidum, such as that of Rehotep, but most of them were emp-

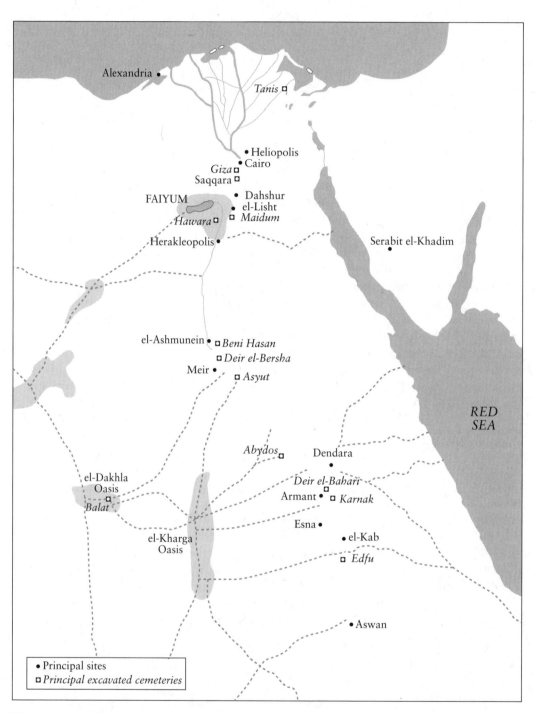

Pharaonic Egypt (Dynasties 3 to 30)

tied of their contents (during Dynasty 4, this niche was replaced by a hole dug in the floor of the chamber).[5]

The practice of evisceration would become rather frequent in Dynasties 5 (2450–2321) and 6 (2321–2140), but it was not the rule, as shown by a female mummy of Dynasty 5 that was found in a tomb at Giza; though it was carefully bandaged and dressed in a linen robe placed around the wrappings, it had not undergone abdominal evisceration, and traces of the viscera were still in place inside the trunk.[6] Most often, the men and women of this period have been preserved only in skeletal state, for the "natron bath" does not seem to have been used for the entire body. In that period, however, Egyptians were already familiar with the technique of packing: the abdominal cavity of Ranefer had been filled with pieces of cloth coated with resin. At Maidum, an entirely exceptional case was found: one mummy showed traces of abdominal and cranial evisceration, in this instance via the foramen magnum. Moreover, the rachis, the sacrum, the shoulder blades, and the kneecaps were separately wrapped in bandages, a practice comparable to the ritual dismemberment practiced in the predynastic era.[7]

A complete example of mummification in the Old Kingdom is that of a Dynasty 5 mummy found in a family tomb at Saqqara: it is that of a man named Nefer, very well preserved, placed in a wooden coffin at the bottom of a sort of funerary shaft. The linen bandages in which it was wrapped had been covered with plaster worked in such a way as to reproduce the contours of the body, including the genitals, which were carefully modeled. The facial features and the mustache were painted on, and there was a false beard made of cloth.[8] This practice of modeling with plaster on the surface of the mummy has also been noted at Giza, at the end of Dynasty 5 and all through Dynasty 6, sometimes on the entire body and sometimes only on the head. The importance of preserving the head was already apparent. A mummy now in Boston shows that the plaster must have been poured onto the body after it was placed in its coffin, for

only the anterior surface and the sides of the body were covered with it.[9] The technique of wrapping the body prefigured, in a sense, that of cartonnage.

Generally, the body was entirely wrapped in shrouds and bandages; still, there was another bandaging technique that consisted of wrapping the limbs separately. Several examples of the latter have been found at Gebelein and Saqqara. Thus, one of the occupants of the "Tomb of the Unknowns" at Gebelein was carefully bandaged, the arms and legs separately, with the facial features painted in black on the cloth (figure 7). It was lying on its left side, the head resting on a headrest, in a wooden coffin.[10] Toward the end of the Old Kingdom we find funerary masks of terra cotta mixed with straw, the facial features outlined with strokes of black and white paint.

With the beginning of Dynasty 4, there was a change in the position of the body in the tomb. The "contracted" position seems to have been rapidly abandoned in the richest tombs: it is quite possible that this position was incompatible with the treatments to which it had to be subjected, in particular, evisceration. From that time on, the body was in extended position, the arms alongside the body and the hands placed on the outside surface of the thighs. Corresponding to the elongated position of the body, the coffin took the form of an oblong wooden crate. In "rich" tombs, this coffin was often placed in yet another, this one of stone. This wealth was also expressed by the material employed, Aswan granite or white limestone from Tura, and in the exterior deco-

Fig. 7. Bandaged mummy. Gebelein, "Tomb of the Unknowns." Old Kingdom. Turin Museum. After A. Donadoni-Roveri.

ration, which was often of the "palace façade" type.[11] But in poor burials, which were evidently the majority, the body, in contracted position, was often simply placed in a terra cotta jar or a wooden box.

FUNERARY ARCHITECTURE

Funerary architecture experienced considerable development during the Old Kingdom, attaining a colossal scale with the royal pyramid complexes, the first example of which was the Step Pyramid of Djoser (second pharaoh of Dynasty 3, c. 2617–2599). The pyramids of the kings of Dynasties 3 to 6 are spread at intervals from Abu Rawash in the north to Maidum (figures 8 and 9) in the south. The Egyptians perfected the technique of stone construction (the pyramid of Djoser is regarded as the first stone monument in the history of the world), and they mastered the art of dressing materials as hard as granite and basalt. The pyramids are monuments of complex architecture, and the largest of them are still viewed as veritable feats of technological prowess. Many theories have been proposed, but there is no agreement as to the methods employed in the various phases of their construction. The layout of the interior of these monuments reveals the care that was taken to protect the funerary chamber, a care that would grow in the course of time and reach its maximum in the Middle Kingdom. Hard materials (mostly granite) were chosen to construct the interior corridors and the burial chamber, materials that were difficult for robbers to penetrate. There were also portcullises, also of granite, immediately in front of the burial chamber (figure 10).

In its subterranean chambers, the pyramid of Djoser has preserved a decor made of small blue faïence tiles, and also bas-reliefs representing the king in the ritual run that occurred during the *heb-sed* festival. Rather similar reliefs have also been found in the subterranean area of the "south tomb" of the same pyramid complex. No interior decoration, however, has been found in the pyramids of Dynasty 4. In the pyramids of Dynasties 5 and 6, the walls of the funerary chambers were entirely covered with religious texts of great importance to us today; the pyramid of Wenis contains the earliest example of these Pyramid Texts.

In fact, the pyramid was only the most visible element—or rather, in most cases, the only element preserved to this day—of the funerary complex. This complex usually included two temples, a lower, "valley" temple and an upper temple, the two of them joined together by a causeway. This causeway, of which that of Wenis is a good example notwithstanding its ruined condition, was covered over and used to transport the sarcophagus from the valley temple to the upper temple. These temples played an important role in the funeral, and afterwards, in the offering cult rendered to the deceased pharaoh. Few remains of these con-

Fig. 8. Pyramid of Snofru at Maidum. Dynasty 4.

Fig. 9. Corbeled vault of the sarcophagus chamber. Pyramid of Snofru at Maidum. Dynasty 4.

buildings. In the Djoser complex (figures 11, 12, and 13), there were special structures intended to perpetuate the celebration of the jubilee festival, the *heb-sed*. These were constructions with a purely symbolic and magical function, making it possible for the deceased pharaoh to continue celebrating this festival for all eternity. Thus, the "chapels" lining two opposite sides of the courtyard were merely false façades that could not be entered, while at the same time, we know that during a *heb-sed* festival, the pharaoh was obliged to "visit" each one of them. The D-shaped structures located in the courtyard in front of the south face of the pyramid recall the hieroglyphs depicted on the bas-reliefs representing Djoser running, and the structures might thus mark the place where the dead pharaoh was believed to have run this course.

Near several of the pyramids, archaeologists have found either stone simulacra of boats, like those built along the Wenis causeway (figure 14), or genuine ships, the finest of which were those of Cheops (figure 15), discovered in 1954.[13] These boats recall the postmortem voyage the king was believed to make in the sun barque, or perhaps the symbolic pilgrimages to Sais and Buto. Some scholars, though, think that the wooden boats could have served to travel on the Nile at the time of the funeral; this would also be the case with the boats found near the pyramid of Senwosret III (Middle Kingdom).[14]

As the custom of constructing a stone ma-

structions have been preserved, with the exception of the valley temple of Chephren, which still preserves a good deal of its wall surfaces and its red granite columns. Here, we must make special mention of the pyramid complexes of Djoser and Sekhemkhet,[12] which feature a huge enclosure wall surrounding the

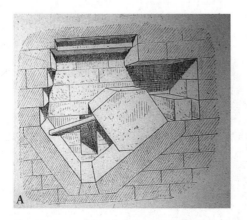

Fig. 10. Portcullis of the Bent Pyramid of Snofru at Dahshur in open (A) and closed (B) position. After Perrot and Chipiez.

Fig. 11. Djoser complex with the *heb-sed* court in the foreground and the Step Pyramid in the rear. Saqqara. Dynasty 3.

staba spread among the upper class, its exterior and interior organization became complex. From that time on, a chapel intended for the funerary cult was the rule (the earliest chapels had made their appearance at Tarkhan under Dynasty 1). At first located outside the mastaba, it was later included within the structure itself, and a narrow corridor connected it to the world outside. This chapel, to which several rooms for storing funerary furnishings could be added, always included an offering chamber in which there was the false door believed to enable the deceased to leave the tomb. The mastaba of Mereruka at Saqqara depicts the deceased, who is standing, exiting via this false door. The interior decoration of the mastaba came to be quite elaborate, with painted bas-reliefs accompanied by hieroglyphic in-

Fig. 12. Djoser complex, south court with D-shaped structures. Saqqara. Dynasty 3.

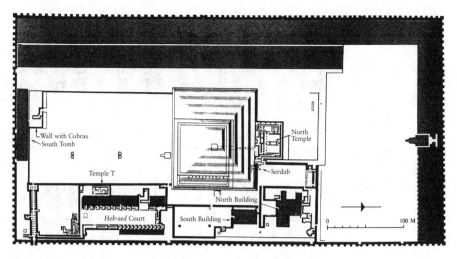

Fig. 13. Plan of the Djoser complex. Saqqara. Dynasty 3. After J. P. Lauer.

scriptions. The funerary statue experienced development. Certain statues were placed in a small space, the *serdab,* where they remained inaccessible and were visible only through one or more narrow openings resembling loopholes, such as what we see in the mastaba of Ty, or in the complex of Djoser, where the statue of the king was found still in place in its

serdab on the north side of the pyramid. As for the burial chamber, it was located beneath the mastaba, directly below the offering chapel. It was usually accessed via a shaft that could begin at the summit of the mastaba or in one of

Fig. 14. The boat-shaped pits south of the causeway of Wenis. Saqqara. Dynasty 5.

Fig. 15. One of the large cedar boats of Cheops, found dismantled in a pit beside his pyramid. Giza. Dynasty 4.

the interior rooms. Often, there were several burial chambers for the various members of the family, each with its own shaft. Sometimes, as in the mastaba of Ty, the shaft led from the peristyle court to the burial chamber. The mastabas were rigorously aligned with one another in rows around the pyramid of the king, who was thus surrounded even in the next life by his relatives and servants. At Giza (figures 16 and 17) and Saqqara, these ensembles constituted veritable cities of the dead.[15]

In this period, tomb furnishings consisted of offering goods, and also of objects of daily use that could be extremely refined, as in the case of the tomb of Queen Hetepheres. The offering materials and the furniture found there are incomplete, for this "tomb" seems to be a reburial after the pillaging of the original tomb, and the body of the queen was not found there. While she might have used cer-

tain objects during her lifetime, most of them must have been made specifically to be placed in the tomb: vases of gold, copper, and alabaster; gold knives, razors, and toilet objects; and especially the bed and the carrying chair, both of which demonstrate the degree of quality attained by the artisans of the Old Kingdom. Diverse furnishings were found in the "Tomb of the Unknowns" at Gebelein, clearly answering to the needs the deceased might have had in the afterlife: ceramic vases for foodstuffs; chests containing fabrics, sandals, and bronze tool blades; and wooden model boats.

The burial places of more ordinary people continued to be extremely rudimentary; they were, in fact, most often pits dug in the ground, some of them with a covering of bricks. Many burials of this type have been found around the mastabas of the rich. They are not fundamentally different from the predynastic graves, and

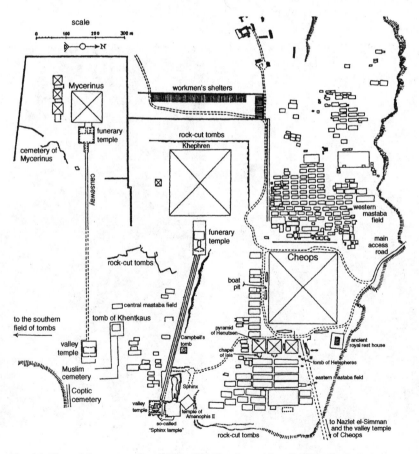

Fig. 16. Plan of the necropolis of Giza. Old Kingdom. After C. Zivie-Coche.

Fig. 17. Pyramid of Cheops. Foreground, entrance to the tomb of Seshemnefer. Giza. Dynasty 4.

for obvious reasons—that is to say, they were cheap—such burials would continue to be made down to the Roman Period.

An example of burials at an "intermediate" level between those of the nobles and those of the most impecunious can be observed in the necropolis of the workmen who built the pyramids of Giza.[16] This cemetery, which was discovered on the plateau, includes two types. The better type consists of about thirty relatively elaborate tombs that were made, it seems, with materials left over from the construction of the pyramids, and on the model of the burials of nobles. The poorer type (about six hundred) consists of extremely simple tombs. Here, too, there is an apparent social differentiation: the overseers and foremen enjoyed a better-quality burial.

FUNERARY BELIEFS

As late as Dynasty 4, the royal sarcophagi (figures 18 and 19) lay in uninscribed chambers. At the end of Dynasty 5, for the first time, texts give us a detailed outline of Egyptian beliefs regarding the fate of the dead. But these texts, the Pyramid Texts, were inscribed in royal tombs and thus concern only the king. A collection of magical formulas, hymns, and invocations, their function seems to be essentially cultic, and their objective is to enable the king to reach the places where he will lead his new life.[17] These highly elaborate and complex texts certainly go back to a period well before the Old Kingdom, but we do not know their origin. Some spells are offering formulas that were undoubtedly recited during the burial ceremony. Others clearly evoke a ritual:

Fig. 18. Sarcophagus of Mycerinus, still in place in the burial chamber of his pyramid. Giza. Dynasty 4. After G. Ebers.

Fig. 19. Sarcophagus of Khephren, in place in his pyramid. Giza. Dynasty 4.

> My mouth is split open for me, my nose is broken open for me, my ears are unstopped for me. (Pyramid Texts spell 407, §§ 712 a–b)

> Horus has adjusted your mouth for you, he has adjusted your mouth to your bones for you, Horus has split open your mouth for you. (Spell 369, § 644 c)

Thus, the Opening of the Mouth ritual, by means of which the priest restored the use of the deceased's senses, and which would become widespread in later periods, was already carried out in this period, at least on the person of the king.

After his death, it was believed that the king boarded the solar barque and accompanied the god Re in his celestial journey, and that he mingled with the gods and with his royal ancestors. He himself became a god in the full sense of the term. This concept of the royal destiny entered into the framework of the solar theology of Heliopolis, which became especially important from Dynasty 5 on. Another tradition attested in these texts identified the king with Osiris, the dead and "resuscitated" god, but it did not contradict the Heliopolitan tradition, as attested by the following text:

> Ascend to your mother Nut; she will take your hand and give you a road to the horizon, to the place where Re is. The doors of the sky are opened to you, the doors of the firmament are thrown open to you, and you will find Re standing as he waits for you; he will take your hand for you and guide you to the two Conclaves of the sky, he will set you on the throne of Osiris. (Spell 422, §§ 756a–757e)

The Osirian tradition would not, however, come into its full force until the New Kingdom. One text clearly affirms that death is not an end, for the king will live again in the world beyond, like Osiris:

> If he (i.e., Osiris) lives, this King will live; if he does not die, this King will not die; if he is not destroyed, this King will not be destroyed; if he mourns, this King will mourn. (Spell 219, §§ 167 b–c)

> O King, you have not departed dead, you have departed alive. (Spell 213, § 134 a)

It was believed that the deceased king sailed across the sky in the barque of Re, and to this belief, we may compare the boats actually discovered near certain pyramids, such as the stone boats of Wenis and the magnificent cedar ships of Cheops.

After his death, the god-king was the object of an offering cult celebrated in his funerary temple, called "temple of millions of years." To this purpose, while still alive, he established a foundation whose revenue permitted the material realization of this cult. This endowment generally consisted of cultivable fields belonging to the king, and eventually, this practice diminished his revenues by reducing the number of his domains.

Originally, the Pyramid Texts were strictly reserved for the king, the priest par excellence; they have also, however, been found in the burial chamber of the pyramid of Queen Ankhesenpepi at Saqqara.[18] No text of this sort has been found in the mastabas of the nobles, which were decorated with painted reliefs representing the deceased surrounded by his family and servants. Texts often accompany the images, but their concern was mainly to enumerate the offerings, to indicate the titles and career of the deceased, or to comment on certain of the scenes. These were in no way texts of a theological character. The scenes in which we see the deceased seated before his abundantly laden offering table, and the harvest scenes and those of livestock raising, however we are to interpret them (evocation of the life of the deceased after death, or of his life on earth, or of his wealth and the activities necessary to produce the offerings), are evidence of belief in life after death, which was considered, even in this early period, to be a passage from one form of existence to another.[19]

In the tombs of this period, there was a widespread custom of depositing funerary statues inscribed with the name of the deceased, a custom that has left us with an extraordinary quantity of sculpture in the round. Those of Rahotep and Nofret, found in their mastaba at Maidum and now in the Cairo Museum, are striking examples of such statues (figure 20). At a time when mummification had not yet

Fig. 20. Head of Nofret (A) and Rehotep (B), from their mastaba. Maidum. Dynasty 4. Cairo Museum.

truly proved itself, the statues could magically take the place of the body and assure the deceased his new life. To the same end, perhaps, sculpted heads called "reserve heads" were often deposited in the tomb, which would again testify to the importance attached to the preservation of this part of the body. In the event of an "accident," they enabled the *ba*, one of the spiritual elements of the personality, to find the material support of the deceased and unite with it. When we study the mummies in a necropolis, we note that one of the most frequent "accidents" was the separation of the head and the body. The custom of reserve heads testifies, in a way, to the poor quality of mummification. Their progressive disappearance at a period when mummification was im-

proving is the proof of this point. A passage from the Pyramid Texts, addressed to the king, clearly indicates the Egyptians' fear of seeing the corpse lose its physical integrity:

> Nut comes, so you will not lack. . . . She will protect you, she will prevent you from lacking, she will give you your head, she will reassemble your bones for you, she will join together your members for you, she will bring your heart into your body for you. (Spell 447, §§ 828 a–c)

With regard to ordinary people, we have no precise information about the fate they were believed to experience after death. The fact that offerings have often been found even in extremely modest tombs leads us to think that in this case as well, there was belief in survival.

3 The Middle Kingdom

THE FIRST INTERMEDIATE
PERIOD

The end of the Old Kingdom (around 2140
B.C.E.) was marked by major social and political upheaval. Increasingly powerful provincial
dynasts carved out veritable little kingdoms for
themselves, weakening the central authority to
the point of an anarchy that was perhaps ag-
gravated by economic problems. During this
period, which would last for at least two hundred years, the tombs, both royal and private,
were wantonly pillaged. In a prophetic text
known as the Admonitions of Ipuwer, which
must have been written in the Middle Kingdom,[1] we read:

> Behold, he who was buried as a hawk (i.e., the
> pharaoh) is (on a stretcher, like any common
> person). What the pyramid concealed is become
> empty. (7, 2)

Written at the beginning of the second millennium, a whole literature depicted this period in
dramatic terms that included, as one of the
signs of general upheaval, the fact that even the
dead were not buried. The Admonitions are
eloquent regarding this topic:

> Forsooth, many dead men are buried in the river.
> The stream is a sepulchre, and the place of em-
> balmment has become stream. (2, 6–7)

> Men do not sail north to [Byblos] today. What
> shall we do for cedars (i.e., to make coffins, or
> perhaps for cedar oil) for our mummies? (3,
> 6–7)

> Forsooth, those who were in the place of em-
> balmment are laid on the high ground. It is the
> secret of the embalmers. (4, 4)

In fact, funerary customs remained unchanged,
and we must take into account the evident fact
that these texts indulge in a rhetorical exag-
geration that we may view as a rewriting of
history.

The few preserved human remains from this
period show that the practice of mummification was still not very elaborate. The mummy
of Pepiseneb, now in Boston, was carefully
bandaged; it had sixteen shrouds separated by
a large quantity of packing[2] and a painted cartonnage mask was placed on the face. A scan
of the mummy, however, revealed that the
"soft tissues" were badly preserved, testifying
to a mummification technique that was still
ineffective, though the wrappings were put together with care. The wooden coffin, anticipating those of the Middle Kingdom, has the
appearance of an oblong crate decorated with
Udjat eyes and with hieroglyphic inscriptions
that included offering formulas, along with the
names and titles of the deceased. Yet although
he was a high-ranking personage, his funerary
furnishings were minimal.

There was no rupture between the tomb furnishings of the Old Kingdom and those of the
First Intermediate Period. In the burial chambers, however, we begin to find painted
wooden models of a type that would become
widespread in the Middle Kingdom, in particular, model boats (figure 21) that are probably
to be connected with the pilgrimage (whether
symbolic or real) to Abydos, where the principal tomb of Osiris was believed to be located.[3]
These models can be viewed as evidence for the
spread of Osirian belief.

It seems that in this period, the funerary rites
that guaranteed survival were extended to

Fig. 21. Model boat. Painted wood. Middle Kingdom. Musée des Beaux-Arts, Lyon.

wider strata of the population. Although this process is often called a "democratization" of funerary practices, this seems to us an improper use of that term.

PROGRESS IN MUMMIFICATION DURING THE MIDDLE KINGDOM

The quality of mummification (figure 22) improved in the Middle Kingdom, thanks to the more frequent use of abdominal evisceration, and especially to the use of natron to treat not only the viscera but also the entire body. Here we must stress the double action of natron, a natural mixture of (mostly) chloride and sodium carbonate, which not only causes the rapid desiccation of the body, thus avoiding the process of decomposition, but also entails the saponification of the fatty tissues, assuring the "chemical stability" of the mummy. This saponification consisted in a transformation of the fatty acids by means of a basic substance (in particular, carbonate of soda), resulting in a mixture of soap and glycerine that would be eliminated from the cadaver. It is thus that certain mummies that give the appearance that the subject was obese during life because of the presence of voluminous cutaneous folds were no heavier than others: they simply lost their fat. Testifying to a reverse process, certain mummies that do not seem to have benefited from the "classic" treatment appear to be covered with spots of a sort of grease, similar to adipocere, that formed when the body lay in a humid tomb. Such seems to be the case with certain "Christian" mummies that have yet to be much studied.

Moreover, the treatment was not always ap-plied in its entirety. The mummies of the princesses of Dynasty 11, whose tombs were discovered nearly intact at Deir el-Bahari, bore no trace of abdominal incision, and the remains of viscera were still visible in the thoraco-abdominal cavity. These mummies might have been treated by anal injection of a solvent or by desiccation with natron, or perhaps both. The rectal wall showed traces of resinous

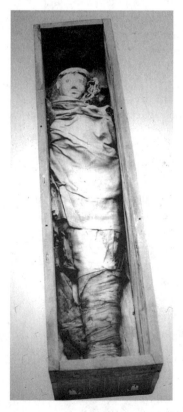

Fig. 22. Mummy in its wooden coffin. Middle Kingdom. © Copyright the Trustees of The British Museum.

products, and the rectum and vagina were considerably dilated. These observations seem to correspond to Herodotus's description of "second-class mummification." Traces of resinous products were visible on the integument, yet the skin was not preserved, and neither was the body hair, the hair of the head, or the nails. The jewels placed on the mummy of Princess Akhayt had left their shallow imprint on the skin. Certain mummies of this period, however, were so well preserved that it has been possible to identify the presence of tattoos. The body of Henhenet, wife of Mentuhotep II, was extremely well preserved. Examination of her body seemed to indicate that she had died young, in labor, probably because of a narrow pelvis. The mummy had not been eviscerated.[4]

Other mummies of Dynasty 11 had been eviscerated, though, such as that of Djehutinakht, nomarch of the Hare Nome in Middle Egypt, which was found in his tomb at el-Bersha.[5] In this tomb, the archaeologists discovered a canopic vase of an unusual sort: it was provided with feet and arms. What remained of the mummy was its head, which had preserved its wavy hair, as well as its facial skin. In a step unusual for this period, the brain had been removed via the ethmoidal and sphenoidal sinuses, though with some damage to the orbits; the person carrying out the operation had penetrated the maxillary sinuses instead of making use of the nasal passages, as would become the usual practice in the New Kingdom. Consider-

able progress was thus made in the mummification process, whose basic elements were known, if not always practiced systematically.

In an unusual instance, we have an intact Dynasty 11 mummy, that of a notable named Wah (figure 23), who lived during the reign of Mentuhotep III.[6] The mummy had the appearance of an enormous package, the body being wrapped in a large quantity of pieces of linen (448.5 square yards of it!). It was not X-rayed until long after it came into the possession of the Metropolitan Museum of Art in New York City. This examination revealed the presence of a large number of jewels and amulets, as well as a mouse and a lizard (surely not included intentionally), between the layers of bandages. Moreover, the well-preserved body had been eviscerated.

Dating to the same period is an embalmer's cache discovered in the Theban region. It contained the leftovers from the embalming of a certain Ipy.[7] This material included pieces of cloth, natron, and oils that were probably considered impure because they had been in contact with the corpse and had to be buried somewhere near the deceased, but not with him. There was also the matter of preventing anyone from using these leftovers for magical ends that could do harm. Among the items found in the cache was an embalming table, a sort of low, four-legged bed. The "liquids" and powdery residues were contained in sixty-seven terra cotta vases. A deposit of the same

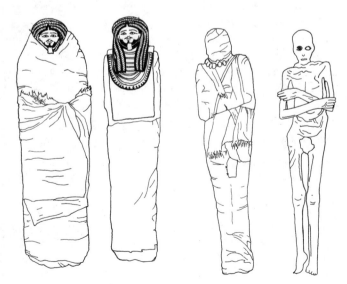

Fig. 23. Stages in the unwrapping of the mummy of Wah. Thebes. Middle Kingdom. Metropolitan Museum of Art, New York.

sort had been found by T. Davis near the tomb of Tutankhamun some years before the discovery of the tomb itself, and it might have been this find that pointed the way to the archaeologists.[8]

All individuals were not treated with equal care, of course, especially ordinary people. The bodies of sixty archers of Mentuhotep II, undoubtedly killed in combat and buried at Deir el-Bahari, had been wrapped in cloth but had not been embalmed according to the usual method. Scholars think that sand, which had adhered to the bodies in large quantity, was used to dry them: its beneficial effect was undoubtedly understood in this period.[9]

In Dynasty 12, the regular presence of canopic vases in tombs seems to indicate that the practice of abdominal evisceration was widespread, though few mummies from this time have been preserved to us. These vases assumed the form of pots with ovoid sides, a shape they would retain for the next two thousand years. The cover was in the form of a human head, often a likeness of the deceased, though sometimes there was simply a convex cover. Later, the covers would take the form of the heads of the four sons of Horus, who were charged with protecting the organs: the human-headed Imset watched over the liver; Hapy, with a baboon's head, over the lungs; the jackal-headed Duamutef over the stomach; and the falcon-headed Qebehsenuf over the intestines. The designation "canopic" vases is particularly ill chosen; it stems from a confusion with the human-headed vase adored late in Egyptian history under the name of Osiris-Canopus, borrowed from that of the city of Canopus, which was itself named after a Greek tradition concerning a helmsman called Canopus. It was Champollion who discovered the exact purpose of these vases.[10] On November 12, 1818, examining the content of a canopic jar, he wrote:

Object wrapped in cloth . . .
Object 4 by 2 inches
Clearly of an animal nature
Fibrous tissue
Held to the lamp: animal odor
Shriveling of the animal part
And boiling of the balm, reduction to black carbon

Found at the bottom of the vase . . .
It is liver, brain, or cerebellum.

Two Dynasty 12 mummies found at Rifa were studied at the Manchester Museum in 1906 by M. Murray.[11] The bodies had been reduced to a nearly skeletal state, but they had been eviscerated, and the viscera were in canopic jars. The skin at the ends of the fingers had been cut and tied around the nails to prevent them from falling out, a procedure that would become frequent in the New Kingdom.

Great care seems to have been taken with the appearance of mummies in this period. "Ocular prostheses" of linen were used to restore a certain volume to the orbital content, as well as plugs, also of linen, in the nostrils to prevent, at least partially, sagging of the nose. The practice of surmodeling was abandoned, along with that of painting facial features on the bandages, both of which had been used in the Old Kingdom. There was, however, a

Fig. 24. Mask of stuccoed cartonnage. Middle Kingdom. Louvre.

growing use of funerary masks. These masks were usually made of stuccoed cloth, and they were often gilded or painted yellow to imitate gold, the "flesh of the gods," the practice thus contributing to the deification of the deceased. A peculiarity of these masks was the depiction of men with bearded jaws and mustaches (figure 24): this must have corresponded to a fashion, doubtless a passing one, contrary to practice in other periods.[12] The placing of amulets between the layers of bandages as a means of protecting the deceased was perhaps not yet as systematic as it would be in the New Kingdom.

BURIAL IN THE MIDDLE KINGDOM

The elongated position was now the rule, and the deceased was often placed in the coffin lying on his left side with his head and neck on a headrest on which magical, protective formulas could be written. The coffins were of the same types as in the Old Kingdom, but they were often better constructed, with boards that were larger, better made, and put together with the help of dowels. In wealthy tombs, both the interior and the exterior of the coffins were decorated. On the exterior were friezes of objects representing offerings and other "goods" belonging to the deceased, along with rows of hieroglyphic texts arranged both horizontally and vertically. On the left side, at the head end, were two painted eyes (the Eyes of Horus were believed to assure the protection of the deceased), often accompanied by the representation of a palace façade with a gate. These eyes were supposed to be in front of the face of the deceased, who could thus magically "see" by means of them and "exit" through the gate (figure 25). Besides the texts of a theological nature that were now written on the coffins, we find the names and titles of the deceased. We thus know the identity of a certain number

Fig. 25. Detail of a painted wooden coffin. The *udjat*-eyes assured the protection of the deceased and enabled him to "look" outside. Middle Kingdom. Louvre.

of them, and we note that they were no longer just major personages, but also provincial bureaucrats, priests, physicians, and scribes, though still of relatively high rank.

Stone sarcophagi, which we find only in the tombs of royals, have sides that are either smooth or of the "palace façade" type. More rarely, they are decorated with scenes of daily life, such as the sarcophagus of Princess Khawyt at Deir el-Bahari.[13]

Anthropoid coffins (figure 26), which had already made their appearance, became widespread toward the end of Dynasty 12. At first no more than "boxes" roughly approximating the shape of a human body, they became more elaborate from Dynasty 13 on. Made of wood or cartonnage, they were carefully modeled so as to evoke the contours of the body. The head

was sculpted on the cover, complemented by a collar and usually also by a vertical strip of hieroglyphs. At first, these anthropoid coffins were placed in sarcophagi lying on their left side, as had earlier been the case with the mummies themselves.

There was little change in the external appearance of royal tombs, which were now located at Dahshur, Lisht, and Hawara, for they maintained their pyramid shape. Their dimensions, though, were much smaller than those of the gigantic monuments of Giza. The quality of their construction was inferior because increasingly their cores were made of brick rather than stone. The interior layout and construction of the funerary chambers and corridors became extremely complex, always in the vain hope of preventing pillagers from penetrating into the sarcophagus chamber. The pyramid of Senwosret II (figure 27), at el-Lahun at the edge of the Faiyum, caused great difficulty for W. M. F. Petrie, who labored for

Fig. 26. Coffin of Inyotef. Gilded wood. Dynasty 11. Louvre.

Fig. 27. Pyramid of Senwosret II: structure of "herringbone"-patterned stone inside the mass of brick. El-Lahun. Dynasty 12.

Fig. 28. Mastabas of the royal family around the pyramid of el-Lahun. Dynasty 12.

months to reach the burial chamber.[14] His principal problem was that the age-old tradition of locating the entrance on the northern face of the monument had been abandoned.

Nobles continued to be buried in mastabas of stone (figure 28), or of brick for those of lesser means. In imitation of the royal tombs, the layout of their chambers and corridors, and other security measures as well, became more complex. Moreover, we witness an increase in the custom of digging tombs into the hillsides bordering the Nile. Such tombs are rather numerous in Middle and Upper Egypt, at Beni Hasan (figures 29 and 30), el-Bersha, Asyut, Qau el-Qebir, and Aswan (figure 31), to cite only the best known. These tombs, mostly

Fig. 29. Entrance to a rock-cut tomb. Beni Hasan. Middle Kingdom. After Perrot and Chipiez.

of princely individuals, have an elaborate plan, somewhat evocative of that of a temple, with a peristyle court, a long axial corridor with a hypostyle hall either in front of or behind the court, and finally, a chapel. The coffin was placed in a subterranean chamber that was accessed via a shaft.

Continuing Old Kingdom traditions, certain Middle Kingdom tombs have sculpted and painted decoration, such as the bas-reliefs of the tomb of Sarenput at Aswan or the paintings in the tomb of Khnumhotep III at Beni Hasan. There was a growing practice of depositing stuccoed and painted wooden models depicting scenes of daily life: butchery, brewing, weaving, carpentry, and so forth. We also find models of groups of soldiers, many types of boats laden with all sorts of cargo, and barques evoking the pilgrimage of the deceased to Abydos. The people depicted still sometimes preserve fragments of the fabrics that once clothed them. A particularly fine example of these models is furnished by the cattle counting scene, now in the Cairo Museum, from the tomb of Meketre at Deir el-Bahari, and there are others of comparable quality in the Cairo Museum and the Metropolitan Museum of Art in New York.[15] In a way, such objects are three-dimensional equivalents of the bas-reliefs of the Old Kingdom mastabas. As in the bas-reliefs, there are models of groups of offering bearers.

The "ka houses" (figure 32) found in the tombs of this period probably had a different function. Made of terra cotta, they reproduce various type of houses in which people actually lived. Because they include channels for the runoff of liquids, similar to those we see on of-

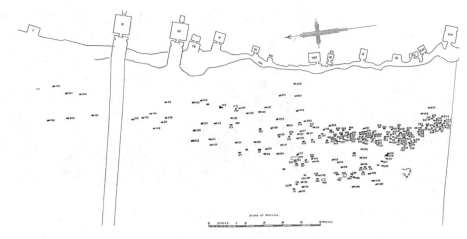

Fig. 30. Plan of the necropolis of Beni Hasan. Middle Kingdom. After J. Garstang.

fering tables, certain scholars (W. M. F. Petrie was the first) have attributed a similar function to them. Others, such as A. Niwinski, think they might be substitutes for offering chapels.

It is also in this period that a particular type of figurine appeared in tombs, female figurines (figure 33) made of wood, faïence, or ivory, improperly called "concubines of the deceased" because they are represented nude, tattooed, and often with accentuated genitals. These are probably images of fecundity and rebirth, all the more so in that they are sometimes accompanied by children, and also because they are also found in tombs of women. Different, however, was the function of the funerary figurines at first called *shawabtis* (or servants of

Fig. 31. The necropolis of the nomarchs of Aswan. Old and Middle Kingdoms.

Fig. 32. "*Ka* house." Terra Cotta. Middle Kingdom. British Museum.

the dead), which began to appear at the end of the Middle Kingdom. Later, they were believed to be able to replace the deceased and to answer for him in the afterlife, which led to their new designation *ushabtis* (answerers). In this

Fig. 33. Female, so-called concubine of the deceased figurine, nude and tattooed. Egyptian faïence. Middle Kingdom. Louvre.

period, these figurines were often uninscribed. Some of them, though, bear an inscription specifying the name and titles of their owner, along with an offering formula. They remained rather rare until the New Kingdom.

In sum, though, funerary equipment became rich and varied. Besides ritual objects, it included objects of daily life, such as jewels, toilet objects, tools for the use of professionals, and even weapons.

In many tombs of the Middle Kingdom, archaeologists have found objects of a rather unusual sort that were meant to assure the protection of the deceased: magical wands made of hippopotamus ivory with incised decoration representing various maleficent beings, as well as protective symbols, such as a frog, the god Bes, and the goddess Taweret (figure 34). A slightly later tomb discovered near the Ramesseum might even be that of a magician; it contained four magical wands, along with amulets, figurines of nude women, a figurine of a woman holding serpents, and a box filled with magical papyri.[16]

Poor tombs were most often simple pits. Sometimes, though, we find vaulted constructions of brick in which the body was placed at the bottom of a shaft. In fact, we observe scarcely any evolution from the Old Kingdom types; such changes as there were related essentially to the rich tombs that persons of humbler status attempted to imitate as their means allowed.

THE COFFIN TEXTS

In the Middle Kingdom, texts were inscribed on the interior surfaces of wooden coffins (figure 35). These were the Coffin Texts, a heterogeneous collection of formulas that varied a bit from one region of the country to another, though the ones considered especially important were used everywhere.[17] These formulas were derived from the Pyramid Texts, and the content of some of them, which are entirely unsuited to nonroyal individuals, can be explained only by positing that they were originally intended for the king. It was in the First

Fig. 34. Magic wand. Hippopotamus ivory. Middle Kingdom. Louvre.

Intermediate Period that scribes had begun to copy texts from the royal tombs for the use of nobles. Most of the Middle Kingdom inscribed coffins have been found in Middle Egypt, in the region between Herakleopolis (Ihnasya el-Medina) and Asyut. This fact undoubtedly has to do with the importance assumed by this region between the First Intermediate Period and the Middle Kingdom.

These texts had rather diverse purposes. These included the protection of the corpse, speculations on the destiny of the deceased,

the "geography" of the world beyond, an enumeration of the dangers there, and prophylactic formulas intended to overcome these dangers.

Certain texts[18] evoke the powers of the deceased in the world beyond:

> The sky belongs to you, the earth has been given to you, you are destined for the double Field of Bliss (i.e., the dwelling place of the blessed) with Osiris, you will ascend to Re in the sky, and the gods who dwell there will obey you, the power of the Foremost of the Westerners (i.e., Osiris) has been given to you. (Spell 764)

This sort of formula seems suited to a king, but in this period, it is clear that every deceased person of high rank had the benefit of it. Another text evokes the journey of the deceased in the world beyond:

> I know the route of the West, I cross the lake, I traverse the firmament, I escape the hall of slaughter, I refresh myself in the cool sky. I am a blessed one. (Spell 344)

Sometimes, though rarely enough, the interior walls of the coffin could include a "map" of the routes that led through this otherworldly realm, as is the case on a Dynasty 12 coffin from el-Bersha. The fate of the deceased in the next world seems to have been envisaged, in this period, under two aspects: that of a voyage in the celestial waters with Re and that of a netherworldly journey through the kingdom of Osiris.

The confidence placed by the Egyptians in these magico-ritual formulas seems to have been absolute:

Fig. 35. Interior of a wooden coffin, with texts. Middle Kingdom. Louvre.

Fig. 36. The *ka* of King Awibre-Hor. Wood, gold leaf, inlaid eyes. Dynasty 13. Cairo Museum.

He who knows this divine word will be in the sky with Re among the gods. Victory will be granted in every tribunal before which he presents himself, he will eat bread in every place to which he directs himself, he will transform himself into anything he desires. It is truly effective. (Spell 651)

Many of these formulas refer to solar beliefs. The goddess Nut, who is often represented on the interior of these coffins, played a highly important role: her function was to assure the re-

birth of the deceased, just as she did for the sun. But from this period on, Osiris occupied a central place. There are many allusions to his dismemberment and to the reconstitution of his body by Isis, and the deceased, henceforth called "Osiris N," was identified with him.

The advantages of immortality, which had been the prerogative of the king and his entourage, thus began to spread into broader strata of society. For these beliefs to be effective, it was of course necessary for them to find expression in the funerary cult, which entailed endowments of land intended to assure that offerings would be made to the *ka* (life force, figure 36) of the deceased. This fact partly explains the growing importance of the priesthood in Egyptian society. But it is probable that only the families of the rich could afford to create such an endowment, above and beyond the expenses, which were surely high, of creating a tomb.

4 The New Kingdom

THE SECOND INTERMEDIATE
PERIOD

The Middle Kingdom was followed by another period of disorder marked by a return to the division of Egypt into two kingdoms. In the delta, the disappearance of a single central power proved favorable to the progressive encroachment of tribes from the Asiatic Near East, whose chiefs ended by adopting Egyptian titularies and behaving like veritable pharaohs. These chiefs would control all of Lower Egypt, along with the valley as far as the Theban region, for a period of a century and a half to two centuries: these were the Hyksos, whose capital, Avaris, has been discovered in the eastern delta at Tell el-Daba–Qantir. Though they were highly Egyptianized, these "invaders" brought and maintained their native funerary customs, as evidenced by the tombs found at Tell el-Daba (figure 37). Placed in shallow rectangular graves, the deceased were not mummified; in certain cases, donkeys were sacrificed, and even servants were put to death just outside the entrance to the tomb of their master. For quite a long time, this type of sacrifice and burial near the tomb of the master had not been a part of the Egyptian tradition.[1]

Otherwise, Egypt retained its traditional funerary customs. We have, however, little information on this subject, given the small number of mummies surviving to us from this troubled era. Found at Deir el-Bahari in 1881, the mummy of Seqenenre Tao II (figure 38) of Dynasty 17, which ruled in Thebes c. 1630–1539, dates to the end of this period.[2] This king had suffered a number of wounds to the head. Several were from a battle ax, so he undoubtedly died in combat, perhaps during the crucial battle between the Hyksos and the Egyptians, the one that must have led to the definitive "liberation" of Egypt. Perhaps because of the tragic circumstances of his death, Seqenenre's body seems to have been treated summarily. The viscera were removed, and the abdominal cavity was filled with cloth, but the head was left untreated. The body, which was found in bad condition, was scarcely more than a skeleton with a few cutaneous remnants. A mummy of the same period, found by W. M. F. Petrie at Qurna, had been quite carefully wrapped in multiple layers of cloth, but the body had been treated ineffectively (if it had even been treated at all), for nothing more than bones remained.[3]

The sarcophagi of this period retained the form of a rectangular box, but often with a convex lid. The coffin placed inside it was anthropoid, and frequently, in rich tombs, it was covered with gold foil. In the Theban region, the coffin was of the type we call *rishi*, characterized by a decoration consisting of one or more pairs of wings that covered the lid. These wings recall those of the goddesses Isis and Nephthys, who protected the dead. Ritual formulas, along with the name of the deceased, were inscribed in the center of the lid, between the wings. The quality of these coffins was often mediocre, with the exception of those of the kings and queens of Dynasty 17. Found at Dra Abu el-Naga, these beautiful royal coffins were gilded, and the eyes were inlaid.

THE DISCOVERY OF THE ROYAL
MUMMIES

The tombs of the New Kingdom have yielded fine pieces of ancient Egyptian art. These include the gilded mask of Tuya (figure 39), *ushabtis* of kings such as Ramesses IV (fig-

Fig. 37. Plan of a Hyksos tomb. Tell el-Daba. C. 1600 B.C.E. After M. Bietak.

ure 40), and the embalming vases of Ramesses II (figure 41).

While the technique of mummification would progress still further at the beginning of the Third Intermediate Period, it was the New Kingdom that furnished us with the most famous and familiar of all the mummies of Egypt: the royal mummies, which were discovered at the end of the nineteenth century. Thanks to these discoveries, Egypt is the only country in the world of which it is true that we can behold nearly all the sovereigns from a period of nearly four centuries, from Ahmose to Shoshenq II (1514–924). Thanks to this extraordinary "pantheon," we can gaze upon the serene expression of Sethos I or the authoritarian look of Ramesses II, to cite only the most famous of these kings. One of these royal mummies, who was not part of this group, recently returned to Egypt, where it is now in the Luxor Museum. This is the mummy of Ramesses I (figure 42), which was identified by its anthropological characteristics. It was residing in the Michael C. Carlos Museum at Emory University in Atlanta after a stay in the

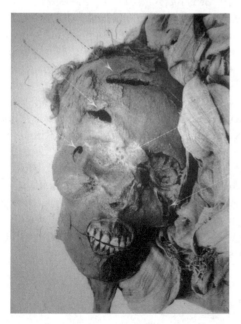

Fig. 38. Head of the mummy of King Seqenenre Tao II: the wounds visible on the skull and face were the definite cause of his death. Deir el-Bahari. Dynasty 17. Cairo Museum.

Fig. 39. Gilded mask of Tuya, mother of Queen Teye. Tomb of Yuya and Tuya (Valley of the Kings no. 46). Dynasty 18. Cairo Museum.

Fig. 40. Ushabti of Ramesses IV. Painted wood. Dynasty 20. Louvre.

Royal Ontario Museum in Toronto, where it had arrived clandestinely in the nineteenth century.[4]

The first discovery was made in 1881, at the end of a police investigation originally requested by G. Maspero, who was at that time in charge of what would come to be called the Egyptian Antiquities Service and curator of the Boulaq Museum. The investigation itself was supervised diligently by the Chief of Police of Luxor. High-quality objects from royal tombs, as proved by the inscriptions they bore (one of these was a papyrus of Pinudjem I), had appeared on the "unofficial" antiquities market, and this attracted the attention of Maspero. Suspicion turned to the Abd el-Rasul family, who lived in Qurna, but it was only after several months of inquiry that family dissension led one of them to reveal the affair to the governor of the province. Ten years earlier, in the mountain of Deir el-Bahari, the Abd el-Rasul brothers had discovered a cache containing a large quantity of mummies and funerary equipment. Prudently, they had dipped into this treasure only three times in the course of the decade. Inspector A. Kamal and the archaeologist E. Brugsch (Mariette's former assistant), who had been dispatched by the Khedive (vice-king of Egypt) in the absence of Maspero, finally penetrated into the cache on

Fig. 41. Four vases used in the embalming of Ramesses II. Egyptian faïence. Dynasty 19. Louvre.

Fig. 42. Head of the mummy of Ramesses I (?). Dynasty 19. Luxor Museum.

July 5, 1881. After receiving their reports, Maspero described the discovery in a text that became famous:

> Mssrs. Emile Brugsch and Ahmed Effendi Kamal were led by Mohammed Ahmed Abd el-Rasul to the very place where the funerary vault opened up. The Egyptian engineer, who had already dug into the cachette, had most capably made the arrangements: Never had a cachette been better hidden. . . .
>
> Mohammed Ahmed Abd el-Rasul's report, which had at first seemed exaggerated, was but an attenuated expression of the truth: where I had expected to find one or two obscure kinglets, the Arabs had unearthed a hypogeum full of pharaohs. And what pharaohs! The most famous, perhaps, in Egyptian history. . . . Monsieur Brugsch believed he was the victim of a dream to have fallen unexpectedly into such an assemblage, and I still wonder, like him, whether I am really not dreaming when I see and touch what were the bodies of so many personages of whom we had thought that we would never know anything more than their names.[5]

Forthwith (and, we must note, a bit precipitously), the content of the cache was emptied in the space of two days with the help of two hundred workmen, and then it was transported to Luxor and finally to Cairo. From Luxor to Koptos, the population, who were informed of the event, reacted as they would for a funeral cortege at the passage of the el-Men-shia, the steamboat that transported the pharaohs, the men shooting rifles and the women letting out cries of mourning. Forty mummies from Dynasties 17 to 21 had just once again seen the light of day:

- Dynasty 17: Seqenenre Tao II
- Dynasty 18: Ahmose, Amenhotep I, Tuthmosis I (?; figure 43), II, and III, Siamun, and ten princesses and queens, including Ahmose-Inhapi (figure 44) and Ahmose-Nofretari (figure 45)
- Dynasty 19: Sethos I (figure 46), Ramesses II (figure 47)

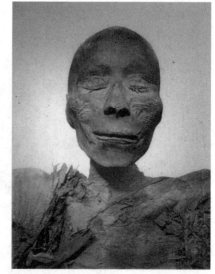

Fig. 43. Head of the mummy of King Tuthmosis I (?). Dynasty 18. Cairo Museum.

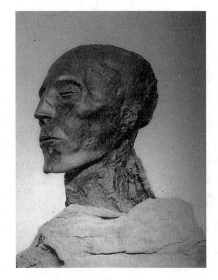

Fig. 46. Head of the mummy of Sethos I. Dynasty 19. Cairo Museum.

Fig. 44. Head of the mummy of Queen Ahmose-Inhapi, wife of Seqenenre Tao II. Dynasty 17. Cairo Museum.

- Dynasty 20: Ramesses III (figure 48) and IX
- Dynasty 21: Pinudjem I and II, Djedptahiufankh, and eight princesses and high priestesses, including Henuttawy
- Eight anonymous, undated bodies

Twenty years later, V. Loret, director of the Egyptian Antiquities Service, discovered the tomb of Amenhotep II in the Valley of the Kings.[6] The king was still resting in his sarcophagus, along with the bow which legend had it he was the only man in the kingdom who could bend it. Excavation of the tomb led to the discovery of fifteen other mummies in two side chapels, ten of which, all royal, had been absent at the earlier roll call! In total, this new discovery uncovered:

- Dynasty 18: Amenhotep II and III, Tuthmosis IV (figure 49), Teye (?; figure 50)
- Dynasty 19: Merneptah (figure 51), Sethos II, Siptah, Twosre (?)
- Dynasty 20: Ramesses IV, V, and VI
- Five anonymous bodies (figure 52)

Fig. 45. Head, front and profile, of the mummy of Queen Ahmose-Nofretari, wife of Ahmose. Dynasty 18. Cairo Museum.

Fig. 47. Head and chest of the mummy of Ramesses II. Dynasty 19. Cairo Museum.

Loret realized he had discovered a cache comparable to that of Deir el-Bahari and that it nearly completed the list of the pharaohs of the New Kingdom. Study of the inscriptions on the bandages enabled him to affirm that these mummies had been reburied at the same time as those in the cache at Deir el-Bahari. In fact, it was under the high priest and pharaoh Pinudjem II, around 950 B.C.E., that in view of the extent of the pillaging whose object had been the royal tombs, the priests decided to collect the bodies. After having duly rebandaged them, they "cached" them securely in various places in the Theban mountain.

By way of gossip, let us recall the final tribulation endured by these unfortunate mummies. When they arrived at the customs house at Cairo, for lack of any idea what to call this rather unusual "merchandise" for tax purposes, they were declared under the category "dried fish"!

In 1907, in the Valley of the Kings, A. Weigall and E. Ayrton discovered a tomb (no. 55) whose doorway was sealed with the seal of Tutankhamun.[7] To this day, the mummy found in the funerary chamber poses problems of identification. It probably belonged to the fam-

Fig. 48. Mummy (full length) of Ramesses III. Dynasty 20. Cairo Museum.

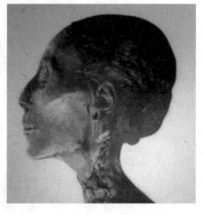

Fig. 49. Head of the mummy of Tuthmosis IV. Dynasty 18. Cairo Museum.

Fig. 50. Bust, front and profile, of Queen Teye (?). Dynasty 18. Cairo Museum.

ily of King Akhenaten. It might be that of Smenkhkare, Tutankhamun's brother, or, perhaps, that of Kiya, one of Akhenaten's wives. The present condition of the remains makes it difficult to arrive at even a definitive specification of the gender. In any event, the blood group of the mummy is identical to that of Tutankhamun.[8]

Later still, in 1922, the spectacular discovery of the tomb of Tutankhamun cast the spotlight on a king who until then had been little known among the sovereigns of the New Kingdom. For the first time, archaeologists found nearly all the furnishings of a royal tomb, and in particular, those of the funerary chamber, which had not been violated. No less than four years of labor were required before H. Carter could open the gilded chapels that contained the king's sarcophagus.

> [T]here, towering above us, was one of the great gilt shrines beneath which kings were laid. So enormous was this structure (17 feet by 11 feet, and 9 feet high, we found afterwards) that it filled within a little the entire area of the chamber, a space of some two feet only separating it from the walls on all four sides, while its roof,

Fig. 51. Bust of the mummy of Merneptah. Dynasty 19. Cairo Museum.

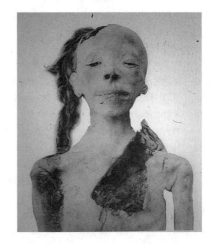

Fig. 52. Bust of the mummy of a young prince. Dynasty 18. Cairo Museum.

with cornice top and torus moulding, reached almost to the ceiling. From top to bottom it was overlaid with gold, and upon its sides there were inlaid panels of brilliant blue faience, in which were represented, repeated over and over, the magic symbols which would ensure its strength and safety. . . . Here, on the eastern end, were the great folding doors, closed and bolted, but not sealed. . . . Eagerly we drew the bolts, swung back the doors, and there within was a second shrine with similar bolted doors, and upon the bolts a seal, intact. . . . [I]n imagination [we] could see the doors of the successive shrines open one after the other till the innermost disclosed the King himself.[9]

With intense excitement I drew back the bolts of the last and unsealed doors; they slowly swung open, and there, filling the entire area within, effectually barring any further progress, stood an immense yellow quartzite sarcophagus, intact, with the lid still firmly fixed in its place, just as the pious hands had left it. It was certainly a thrilling moment, as we gazed upon the spectacle enhanced by the striking contrast—the glitter of metal—of the golden shrines shielding it. Especially striking were the outstretched hand and wing of a goddess sculptured on the end of the sarcophagus, as if to ward off an intruder.[10]

The great number of objects to be inventoried and the considerable disorder in which thieves had left them were in part the reason for the slow speed of the work, but we must also bear in mind the need to reinforce, or even to restore on the spot, this multitude of highly fragile objects. Some of these had purely ritual functions, but others—furniture, weapons, clothing—might have been used by the pharaoh during his lifetime.

The richness and the quality of these furnishings demonstrate the high technical and artistic level attained by the jewelers and artisans of this period, and they leave us to imagine the treasures that might have been contained in the tombs of rich and powerful pharaohs such as Tuthmosis III and Ramesses II. The discovery of the tomb of Tutankhamun yielded our most complete example of a royal burial at the apogee of Egyptian power.

The quartzite sarcophagus was enclosed in four gilded wooden chapels nested inside one another; this arrangement led to the correct interpretation of the papyrus in the Turin Museum that bears a plan of the tomb of Ramesses IV (figure 53).[11] The quartzite sarcophagus itself contained three nested coffins: the first two were of gilded wood with inlays of faïence and glass paste (figure 54), while the third, which was solid gold, weighed nearly 245 pounds. These coffins were anthropoid, with the king depicted in the Osirian pose and provided with the god's *heqa*-crook and flabellum. The surprises did not stop there, for when the innermost coffin was opened, the archaeologists saw a funerary mask of solid gold weighing almost twenty-five pounds, a veritable marvel of the jewelers' art, resting directly on the mummy. The second coffin was entirely covered by a piece of cloth on which garlands of flowers had been laid; the "crown of justification," also of real flowers, was placed on the brow. A huge collar of flowers and beads also lay on the breast area of the outermost coffin. The unwrapping of the mummy revealed a large number of high-quality jewels and amulets, but the unwrapping process was extremely frustrating, for the abundance of unguents had literally burned and stuck to the

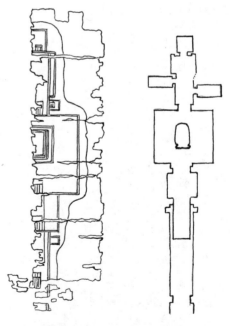

Fig. 53. Plan of the tomb of Ramesses IV. (Valley of the Kings, no. 2). Dynasty 20. Modern plan (right) and ancient plan on a papyrus in the Turin Museum (left).

Fig. 54. Second coffin of Tutankhamun. Gilded wood with inlays. Dynasty 18. Cairo Museum.

walls of the coffin. Each finger and toe was encased in gold.

The king had died young, between the ages of seventeen and nineteen, but examination of the mummy did not reveal the cause of death. Certain writers have raised the possibility of the idea of death by assassination, a hypothesis based on the presence of multiple fractures observed in 1968, when the mummy was X-rayed. In fact, it seems more likely that the abundance of unguents gluing the body to the coffin was the indirect cause of fractures that occurred when the mummy was removed from its coffin. The controversy was finally ended by the CAT scan of the remains of the pharaoh, which eliminated the hypothesis of an assassination.[12] Tutankhamun's mummy remains in his tomb in the Valley of the Kings, where at present, pending the discovery of yet another royal tomb, it is the only one still in its final resting place.

Since the day of their discovery, the study of the royal mummies has been a driving passion for scholars. In the autumn of 1881, Maspero and Brugsch published a photographic album of the mummies found in the cache at Deir el-Bahari. Next, in 1912, G. E. Smith published an atlas containing photographs and descriptions of all the royal mummies in the Cairo Museum.[13] Detailed X-ray study of these mummies was done in 1967 by J. E. Harris, who published his results in 1973, under the title *X-raying the Pharaohs,* with K. Weeks; later, in 1980, he and E. F. Wente published *X-Ray Atlas of the Royal Mummies.*[14] More recently, several royal mummies were once again X-rayed to clarify certain points. The mummy of Ramesses II was taken to France in 1976, where it was exhaustively investigated and carefully restored.[15] Study of the mummy confirmed that the pharaoh died at a highly advanced age, suffering from osteoarthritis of the hips in particular, as well as from an ankylosing spondylitis, of which his spinal column bore marks. The blood vessels displayed atheroma lesions. The teeth were in bad condition. Finally, the cervical column had been broken by the embalmers when they poured resin into the skull.[16]

In the New Kingdom, mummies of important persons became more numerous, and their quality, like that of the mummies of the pharaohs, improved, as shown by the mummy of an unknown lady and that of Nebseni found in the cache at Deir el-Bahari (figures 55 and 56). Another good example is afforded by those of the couple Yuya and Tuya, the parents of Queen Teye, wife of Amenhotep III. Preserving nearly their exact appearance during life, these mummies testify to the quality attained by the embalmers during this period.[17] Abdominal evisceration was the rule for the best prepared mummies. We must note the displacement of the opening for the evisceration: at first vertical, at the level of the left hypochondrium, from Dynasty 18 on, it was made parallel to the left iliopubic line. Similarly, excerebration became nearly systematic:

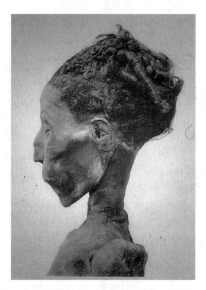

Fig. 55. Head of the mummy of an unknown lady ("D"). Dynasty 19. Cairo Museum.

it was usually carried out via the ethmoidal cavity.

The mummies, always in elongated position, had their arms arranged in more than one way. They could be placed along the body, the palms touching the thighs, or placed (in the case of men) in front of the genitals. In what is called the "Osirian" position, with the arms crossed in front of the thorax, the hands either grasped the shoulders, or they were simply placed flat on the upper part of the thorax.[18]

In certain cases (as in that of King Merneptah), the fingers are still wrapped in the position they once had around the handles of the *heqa*-crook and the flabellum, which have in the meanwhile disappeared.

COFFINS AND SARCOPHAGI

In the New Kingdom, the use of anthropoid coffins became the rule, but their decoration varied considerably. At the beginning of Dynasty 18, they were relatively simple and massive, depicting a bandaged mummy wearing a mask. Stripes imitating bandages were painted on the cover, generally in white, and texts were written on these stripes. Later, coffins of this type more nearly resembled a human form (figure 57); the mask often had eyebrows and eyes inlaid with glass paste, while the hands were sculpted in relief. Between the stripes, the decoration included vignettes depicting scenes in the world beyond. Such was the case with the coffins of Yuya and Tuya in the reign of Amenhotep III. Later, more space was reserved for texts, and the decorative motifs were divided into registers and pictures representing funerary deities and scenes: Nut, Isis and Nephthys flanking Osiris, the Sons of Horus, and so forth. The coffin could sometimes represent the deceased dressed as in daily life, as in the

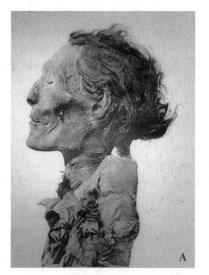

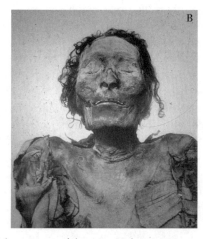

Fig. 56. Head in profile (A) and front view (B) of the mummy of the priest Nebseni. Dynasty 18. Cairo Museum.

Fig. 57. Coffin of the lady Madja. Stuccoed and painted wood. Deir el-Medina. New Kingdom. Louvre.

case of Sennedjem and his daughter-in-law, the lady Isis (Dynasty 19). Isis also has her left arm bent in front of her waist and her right arm stretched along her thigh (figure 58), an arrangement of the arms sometimes found on the coffins (and the mummies) of this period.[19]

According to the means of the deceased, their coffins were more or less numerous and elaborate. The pharaohs, as in the case of Tutankhamun, seem to have had three anthropoid coffins, of which the innermost, which

Fig. 58. Coffin of the lady Isis. Stuccoed and painted wood. Tomb of Sennedjem (Deir el-Medina no. 1). Dynasty 19.

contained the body, was of pure gold, while the other two were of cedar wood richly covered with gold and with motifs in glass paste. These three nested coffins were placed in a stone sarcophagus, which was itself encased in several chapels of gilded wood. Such equipment was undoubtedly reserved for the king, of course, but wealthy private persons often had three coffins inside a sarcophagus that could be of stone or wood. Royal sarcophagi evolved from a rather simple type similar to those of the Middle Kingdom (with flat sides and lid) into more complex forms; that of Amenhotep II, for example, had a convex lid (figure 59). In the case of Ramesses III, the sarcophagus took the form of a cartouche. The stone used for royal sarcophagi was quartzite or granite. The decoration was almost always the same, with *udjat*-eyes on the left side, the goddess Isis at the head, and the goddess Nephthys at the foot of the sarcophagus. The texts were taken from the Coffin (or Pyramid) Texts. Progressively, these were replaced by new formulas that were also reproduced on papyri for private persons; these collections are today called the Book of the Dead.

A new type of sarcophagus made its appearance at the end of the Amarna Period, with four goddesses carved in relief on its corners: Isis, Nephthys, Neith, and Selkis. Good examples are the sarcophagi of Tutankhamun and Haremhab.[20]

During Dynasties 19 and 20, the royal sarcophagi were generally of granite, and the lid could be sculpted in the image of the king, as in the case of Merneptah. The inscriptions,

Fig. 59. Sarcophagus of Amenhotep II, in place in his tomb in the Valley of the Kings (no. 35). Red quartzite. Dynasty 18.

which were more abundant and varied than in the preceding period, were drawn from new theological compilations, such as the Book of Gates.

TOMB FURNISHINGS

Since pillaging cemeteries has always been a "national sport" in Egypt, few tombs have survived to us intact. Even that of Tutankhamun had been "visited" twice, and it was probably the construction of the tomb of Ramesses VI just above it that subsequently protected it, for the rubble covered the entrance to that of Tutankhamun. Even so, this tomb affords us an excellent example of what the furnishings of a royal burial could include.

Among the ritual objects, we find a magnificent collection of *ushabtis* of cedar wood or Egyptian faïence. The alabaster canopic chest, which had four compartments, contained the canopic vessels, whose lids depicted the king; the vessels contained little mummiform coffins of solid gold in which the viscera were placed. This canopic chest was placed in a gilded wooden chapel, each side of which was protected by a goddess (Isis, Nephthys, Neith, Selkis). Statues, mostly of gilded wood, represented either deities (Anubis, Hathor, Ihy) or the king himself in various poses and with various attributes. Several beds decorated with the head of a lion, cow, or hippopotamus (figure 60) were typically funerary, while another bed, a folding one, might have been used by the king

Fig. 60. Hippopotamus head decorating a funerary bed. Gilded wood. Tomb of Tutankhamun. Dynasty 18. Cairo Museum.

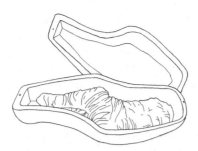

Fig. 61. Piece of mummified beef in its "coffin." Tomb of Yuya and Tuya (Valley of the Kings 46). Dynasty 18. Cairo Museum.

during his lifetime. Model boats recalled the pilgrimages the king was believed to make after death. Also ritual in intent were mummified food offerings, some of them in boxes shaped like their content: haunches of meat, ducks, loaves of bread, and so forth (figure 61).

Other objects were not funerary in nature but related to the royal office. Examples of these are certain seats or thrones, a painted chest depicting the pharaoh in scenes of hunting and warfare, ceremonial chariots (probably never used), a fly-whisk, staffs, and scepters.

Finally, a number of objects apparently had to do with the daily life of the king. Some of them had been used, while others were probably made to be placed in the tomb: a folding bed for travel, chairs, chests, games (*senet*), everyday and ceremonial clothing, sandals, wigs, and so forth. Besides the jewels found on the mummy, others were stored in chests. Some of these must have been stolen, for jewels were found on the ground, dropped by the thieves when their "work" was interrupted. The objects also included weapons, such as "boomerangs,"[21] lances, and a dagger with a blade of iron, a metal rare in that period.

The tombs of private persons did not contain such riches, of course. Still, the tomb of the architect Kha, found intact at Deir el-Medina in 1906 and dating to around 1400 B.C.E., contained a large quantity of funerary furnishings that are now in the Turin Museum.[22] Among them we may cite the funerary beds with lion paws and a frame of woven plant fibers; the bed of Meryt, Kha's wife, was adorned with sheets, a fringed blanket, and a headrest

wrapped in cloth to make it more comfortable. Other furniture was found, including chairs, one of them a folding chair, little tables (one of them, made of rushes, still bore loaves of bread), a number of chests containing toilet objects (figure 62), linens, and Meryt's wig. The sarcophagi were draped with large pieces of cloth, and many items of fabric were placed in chests, including tunics, shawls, G-strings, sheets, and rugs. Meryt's "sewing box" still contained needles. There was abundant pottery: large amphorae, both decorated and undecorated, contained foodstuffs (salted meat, wine, flour), while small vases of terra cotta, faïence, or alabaster contained perfumed oils and kohl. The basketwork was especially well preserved, most of it made of palm fibers or woven reeds. Finally, we may cite Kha's professional implements, which included cubit rods (one of them folding), a scale case, an ax, and a chisel.

We can observe a change in tomb furnishings between Dynasty 18 and Dynasties 21–22: the quantity of specifically funerary objects became much greater, while objects of daily life became fewer.[23] In Dynasty 18, tombs included many pieces of furniture, toilet objects, vases, and fabrics; such objects seem to have decreased in number around 1300 B.C.E., and they nearly disappeared toward 1100 B.C.E. In Dynasties 21–22, the tombs contained essentially *ushabtis*, funerary papyri, and sometimes

Fig. 62. Box with toilet objects of the lady Meryt. Tomb of Kha (Deir el-Medina 8). Deir el-Medina. Dynasty 19. Turin Museum.

wooden statuettes of Osiris. These changes occurred especially in private tombs but also, it seems, in the tombs of kings: the furnishings of the kings of Tanis are much less varied than those of Tutankhamun. These changes do not seem, however, to reflect conceptual changes regarding life in the world beyond.

THE TOMBS

After nearly a thousand years of custom, the pyramid tomb was abandoned by the pharaohs of the New Kingdom. Too ostentatious and too apt to attract tomb robbers, it was replaced by rock-cut tombs dug into the desolate wadis. As Ineni affirms in an inscription in his tomb:

> I supervised the excavation of the cliff-tomb of his majesty, alone, no one seeing, no one hearing.[24]

Ineni was the architect who constructed the tomb of Tuthmosis I, the first to be located in what would become the Valley of the Kings. We must recall, moreover, that this valley is situated at the foot of the Theban peak, which in many respects resembles a pyramid. This choice to hide the tomb entailed its separation from the funerary temple, which from that time on would be constructed in the valley, often at a great distance. The entrances to the tombs of the pharaohs of Dynasty 18 answer well to this desire for secrecy, but later, they would become monumental, undoubtedly because Egyptians were by then convinced of the uselessness of hiding them. In fact, only completely fortuitous circumstances made it possible for the tomb of Tutankhamun to have been the object of only some initial pillaging. From that time on, security would depend essentially on the presence of guards at each of the access routes to the Valley of the Kings. Without doubt, the interior layout of the tombs was conceived so as to discourage robbers: there were vertical shafts opening up in the descending corridors, pseudo-funerary chambers, and changes in the axis of the corridors. When all was said and done, however, these measures proved ineffective. In fact, in Dynasty 20, under Ramesses IX (c. 1110), those in charge of the royal necropolis turned into robbers, or at least into accomplices of robbers, and one by one all the tombs were violated. By chance, we have part of the proceedings of the judicial inquiry that was carried out on this occasion, which demonstrates that the corruption probably went all the way up to the mayor of Thebes:

> We left to commit thefts in the funerary monuments in the manner to which we quite regularly conformed. . . . We found the god (= the dead pharaoh) lying in his grave. . . . We found the grave of the royal wife . . . in the space beside him. . . . We opened their sarcophagi and their coffins, in which they were. We found . . . that the venerable mummy of this king was entirely covered with gold. . . . We collected the gold that we found on this august mummy of this god, as well as the amulets and jewels which were on his neck and the coffins in which he rested. . . . We set fire to their coffins; we took their accessories, which we found with them and which consisted of utensils of silver and copper. We made a division among ourselves.[25]

The passage continues, "It is thus that with the thieves, my companions, we continued to this day our practice of pillaging the tombs of the nobles and the people of the land who rest in the west of Thebes. And a great number of the men of the land were pillaging them like us and our accomplices."[26]

This pillaging is what led the Theban priests, under Herihor and Pinudjem, to collect the royal mummies in caches, as at Deir el-Bahari, or in tombs they regarded as more secure, such as that of Amenhotep II.

The tomb of Sethos I (figure 63) is an excellent example of the funerary architecture of the New Kingdom.[27] A series of downward sloping corridors alternating with staircases leads to the shaft room, which is decorated with scenes of the pharaoh in the presence of various deities. The visitor then penetrates into a first pillared hall that simulates a burial chamber. From there, a new corridor leads down toward another pillared hall, at the back of which, under a vault, lay the sarcophagus.[28]

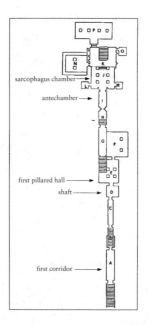

sarcophagus chamber

antechamber

first pillared hall

shaft

first corridor

Fig. 63. Plan of the tomb of Sethos I. Valley of the Kings, no. 17. Dynasty 19.

The adjacent rooms must have contained funerary furnishings. Though it was not completed (in places, we can still see sketches in red ink), the decoration of this tomb is rich indeed, and its style recalls that of the temple the king constructed for himself at Abydos. Many scenes are taken from the Amduat and the Book of Gates. This tomb is one of the largest in the Valley of the Kings.

Some years ago, K. Weeks rediscovered a tomb (KV 5) in the Valley of the Kings.[29] It had been briefly explored in 1825 by J. Burton, who considered it to be of no interest. What is more, in 1922, H. Carter had used it to dump the rubble from his own excavations. In 1988, there was a plan to construct a parking lot nearby and to use it again to store rubble. Before this work began, Weeks requested authorization to explore the tomb, and he discovered that it was of huge dimensions: this was the tomb of the sons of Ramesses II. Located just opposite the latter's tomb, this one is probably the largest in the Valley of the Kings, and even in all Egypt. It contains at least a hundred chapels and perhaps the same number of burial chambers. Its investigation is still under way.

The tombs of private persons were also usually cut into the rock, but they often had a su-

perstructure consisting of a chapel made of stuccoed brick. Though the kings had abandoned the pyramid form, the artisans of the village of Deir el-Medina kept the memory of it alive: their funerary chapels were surmounted by little pyramids, of which there are still some examples (restored in modern times by B. Bruyère, figures 64, 65, and 66).[30] In this period, there were many other cemeteries of private persons in the Theban region, including those of Qurna and Qurnet Murai. The tombs were often well constructed and decorated with care, especially when they belonged to high-ranking individuals but also when they were constructed by the workmen of Deir el-Medina for their own use: those of Sennedjem (figure 67), Inkhau, and Pashed are especially fine examples of decorated tombs.

Moreover, ongoing excavations in the Memphite region, especially at Saqqara, have brought to light a rather large number of tombs of important individuals from the New Kingdom. Examples are the tomb of General Haremhab (figure 68), which was abandoned when he became king; the tomb of the vizier Aper-El, who lived under Amenhotep III; and, discovered more recently still, that of Maya, the "nurse" of Tutankhamun. The tombs of Aper-El and Maya are located in the "hillside" of the Buba-

Fig. 64. The necropolis of the artisans. Deir el-Medina. New Kingdom.

Fig. 65. Pyramid-entrance to a tomb. Necropolis of the artisans. Deir el-Medina. New Kingdom.

steion, and they were discovered and excavated by A. Zivie.[31]

Also at Saqqara, certain New Kingdom tombs located near that of Haremhab were mastabas with little pyramids attached to them (figure 69). The majority of the population, however, continued to be buried in simple pits.

OSIRIAN IMMORTALITY

It was in the New Kingdom that Osiris (figure 70) came to play a major role in funerary belief. The myth of Osiris was already present in the Pyramid Texts, but only now, a millennium later, did it assume more elaborate and

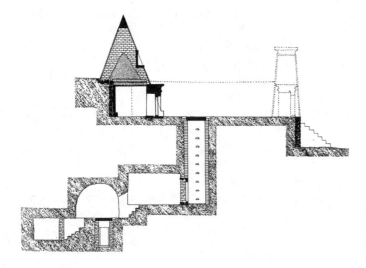

Fig. 66. Section of the tomb of Sennedjem (Deir el-Medina 1). Deir el-Medina. Dynasty 19. After B. Bruyère.

Fig. 67. Activities of the deceased and his wife in the afterlife (A), the deceased conducted by Anubis (B). Paintings from the tomb of Sennedjem (Deir el-Medina no. 1). Deir el-Medina. Dynasty 19.

complex forms. Originally, it seems, Osiris had a double function, royal and agrarian. He was in fact the principle behind the growth of the plant world and incarnate in the grain that sprouted; this role would be recalled by the "Osiris beds" (figure 71) placed in tombs from the New Kingdom on. At the same time, already in the Old Kingdom, he was the model with whom the deceased king was identified.

While there are various versions of the leg-

Fig. 68. Haremhab before his offering table. Bas-relief in limestone from his Memphite tomb. South Saqqara. End of Dynasty 18.

end of Osiris, late sources, mostly Greek, enable us to reconstitute a "mythic core" to which diverse and heterogeneous traditions came to be attached. King of Egypt at a time in the remote past, before the beginning of history, Osiris incurred the jealousy of his brother Seth, who resolved to usurp his power. Treacherously, Seth succeeded in killing him, and he cut his body into pieces, which he scattered throughout the nomes of Egypt (or into the Nile, according to one version). The number of pieces varied, according to the traditions, from

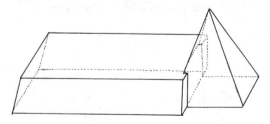

Fig. 69. Restoration of a mastaba with an adjoining pyramid. South Saqqara. New Kingdom.

fourteen to forty-two, the latter number corresponding in theory to the number of nomes (and to that of the forty-two gods who played the role of Osiris's assistants in the next world). Isis, Osiris's wife, searched through all of Egypt for the scattered pieces of her husband's body, and then she magically put him back together and brought him to life, with the result that he was able to impregnate her with a child. This child would be the god Horus, the avenger of his father and his successor on the throne of Egypt (figure 72). In another version, which somewhat contradicts the one just summarized, Isis succeeded in collecting all of Osiris's members except for his phallus, which had been devoured by fish in the Nile. We find an echo of this tradition in the practice, which was frequent, of emasculating mummies: Sethos I and Ramesses II are well-known examples.[32]

As a dead god, Osiris quite naturally became god of the dead, though he retained his agrarian dimension. It was always he who was responsible for the rise of the waters at the time of inundation and for the growth of the grain (figure 73). In consequence, the pharaoh, who was his successor, was also a guarantor of the fertility of the soil. In the Greek interpretation of Egyptian myths, Osiris appears as the inventor of agriculture, which he taught to humankind, who had previously practiced anthropophagy.[33] From the New Kingdom on, Osiris played a preponderant role in Egyptian beliefs about the afterlife. Henceforth, the place where the dead resided was viewed as a subterranean realm over which Osiris ruled with the help of his "assistants."

After the funeral rites were performed—in particular, the Opening of the Mouth ceremony that was believed to restore the use of the senses—the deceased was placed in his tomb. This was the beginning of his "new life," which regular offerings would help to assure. For even more assurance, the offerings were also represented on the walls of the tomb. It is clear that for the Egyptians, death was not a definitive state but rather just a passage between two forms of existence. This second life began with a veritable journey in the next

Fig. 70. The god Osiris. Wall painting from the tomb of Sennedjem (Deir el-Medina no. 1). Deir el-Medina. Dynasty 19.

Fig. 71. "Grain Osiris." Wooden mold for making "Osiris gardens." Cairo Museum.

world. The first and most important step was the Judgment of the Dead (this was an individual judgment quite different from the Last Judgment of Christians and Muslims, which is collective and will take place at the end of time). Holding the deceased by the hand, Anubis conducted him to the scale on which his heart would be weighed. It was undoubtedly at this moment that the deceased was believed to address his declaration of innocence, or "negative confession" to Osiris:

> I have not killed, I have not commanded to kill, I have not made suffering for anyone. . . . I have not laid anything upon the weights of the hand-balance. . . . I have not taken the milk from the mouths of children.

The deceased also addressed the forty-two assistants of Osiris to affirm his innocence:

Fig. 72. Horus (left) and Osiris. Bas-relief. Funerary temple of Sethos I. Abydos. Dynasty 19.

> O Swallower of Shades who came forth from Kernet, I have not slain people . . . , O Breaker of Bones who came forth from Heracleopolis, I have not stolen food . . . , O He-who-is-Blood who came forth from the place of slaughter, I have not done grain-profiteering.[34]

The heart was placed on one pan of the scale, while the feather of Maat, symbolizing truth and justice, rested on the other. The heart had to be lighter than the feather, or it would mean that the bad deeds of the deceased would prevail over his good ones, in which case he would be fodder for Amyt (the Devouress), who was sitting by the scale, ready to swallow him. This possibility (scarcely to be imagined, it would seem) would have condemned the deceased to a "second death," this one definitive. The god Thoth, in the form of an ibis-headed man, recorded the results of the weighing on a sheet of papyrus; in the form of a baboon, he could also be present atop, or beside, the scale. This presence recalled the wisdom that Thoth

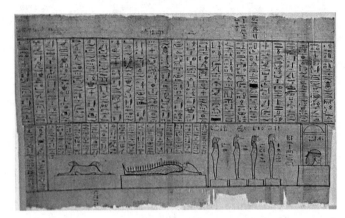

Fig. 73. Grain sprouting from the mummy of Osiris. Papyrus Jumilhac. Ptolemaic Period. Louvre.

Fig. 74. The tribunal of Osiris. Book of Gates, fifth hour. After E. Hornung, 1999.

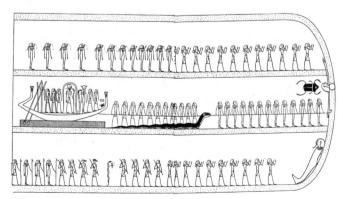

Fig. 75. The nocturnal journey of the deceased. Amduat, twelfth hour. After E. Hornung, 1999.

incarnated, and it guaranteed the integrity of the procedure.[35] Otherwise, the baboon could be replaced by Maat herself.[36] Having at this point been "vindicated," the deceased was led before Osiris, who was accompanied by Isis, Nephthys, and the four Sons of Horus. From that time on, having become the equal of the god, he was "the Osiris N," and he could continue to exist in the life beyond. But before this could happen, he had to undertake a journey strewn with traps: he had to pass through gateways guarded by redoubtable genies armed with knives, and he had to confront all sorts of hybrid monsters. To reach his destination, he had to know and recite the propitiatory formulas written down in the Book of the Dead.

The texts describing this process were consigned to rolls of papyrus, decorated with vignettes. These papyri were placed in the tomb, either directly on the mummy, like a vade mecum, or in a little box that was sometimes surmounted by a wooden statuette of Osiris. These texts played the same role as those carved or painted on coffins in the Middle Kingdom or, in the Old Kingdom, inside the pyramids. But on the walls of the funerary chambers of the royal tombs of the New Kingdom, artisans painted or carved texts evoking the destiny of the deceased king in the realm of the dead: the Book of Gates, the Book of Caverns, the Amduat, and others (figures 74 and 75). These were texts with complex theological content, in which cosmogonic elements played an important role. Representations of the heavens, such as those on the ceiling of the burial chamber of Ramesses VI, were in accordance with ancient belief in a celestial destiny of the king among the stars.

5   The Later Stages of Pharaonic History

After the New Kingdom, there were several periods of history that were politically and culturally rather distinct from one another. The first millennium was the era of invasions and foreign dominations, yet the succession of dynasties continued without interruption down to the conquest of Egypt by Alexander the Great in 332.

The Third Intermediate Period (Dynasties 21–25, 1069–664 B.C.E.) represented a continuity with the civilization of the New Kingdom. Thebes remained an extremely important religious center and thus a center of political power, though another power center was founded at Tanis in the delta by the sovereigns of Dynasty 22. The "Libyan" Dynasty 23 began a period of upheaval that included territorial division and competition for power among rival dynasties, and even Assyrian invasions. There was then a return to a strong and centralized kingdom with the Saite sovereigns of Dynasty 26 (664–525 B.C.E.). Independence was finally lost with the two episodes of Persian domination (525–398 and 341–332 B.C.E.), which would come to an end with the "liberation" represented (in the eyes of the Greeks, that is) by the conquest of Alexander.

THE THIRD INTERMEDIATE PERIOD

At the beginning of the first millennium, under Dynasty 21 (1069–945 B.C.E.), there was further progress in the technique of mummification, at least as concerns the appearance of the mummy. A particularly striking example is that of Queen Henuttawy (figure 76), wife of Pinudjem I, whose mummy was found in the cache at Deir el-Bahari: packets of sawdust were placed under the skin of her face via the interior of the mouth in such a way as to restore a volume comparable to that during life. Unfortunately, with time, the skin cracked, which ran counter to the intended goal; in modern times, the mummy was restored by Professor N. Iskander.[1] In the arms, the neck, and the back, incisions were made in order to introduce packing; the evisceration incision was also used for this purpose. This procedure of subcutaneous packing seems to have been rather widespread in this period. Besides sawdust, other ingredients were used, including clay, sand, resin, and linen. There were further means of improving the appearance of the mummies, such as the insertion of artificial eyes in the orbits. The skin was often painted with yellow (for women) or red (for men) ocher. The mummy of Nedjmet (figure 77), wife of Herihor, high priest of Amun at the end of Dynasty 20, was provided with false eyebrows made of human hair. The "treatment" she received conferred a youthful appearance, though she was a relatively old woman at the time of her death, and a wig served to mask the onset of baldness. Her mummy was further "embellished" by the addition of sawdust between the bandages.[2] Masaharta (figure 78 now on exhibit at the Museum of Mummification in Luxor), son of Pinudjem I, high priest and general during the reigns of his father and of Smendes, has a swollen appearance characteristic of the mummies of this period.[3] A little later, in the case of Djedptahiufankh (figure 79), priest of Amun and perhaps related to the royal family, whose mummy was also found in the cache at Deir el-Bahari, the face looks won-

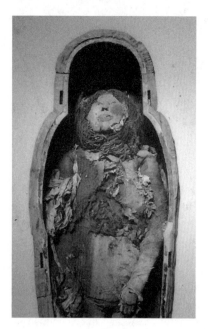

Fig. 76. Mummy of Queen Henuttawy, wife of Pinudjem I, in its coffin. Dynasty 21. Cairo Museum.

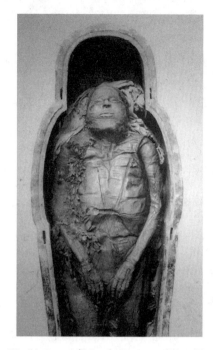

Fig. 78. Mummy of Masaharta, son of Pinudjem I, in its coffin. Dynasty 21. Museum of Mummification, Luxor.

derfully vivacious, though the results of the treatment of his limbs were less successful.[4] But the mummies buried in the royal necropolis of Tanis, which of course must have received especially painstaking treatment, were found in extremely bad condition because of the dampness of the ground in the delta. This fact

once again illustrates the principle that good treatment was not sufficient to assure the preservation of the body: it was necessary for the burial chamber or the place of burial to assure a constant aridity.[5]

The viscera, which had previously been placed in canopic vases, were now reintroduced into the abdominal cavity after having

Fig. 77. Head of the mummy of Queen Nedjmet, wife of Herihor. Dynasty 20. Cairo Museum.

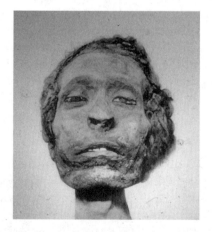

Fig. 79. Head of the mummy of Djedptahiufankh, son-in-law of Pinudjem II. Dynasty 21. Cairo Museum.

been mummified and wrapped in linen; we call these "canopic packets." They were accompanied by amulets representing the four Sons of Horus, recalling, as had the sculpted lids of canopic vases that preceded them, the protective role these four figures played with regard to the mummified organs. Despite this innovation, canopic vessels continued to be sculpted, but these were imitations, blocks of solid stone whose presence was merely a nod to tradition.

This "standard" of mummification would continue down to the end of Dynasty 22. There were the usual variations in quality, of course, according to the resources of the individuals concerned; the royal mummies continued to exemplify the highest quality as regards wrappings and mummification techniques (figures 80 and 81).

Stone sarcophagi were rare, even among the ruling class, which had used them often in earlier periods. As for the pharaohs, they often contented themselves with reusing sarcophagi made for their predecessors. Thus, in the royal tombs of Tanis (figure 82), eight of the thirteen sarcophagi discovered were reused, and the original inscriptions had not been entirely erased, making it possible to identify, among their previous "owners," King Merneptah and a priest named Amenhotep; the latter had been buried at Thebes in the New Kingdom.[6] Still others had been fashioned from architectural fragments or even statues. Inside these stone sarcophagi, the pharaohs were encased in coffins of silver, such as those of Psusennes and Shoshenq II (we must note that in Egypt, silver had long been more precious than gold). Moreover, funerary masks of solid gold were still in use, as evidenced by those of the pharaohs Amenemope, Psusennes (figure 83), and Shoshenq II, as well as that of General Undebaunded, also from Tanis.

Private persons continued to be provided with wooden anthropoid coffins (figure 84), as in the New Kingdom. A huge group (in the hundreds) of coffins of the high priests of Amun at Thebes was found at Deir el-Bahari beneath the first court of the temple of Hatshepsut, a site bearing the name of Bab el-Gusus.[7] In many cases, the mummy bandages

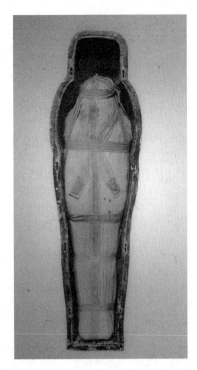

Fig. 80. Mummy of Queen Isetemkheb, wife of Pinudjem II, in its coffin. Dynasty 21. Cairo Museum.

were inscribed, making it possible to identify their occupants. Many of these mummies, covered by a sculpted and painted wooden board (a practice already in use in the Ramesside Period), were placed in an anthropoid sarcophagus, which was itself inside a second sarcophagus of the same type.[8] The exterior decoration of the sarcophagi largely recalls

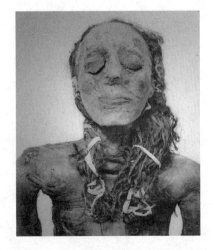

Fig. 81. Head of the mummy of Queen Nesikhons, wife of Pinudjem II. Dynasty 21. Cairo Museum.

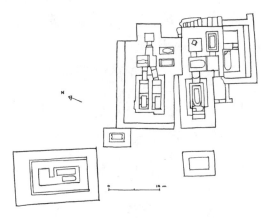

Fig. 82. Plan of the royal necropolis of Tanis.

divided into registers decorated with various religious motifs and texts. The interior of the trough is entirely occupied by representations of funerary deities. Sarcophagi of the period also display some unusual depictions, as in the case of the sarcophagus of Amenemone (figure 85).

At the end of Dynasty 21, there seem to have been changes in this decoration, which became more and more ornate. The principal motifs were borrowed from the Book of the Dead: the journey of the deceased in the world beyond and the Judgment before Osiris. Other motifs are from solar mythology or depict cosmogonical themes, such as the separation of Geb and Nut. Many have to do with the resurrection of the deceased. There are, however, significant variations in the decoration, a fact that leads us to think that the artisans had a relative free-

that in use at the end of the Ramesside Period: the motifs are painted in vivid colors on a yellow background, and the head of the deceased is usually depicted on the lid, most of which is

Fig. 83. Gold mask of Psusennes I. Tanis. Dynasty 21. Cairo Museum.

Fig. 84. The two nested coffins, with a board covering the mummy, of Sutymes. Late Period. Louvre.

dom of choice. We note that often the sun god predominates and that he is invoked, instead of Osiris, in the offering formulas. It seems that in this period, private persons appropriated what had earlier been a royal privilege, that is, assimilation to the sun. The interior of the sarcophagus often includes, on the floor, a representation of the Goddess of the West or of the *djed*-pillar, a symbol of Osiris that signifies sta-

bility. Some scholars have identified this pillar as a spinal column, which would explain its presence just below the back of the deceased. The goddess Nut is often represented inside the lid (or sometimes on the floor of the trough).[9] Otherwise, a large number of sarcophagi, probably intended for less important individuals, are of a rather mediocre quality and have stereotyped decoration.

In Dynasty 22, there were important changes in the equipment of the mummy, and these can be noted in all classes of society. In particular, there was growing use of a new type of container: the cartonnage (figure 86). Though attested in the Middle Kingdom—at least, in the form of a mask—it was not until this later period that it was more commonly used. A cartonnage was a sort of mold that entirely enclosed the mummy; it was made of compressed and stuccoed cloth. This mold was made by placing the material on an anthropoid core of clay mixed with straw. Once it dried, a longitudinal cut though the dorsal portion made it possible to separate the cartonnage from its "mannequin." The result was a sort of box in which the mummy was placed. The two parts of the cartonnage were then held together by lacing. The name "cartonnage" has been given to these objects because in the Ptolemaic Period, compressed papyri were often used instead of cloth, creating the appearance of cardboard (in French, "carton"). It

Fig. 85. Detail of the coffin of Amenemone, exterior surface of the trough: horse-headed serpent. Third Intermediate Period. Louvre.

was only after the mummy was placed in its "box" that the cartonnage received its painted decoration. It is likely that the manufacture of a cartonnage was much less costly than that of a wooden coffin, given the relative rarity of wood in Egypt. Certain persons, of course, were provided with both a cartonnage and a coffin, but the cartonnage was often the sole outer container of the mummy.[10]

There were changes in the royal tombs and in those of high-ranking individuals. The Valley of the Kings was officially abandoned, for its vulnerability had been proved. Ramesses XI was the last pharaoh known to have been buried there. In Dynasty 21, under Pinudjem II (figure 87), the royal mummies of Dynasties 18 to 21 were secretly hidden in the cache at Deir el-Bahari (DB 320), and in the tomb of Amenhotep II (KV 35), as well. After that, the custom arose of constructing tombs near temples, within the sacred enclosures, in the hope of assuring them a heightened security. Thus, the royal tombs of Tanis were constructed in the enclosure of the temple of Amun. These tombs have for the most part lost their superstructures, but scholars think they were of the same type as those built later, at Medinet Habu, for the Divine Adoratrices of Amun: tombs in the form of a temple with a pylon at the entrance,

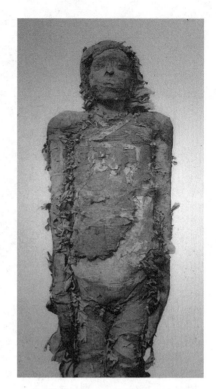

Fig. 87. Mummy of Pinudjem II. Dynasty 21. Cairo Museum.

an open-air court, and a roofed chapel. The subterranean burial chamber was accessed via a shaft dug under the chapel.[11] While some of the royal tombs of Tanis had been "visited," though not completely, others had escaped pillaging. In the case of the tomb of Shoshenq III, the thieves had succeeded in digging a tunnel that took them directly into the burial chamber, next to the sarcophagus. The opulence of the funerary furnishings discovered in the majority of these tombs demonstrates that the pillaging had been anything but complete.

One of the most important funerary assemblages from this period is the large collective tomb of the Dynasty 21 priests and priestesses discovered in 1891 at Deir el-Bahari (figure 88).[12] A corridor about 330 feet long leads to two contiguous burial chambers. A little in front of these chambers, a second corridor branches off at a right angle; it is about 165 feet long, and it descends to a depth of about 330 feet. The tomb contained 254 sarcophagi (153 mummies, 101 of them with two sarcophagi), often in a remarkable state of preser-

Fig. 86. Cartonnages of two Theban priestesses. Bab el-Gusus. Dynasty 21–22. © Copyright the Trustees of The British Museum.

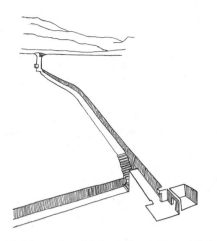

Fig. 88. The cache of Bab el-Gusus. Deir el-Bahari. Dynasty 21. After R. Czerner.

vation, piled up in the corridors and chambers. For the priests, this collective tomb was the counterpart of the royal cache at Deir el-Bahari. It was probably under Psusennes II, at the end of Dynasty 21, that this tomb was dug to shelter the sarcophagi and what remained of the equipment (*ushabtis,* canopic vases, statuettes of Osiris) of the priests and priestesses of Amun, who had originally been buried in various tombs in the Theban necropolis. This kind of equipment was rather similar to that of the kings (figure 89).

As for private persons in this period, most tombs in the Theban region were composed of a simple chamber excavated into the cliffside. It must be noted that the Theban mountain, which was steep and rocky, offered far more

opportunities to dig tombs that were likely to endure than did the flat, sandy delta region. In fact, few tombs found in the delta go back to this period.

THE KUSHITE, SAITE, AND PERSIAN PERIODS

From Dynasty 25 (715–656 B.C.E.) on, there was no great change in the mummification process. The "canopic packets," though, were now placed next to the mummy, or even between its legs, or, much more rarely, following old tradition, in canopic jars. In this period, there was a custom of coating the body with a black substance, glistening like pitch, brittle and with vitreous reflections; this substance is habitually called "bitumen," though its chemical composition could vary. Still, the term continues to be used, because its Arabic equivalent, *mumia,* is the origin of our word "mummy." Bodies thus treated have often been called "black mummies," as opposed to those prepared according to the traditional method; the latter are sometimes called "white mummies," though they are actually chamois in color. It seems that this black product had antiseptic properties and that it also made bodies more rigid. In the same way, a black substance was often used to coat the mummy bandages, doubtless to help the various layers of cloth to stick together. Certain coffins were also daubed with black, but it is uncertain whether this was the same substance: it might

Fig. 89. Ushabti box of Pinudjem I. Stuccoed and painted wood. Dynasty 21. Cairo Museum.

have been a transparent product (varnish, perhaps) that blackened over time, for in many cases, its presence masks painted decoration.

The care with which certain mummies were prepared contrasts with the bad quality of many others. Among the factors explaining the existence of "bad" mummies, we must perhaps make reference to what Herodotus reports:

> When the wife of a distinguished man dies, or any woman who happens to be beautiful or well known, her body is not given to the embalmers immediately, but only after the lapse of three or four days. This is a precautionary measure to prevent the embalmers from violating the corpse, a thing which is said actually to have happened in the case of a woman who had just died. The culprit was given away by one of his fellow workmen.[13]

Of course, a delay in beginning the mummification process, which must often have been the cause of mummies of bad quality, could be explained in many other, more plausible ways—for instance, a sudden increase in the number of bodies needing to be treated, as would have been the case during an epidemic.

A mummy found by W. M. F. Petrie in an unviolated tomb in the necropolis of Tell el-Nebsha (eastern delta), dating to a period between Dynasties 26 and 30, enables us to form an idea of where amulets were placed on mummies. In this period, in fact, amulets were particularly abundant. There were forty amulets in place on the mummy, in particular on the upper torso, near the heart, and in the pelvic area. These were mostly symbolic objects intended to guarantee the deceased his food (*udjat*-eye), his stability (*djed*-pillar, mason's level), his protection (*tit*-knot of Isis), his resurrection (scarab, frog), and his eternal youth (papyrus scepter).[14]

As in the preceding periods, the "leftovers" from the embalming process—that is to say, the material that had served to embalm the deceased, along with the "biological residues"—were buried near the tomb. A cache dating probably to the Saite Period has been found near Giza. It contained thirty ceramic vessels of various sorts, the inscription on one of them indicating that it contained a "cleansing" product. Another pot was a container for na-

tron. Also found in tombs of these later periods were instruments used in the embalming process: tongs, knives, hooks, and a special, two-spouted funnel that was inserted into the nostrils to help fill the cranial cavity with resin.[15]

The sarcophagi of Dynasty 25 represent a transitional phase: cartonnages, now less numerous, were replaced by anthropoid wooden coffins with a rectangular base and a dorsal pillar, all this covered with inscriptions. It is possible that this form of sarcophagus was conceived of to facilitate setting the mummy upright, which was indispensable to the Opening of the Mouth ritual during the funeral ceremonies. In certain cases, the deceased was provided with an external coffin in the form of a box with a convex lid and, at the corners, four pillars on which falcons could be placed, as on the coffin of Djedthothiufankh (figure 90), found at Deir el-Bahari.[16] This type of coffin in the form of a chapel had affinities with certain examples from the Old Kingdom. In Dynasty 25, as later, in the Saite Period (which was marked by the rise to power of Dynasty 26, from Sais), we observe a clear archaizing tendency in the decoration of the funerary furnishings. Thus, the motif of the two eyes reappeared on the external wall at the head end of the coffin, with its double function of magical protection and a "window" to the exterior.

In the most complete cases, the Saite Period saw the use of ensembles including an interior anthropoid coffin with pedestal that was nested in a second anthropoid coffin, both contained

Fig. 90. Coffin with pillars of Djedthothiufankh. Deir el-Bahari. Dynasty 25. Oxford, Ashmolean Museum.

in an outer coffin that could be either anthropoid or in the form of a "box." The decoration of certain anthropoid sarcophagi consisted especially of bands of text surrounding copies of scenes from the Book of the Dead. The trough of the inner coffin was usually decorated on the outside with either a *djed*-pillar or columns of text, while the interior often bore a representation of Nut, as in the preceding period (figure 91), or Hathor. The exterior of the foot end of the trough was often decorated with a running Apis bull carrying the deceased on its back (figure 92), a motif that had already made its appearance in the Libyan Period. This type of sarcophagus was used throughout the Saite Period, both at Thebes and in the Memphite region. A characteristic example is the coffin of Peftjauneith from Saqqara, now in the Leiden Museum.[17] The outer surface of the lid is mostly covered with bands of texts carefully written below an image of a winged Nut, while another image of a nude, standing Nut giving birth to the sun is painted on the inner surface. As can happen in this period, the mask is painted green to stress the identification of the deceased with Osiris. The color green evokes the connection of the god with the forces of vegetation.

In the Saite Period, we note a return to the use of stone sarcophagi, in private as well as in royal tombs. While the mummies they contained usually had one or two wooden coffins, they were placed directly in the stone trough. These sarcophagi could be rectangular with palace façade panels in Old Kingdom style, though this motif was relatively rare. We know

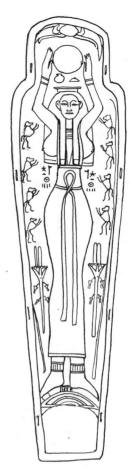

Fig. 91. The goddess Nut. Internal surface of the lid of the coffin of Hetepamun. Stuccoed and painted wood. West Thebes (?). Dynasty 25. Heidelberg, Universitäts-Sammlung.

Fig. 92. Apis bull carrying a mummy. Foot of a coffin. Stuccoed and painted wood. Late Period. Vienna, Kunsthistorisches Museum.

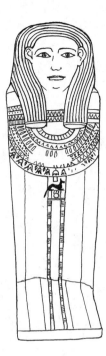

Most often, Saite sarcophagi are anthropoid in form (figure 93), rather massive and with thick walls, and they are made of hard stone, such as basalt, for reasons of security. The texts on the sarcophagi are taken from the Pyramid Texts, another example of the archaizing taste of this period. As for nonanthropoid sarcophagi, they reproduce models of the New Kingdom, with the head end rounded and the width of the trough tapering toward the feet. The decoration could also be inspired by old models; thus, the decoration of the sarcophagus of Hapymen, now in the British Museum, faithfully copies that of the sarcophagus of King Tuthmosis III, though the shape of the latter has not been reproduced.[19]

Certain tombs of Dynasties 25 and 26 are especially well preserved. This is the case with those of the Divine Adoratrices of Amun, which were built near the temple of Medinet Habu and present the appearance of miniature temples (figure 94). The same is true for the tombs of high-ranking personages built in the Asasif, one of the Theban cemeteries, in particular that of Mentuemhet, mayor of Thebes. The proportions of the chapels are often monumental, and the subterranean parts excavated into the rock recall the royal tombs in their size and complexity.

The tombs discovered by A. Fakhry in Bahriya Oasis provide a highly representative example of the architecture and the decoration of private tombs in the Saite Period. The tombs of Djedamuniufankh and his grandson Bannentiu display an elaborate decoration evoking the funeral ritual, along with representations of the next world, including, in the tomb of

Fig. 93. Coffin of Sepdet, Songstress of Amun. El-Hiba. Saite or Persian Period. Florence, Museo Archeologico.

that in this period, there was a growing tendency toward archaizing, with copying of Old Kingdom creations. It was in this period that an open-air descending path was dug under the southern face of the pyramid of Djoser in order to remove the blocks obstructing the central shaft that gave access to the burial chamber. The objective of this "archaeological" undertaking might have been to study the internal layout of the tomb, and perhaps even to copy certain bas-reliefs, as seems to be shown by the drawing of "grid lines" on a number of old stelae during this period.[18]

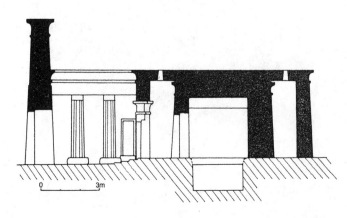

Fig. 94. Section of the tomb of Amenirdis, Divine Adoratrice of Amun. Medinet Habu. Dynasty 25.

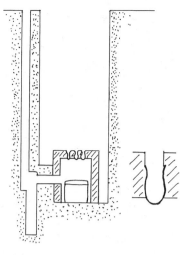

Fig. 96. Section of the protective system of a Saite Period tomb. After A. J. Spencer, 1982.

Fig. 95. Interior of a Persian Period tomb with an anthropoid trough dug into the rock. South Saqqara.

Bannentiu, an extremely rare image of the voyage of the barque of the moon god.[20]

At Memphis, during Dynasty 26 and then in the Persian Period, the tombs with extremely deep shafts must have had superstructures of brick. In some tombs, sarcophagi are cut directly into the stone floor of the funerary chamber (figure 95). The tombs of these periods represent the acme of an ingenious security system (figure 96) whose effectiveness enabled three tombs to survive to us intact. The funerary chamber was constructed at the bottom of a wide shaft. This shaft was filled with sand after the sarcophagus and the tomb furnishings had been placed in the chamber. In the ceiling of this funerary chamber, there were ceramic

Fig. 97. The temple-tomb of the high priest Petosiris. Tuna el-Gebel, cemetery of Hermopolis. End of the fourth century B.C.E.

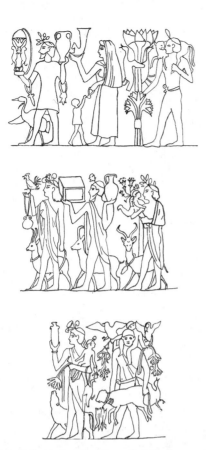

jars whose bottoms were broken when the burial was completed, permitting the sand to flow into the chamber. The last officiants escaped via a second, lateral, narrow shaft; this shaft was also filled with sand after they returned to ground level. It was thus impossible to penetrate into the burial chamber by whatever route was taken, whether the existing shafts or a robber's tunnel, because it would have been filled with sand as soon as anyone tried to clear it.[21]

A beautiful example of funerary architecture, probably dating to the first years of the conquest of Alexander, is the tomb of Petosiris (figure 97) at Tuna el-Gebel, the cemetery of Hermopolis.[22] It has the appearance of a miniature temple, and the "screen walls" of its façade follow a model that would also be used in the Ptolemaic temples. The actual chapel where the offering ritual was carried out is preceded by a columned pronaos. A shaft in the floor of the chapel gives access to the burial chamber, in which was found Petosiris's magnificent coffin (today in the Cairo Museum), whose hieroglyphic inscriptions are made of glass paste inlaid in black-painted wood. The decoration of the tomb (figure 98) is entirely exceptional, displaying changes in the style of

Fig. 98. Offering bearers. Bas-reliefs in the tomb of Petosiris. Tuna el-Gebel, cemetery of Hermopolis. End of the fourth century B.C.E.

Fig. 99. The necropolis of Gebel el-Mawta. Siwa Oasis. Late Period and Ptolemaic and Roman Periods.

representing themes that are otherwise entirely Egyptian (work in the fields, processions of offering bearers, etc.). Greek influence is noticeable in scenes resembling those which decorate Greek funerary stelae; but the sheer quantity of decoration and the movement of individuals, who are often represented frontally, might correspond to a new trend in Egyptian art.

At this time, many tombs were excavated into the hillsides that border the valley. These were often simple, undecorated burial chambers. Such was the case in the necropolis of Siwa Oasis (figure 99), where archaeologists found many tombs dating from Dynasty 26 to the Ptolemaic Period.

It seems that at this time the image of the afterlife took on a decidedly "moral" coloration, as emerges from texts in the tomb of Petosiris:

Amenti is the dwelling of the one without sin: happy is the man who arrives there! No one reaches it save the one whose heart is exact in practicing equity. There, there is no distinction between poor and rich, except in favor of the one who is found to be without sin when the scale and the weight are in front of the Lord of Eternity.[23]

6 The Graeco-Roman Period

The conquest of Egypt by Alexander in 330 B.C.E. marked a turning point in the history of the land. A new dynasty, the Lagide dynasty, assumed the reins of power, and a new capital, Alexandria, was founded. Many of the Graeco-Macedonian immigrants who settled in Egypt, especially during the third century B.C.E., played a dominating role in this period, imposing Greek as the administrative language. Progressively, a double culture established itself in Egypt.

Indigenous revolts and dynastic wars would on several occasions disturb the stability and prosperity of the land; still, the economic and administrative organization undoubtedly changed less than we might think, and religious and cultural traditions remained lively. The foreign communities that settled in Egypt (Greeks, Jews, Persians, Syrians, etc.) practiced their cults without entering into conflict with the traditional religion. Moreover, many foreigners came to practice the Egyptian religion. In the area of funerary practices, in the beginning, Greek immigrants continued to have themselves cremated in conformity with their own customs, but over time, we see them adopting the customs of the land.

Beginning in the thirties B.C.E., the Roman conquest and occupation led to far more profound changes in the society and economy; the temple lands were confiscated, and the clergy was closely supervised. Still, down to the third century of our own era, we find no decline either in the traditional religion or in the funerary practices connected with it. We even see Romans adopting the practice of mummification, a fact that well demonstrates the force and the attraction of the Egyptian model of death.[1]

MUMMIFICATION IN THE GRAECO-ROMAN PERIOD

The dominant phenomenon in the Graeco-Roman Period was not technical progress, which was in fact limited, but rather the extension of mummification to the whole of society. Also well attested is demographic growth: at the beginning of our own era, the population of Egypt has been estimated as about seven million.[2] There was thus a considerable increase in the number of mummies. We also observe a veritable "run" on the cemeteries, with much reuse of old tombs. In the Theban region, many New Kingdom tombs at Deir el-Medina and in the Valley of the Queens were literally stuffed with mummies, mostly anonymous, during the Roman Period. Being less ancient, these mummies had more chance than earlier ones to survive intact, a fact that partly explains the great number of mummies dating to this period.

The techniques of mummification did not change. What changed was the respective proportion of the different categories of treatment that were employed. Use of the simplest and most expeditious techniques made it possible to extend the practice to the poorest levels of the population. For a long time, modern scholars claimed that the quality of mummification had sunk, but nothing could have been further from the truth: there are many examples of high-quality treatment, as shown by studies of the mummies in museums,[3] as well as by the

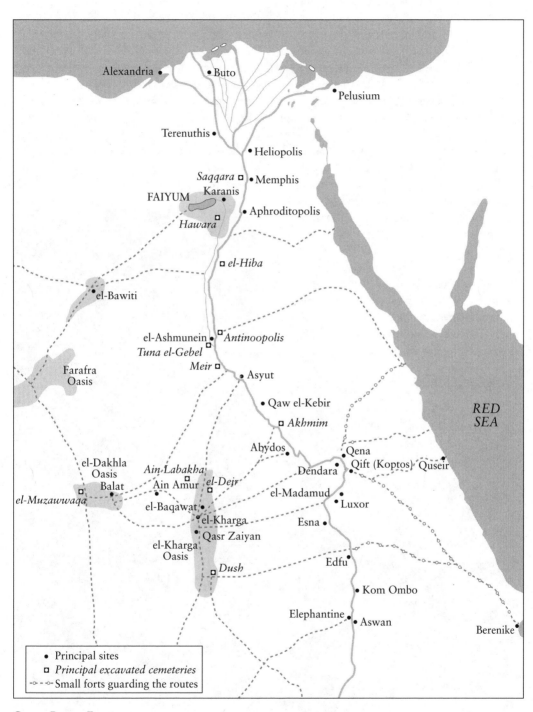

Graeco-Roman Egypt

more recent studies of the mummies in the field.[4]

The procedure used most often in this period was the one that resulted in "black mummies" and that undoubtedly corresponded to the "second class" mummification described by Herodotus. The color black was sometimes used to represent the body of the deceased in vignettes of the Book of the Dead (figure 100) or in tomb paintings in the New Kingdom, a fact that speaks in favor of the antiquity of this technique.[5] This type of image is rather rare, however, the deceased most often being depicted as though still alive. The product responsible for the black color, whose chemical nature and provenance are still debated, might have varied according to region and period. Chemical analyses have shown that in certain cases, it was bitumen, which would have been imported from the Dead Sea, while other studies have revealed the exclusive presence of vegetal products whose black color was presumably due to chemical changes that occurred in the course of time.[6] The use of vegetal materials from the Middle East (cedar oil, for example) is attested

in Ptolemaic Period documents, indicating that the state furnished a determined quantity of them to the embalmers, who were to divide it among their "customers." Though these black mummies have a relatively unflattering appearance, the quality of their preservation is rather good, even when they were not eviscerated. Our experience in the cemeteries of el-Kharga Oasis (figures 101 and 102) has shown that nearly all the mummies there were of this type. The nails and hair (both head and body) are in good condition (figure 103), while the organs still in place, such as the lungs and the liver, are identifiable, making it possible, among other things, to diagnose schistosomiasis, and even

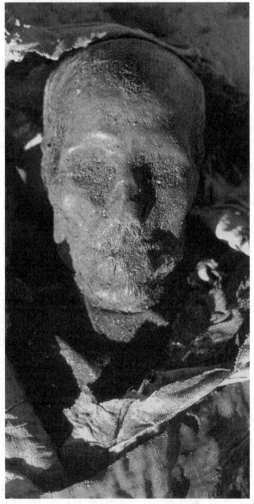

Fig. 101. Head of the mummy of a middle-aged man with its funerary wrappings preserved. Necropolis of Dush, T20 (el-Kharga Oasis). Fourth century C.E.

Fig. 100. Black mummy with its *ba* fluttering above it. Book of the Dead of Tehenna. New Kingdom. Louvre.

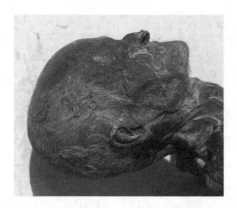

Fig. 102. Head of an old, half-bald man, hair and beard dyed. Necropolis of Ain Labakha, T6 (el-Kharga Oasis). Ptolemaic or Roman Period.

tuberculosis, in a certain number of cases.[7] X-ray study has made it possible to determine these facts and also to refine the comparison of these mummies with those obtained by the "first class" method also represented in these cemeteries.

One of the special characteristics of the mummies of this period is their sometimes "puffy" appearance (figure 104), which gives them a volume almost identical to that during life.[8] The integument is separated from the skeleton, the space thus created being empty, as confirmed by X-ray. This relatively rare situation is perhaps the result of an onset of decomposition that was interrupted by the pro-

cess of desiccation. This particular appearance recalls to a certain extent that of the "natural" mummies of the Predynastic Period. In arid lands, it is not rare to encounter dead animals in the desert that also present this appearance. We may speak of a veritable "foot race" between desiccation and decomposition.

Otherwise, many mummies show signs of a hasty, incomplete treatment that can be explained by the great number of bodies to be treated at one and the same time. It is also possible that treatment had been undertaken too late, the family having been late in delivering the body to the embalmers (figure 105). We no longer try to count the mummies whose heads were detached, an accident that occurred during treatment, as shown by the presence, in the spinal column and in the cranial cavity, of *gerid* intended to reattach (with more or less success) the head to the trunk.[9]

At the very bottom of the quality scale, we find pseudo-mummies of a pleasing but deceptive outward appearance, for once the funerary wrappings are removed, we find ourselves faced with an incredible mixture of bones, sometimes from several individuals, which does not even deserve to be called a mummy.

Finally, it happens that "mummies" of satisfactory appearance turn out to contain nothing but nonhuman artifacts. These false

Fig. 103. Head of the mummy of a little girl with abundant hair. Necropolis of Ain Labakha, T6 (el-Kharga Oasis). Ptolemaic and Roman Periods.

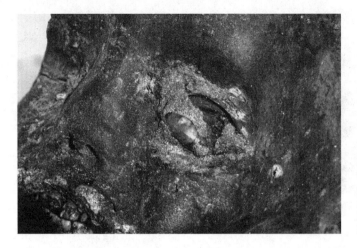

Fig. 104. Head of the mummy of a very young child, retaining his appearance during life. Presence of a nail in the left orbit. Necropolis of Dush, T54 (el-Kharga Oasis). Roman Period.

mummies might have been put together by the embalmers because of the loss or destruction of the body they were supposed to treat: such substitutes were intended to pull the wool over the eyes of the family of the deceased. These false mummies are sometimes difficult to distinguish from false modern examples made for commercial ends when the fashion of antiquities began to spread. We know that in the seventeenth century, certain travelers brought mummies from Egypt that were intended to adorn their "cabinets of curiosities."

There was little variation in the outward appearance of mummies. The arms and legs were usually extended, with the arms placed along the outside surface of the thighs. The hands of young boys were often placed on the genital area. In the case of adults, we also sometimes see the arms crossed in the Osirian position or, alternatively, the right arm extended along the

Fig. 105. Mummies reduced to skeletal state: stalks of *gerid* hold the spinal column and the legs together. Necropolis of Dush, T27 (el-Kharga Oasis). Roman Period.

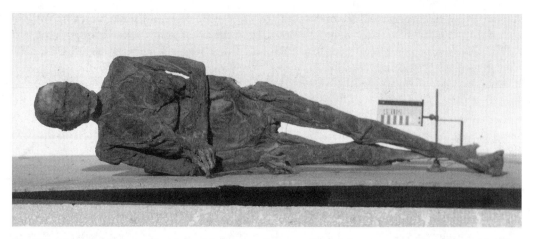

Fig. 106. Mummy of a woman with her left arm bent in front of her abdomen and her legs crossed. Necropolis of Dush, T49 (el-Kharga Oasis). Roman Period.

body and the left arm bent at a right angle in front of the abdomen (figure 106). The latter is already to be seen in the New Kingdom, at least on the lids of coffins—for example, that of the lady Isis from the tomb of Sennedjem at Deir el-Medina.[10]

A practice that seems specific to the Graeco-Roman Period is that of gilding the body (fig-ures 107 and 108). Already in the Hellenistic Period, the eyelids, lips, and nails of certain mummies were occasionally gilded; there are examples of this practice in the necropolis of the priests at Philae.[11] In the Roman Period, small leaves of gold were applied directly to the skin so as to cover, at least partially, the head and the hands and feet. Mummies of this type have been found at Antinoe, in the Theban necropolis, and in some of the cemeteries of el-Kharga Oasis. At Dush, this practice seems not to have been widespread: out of 345 mummies inventoried, only 12 bore traces of gilding.[12] But our study of the Roman Period cemetery of

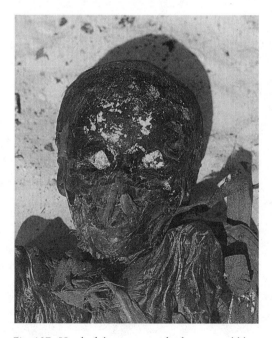

Fig. 107. Head of the mummy of a four-year-old boy presenting numerous traces of gold on the face. Necropolis of Ain Labakha, T6 (el-Kharga Oasis). Ptolemaic and Roman Periods.

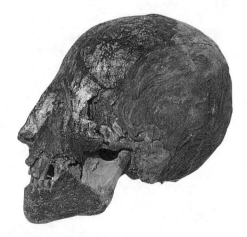

Fig. 108. Head of the mummy of an adult male presenting numerous traces of gold on the face. Necropolis of Dush, T20 (el-Kharga Oasis). First century C.E.

Ain Labakha, twenty-five miles north of the city of el-Kharga, enabled us to count 12 mummies bearing traces of gold out of a total of 70 studied, which is a much larger ratio. The ratio is probably higher still because, of the mummies at this site kept for study, the bandages of a dozen were completely preserved, for the time being preventing a definitive evaluation.[13] We have also found mummies bearing traces of gilding among the human remains at the site of el-Deir, which is currently under study. The use of gilding usually went hand in hand with high-quality mummification and relatively rich funerary furnishings. We may thus assume that gilding was a usage reserved for notables.

This practice was not exclusive to adults; it is found, and not rarely, on mummies of children, in particular on two mummies in the British Museum, one mummy from Dush, and three from Ain Labakha.[14] The significance of gilding was religious: gold was the "flesh of the gods," and for this reason, it conferred a divine quality on the deceased. We may consider that this gilding of the body was the equivalent of the gilded masks that were frequent in the New Kingdom, themselves substitutes for the golden masks of the pharaohs. The Embalming Ritual, which was still being copied in the Roman Period, promises the deceased: "You will appear as a golden being, you will shine like electrum."[15]

Bandaging was particularly careful in the Ptolemaic Period, and especially in the Roman Period. The bandages are often quite narrow, only an inch or so wide, with selvages, and thus woven intentionally for this use. Often, too, ripped cloth was used; a narrow bandage was obtained by folding the cloth lengthwise, and the frayed edge was hidden by the bandage placed directly above it. This method made it possible to create complex geometric motifs—lozenges, squares, "staircases"—whose decorative effect was heightened by the use of different-colored cloths, mostly white, black, and red (ranging from light red to a dark brick red). Medallions of gilded stucco were often placed in the center of these motifs. The Roman Period mummies found at Hawara by W. M. F. Petrie are excellent examples of this type.[16]

In certain cases, the mummies were covered with cloth that tightly followed the contours of the body, with the limbs wrapped separately. One Roman Period mummy in the British Museum, which is quite carefully wrapped, is an especially striking example (figure 109).[17] This technique to some extent recalls the outward appearance of certain mummies of the Old Kingdom.

In many cases, though, the "packaging" of the mummies was rather perfunctory. The body was wrapped in several shrouds that were held in place by bands of cloth of varying widths, the "bandages" in this case being nothing more than strips of ripped, unhemmed cloth. While the cloth on the outside is generally of good quality, with openwork, fringes, and selvages, the pieces of cloth that are not visible are often quite mediocre, patched together with rough-and-ready stitching. Between the shrouds, there were packets of crumpled cloth, shreds, and old clothing intended to lend some volume to the "package" that was called a mummy. Thus, at Dush, between the shrouds of a seven-year-old girl, we found a used embroidered gown that had belonged to an adult, perhaps the child's mother (figures 110 and 111).[18] Another example of the "recycling" of used cloth was furnished by

Fig. 109. Mummy with very elaborate bandaging, arms and legs bandaged separately. Roman Period. © Copyright the Trustees of The British Museum.

Fig. 110. Embroidered tunic reused as packing tissue in a mummy (fourth century C.E.). Necropolis of Dush, T20 (el-Kharga Oasis). Roman Period.

the unwrapping of a mummy in the Lyon Museum of Natural History by J. C. Goyon and P. Josset, which uncovered large fragments of the sail of a boat, though of course, this need not mean the deceased had been a sailor.[19]

As in previous periods, we still find amulets intended to assure the protection of the members of the deceased's body inserted between the layers of cloth. The heart scarab was always used. More generally, though, the num-

Fig. 111. Winged Victory, element of the decoration of an embroidered tunic (fourth century C.E., see fig. 110). Necropolis of Dush, T20 (el-Kharga Oasis). Roman Period.

ber of amulets seems to decrease: most recent excavations in Graeco-Roman cemeteries have failed to signal their presence. Yet among the many examples of amulets in museums and private collections, many can be dated to this period and come from pillaged tombs.

The finery of a mummy could be complemented by a net of elongated faïence beads, usually green or turquoise blue. In the network of lozenge-shaped stitching, artisans could insert more elaborate polychrome motifs made either of beads or of small faïence plaques depicting the Sons of Horus, the *djed*-pillar, the Khepri scarab, or Anubis in the form of a jackal. This usage seems to go back to Dynasty 25, or perhaps even to Dynasty 21. More often, especially in the later periods and for reasons of cost, individuals contented themselves with painting a network of beads on the cartonnage or on the outermost shroud. Representations of Osiris in these later periods often depict him wrapped in a shroud decorated with lozenges.

Fig. 112. Coffin with sliding door. Necropolis of el-Baqawat (el-Kharga Oasis). Fourth century C.E. Archives of the Metropolitan Museum of Art, New York.

COFFINS AND CARTONNAGES

Coffins remained in use. Down to the Roman Period, we find wooden anthropoid coffins, but they tend to diminish in number. The shape of coffins was generally that of a box with a cover that was flat, rounded, or in the form of a double-pitched roof. Inside and out, the coffins could be decorated or undecorated. In certain cases, the short end was in the form of a temple façade with a sliding door flanked by columns and surmounted by a cornice (figure 112). This door made it possible to open the coffin and insert, for example, the mummy of a baby next to its mother, as is the case with one of the two coffins found in a "pagan" tomb in the Christian cemetery of el-Baqawat, dating to the fourth century of our own era.[20]

The decoration consisted most often of traditional motifs (figure 113): Anubis in the form of a crouching or recumbent canine, the Sons of Horus, Osiris enthroned, the deceased on his funerary bed surrounded by mourning women. On the inside surface of some coffin lids, the goddess Nut is depicted standing frontally (figure 114), this motif having already appeared in Dynasty 22. The same motif appears on the coffin lid of Pollios Soter, governor of Thebes in the reign of Trajan, but the goddess is surrounded by a typically Roman zodiac.[21] The association of Egyptian and Graeco-Roman motifs is quite striking: the deceased could be represented in Greek style, clothed in a tunic and crowned with flowers, but flanked by Isis and Nephthys. On a coffin from Magdola in the Faiyum, we see representations of baboons and Anubis on the ends, and Greek motifs—garlands and bucrania—on the sides.[22] At the same time, we find, especially at Alexandria, purely Greek stone sarcophagi, sometimes undecorated, and sometimes adorned with motifs borrowed from Greek mythology. Thus, on a beautiful sarcophagus found at Mex (one of the quarters of Alexandria), the legend of Dionysus and Ariadne is depicted.[23]

In the Roman Period, there was also use of "mummy cupboards": these were cupboards of a sort, with a double door; sometimes, only the upper part could be opened, enabling the viewing of the mummy (or only its head) cov-

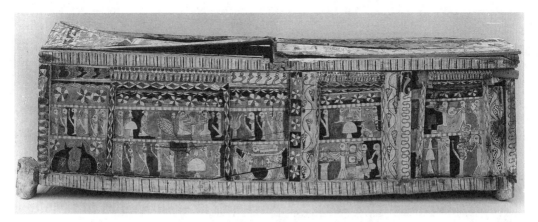

Fig. 113. Same coffin, with traditional decoration. Painted wood. Necropolis of el-Baqawat (el-Kharga Oasis). Fourth century C.E. Archives of the Metropolitan Museum of Art, New York.

ered in its cartonnage. It seems that this type of cupboard was not intended to be placed in the tomb but rather in the house, until the burial could take place. For shock value, certain classical authors, such as Diodorus Siculus and Cicero, evoke this Egyptian custom of keeping the mummies of one's parents at home. Cupboards of this type have been found at Abusir el-Meleq.[24]

Cartonnage was widely used in the Ptolemaic and Roman Periods. In the Ptolemaic Period, instead of being enclosed in its wrappings of cloth or stuccoed papyri, the mummy was usually provided with cartonnage plaques (figure 115) that were sometimes cropped around the outline of the decoration, producing a veritable cutout of the motif. These plaques, which could be quite small, were held in place with string, or simply by the mummy bandages, or glued in place with resin, in the places prescribed by the ritual: thus, the *usekh*-collar (a large floral collar with falcon's heads) was placed at the base of the neck, while the image of the winged Nut was placed lower, at the level of the anterior wall of the thoracic cage. The head was covered by a mask that could be gilded, and the feet were placed in a "foot box" that was generally decorated on its upper surface with a crouching Anubis and on its sole with representations of prisoners, or more often, with geometric motifs (polychrome checkerboard, scales, etc.).

In this period, cartonnages were often made of several layers of papyrus tightly pressed to-

Fig. 114. Sarcophagus with an image of the goddess Nut inside the cover. Basalt. Ptolemaic Period. Louvre.

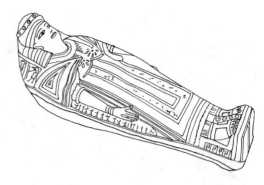

Fig. 115. Plaque depicting the winged goddess Nut, part of the adornment of a mummy. Stuccoed and painted cartonnage. Necropolis of Dush, T70 (el-Kharga Oasis). Ptolemaic Period.

Fig. 116. Coffin of Tamin. Stuccoed and painted cartonnage. Akhmim. Second century C.E. London, British Museum.

gether, giving the material its characteristic "papier-mâché" consistency. This practice has led archaeologists to recover the papyri constituting the cartonnage in order to read the texts preserved on them, though unfortunately to the detriment of the object itself. One mummy from the necropolis of Dush was an entirely exceptional case; stuck to its thorax was a large fragment of a Greek papyrus whose presence remains unexplained. This papyrus contains a list of in-kind taxes paid by the inhabitants of the village of Dush at the beginning of the second century C.E.[25]

In the Roman Period, there were new changes. The cutout cartonnage plaques disappeared, giving way to complete cartonnages that often looked like a sort of box. The face, the arms, and the hands of the deceased were modeled in stucco, and sometimes the entire body seems to be sculpted in the round: such is the case with a cartonnage from Abusir el-Meleq dating to the first century of our own era, which realistically depicts the deceased dressed in a tunic and a tight-fitting cloak.[26] In a later series of examples, coming especially from Akhmim (figure 116), the deceased are presented in everyday garb, the women dressed in robes with geometric motifs and the men in sleeved tunics and cloaks draped over the left shoulder.[27] Otherwise, only the bust of the deceased man or woman, modeled according to the same technique, is bound into the bandages. The best examples are the busts from Meir, now in the Cairo Museum, with their

outrageously made-up faces.[28] In still other cases, the mask is prolonged by a painted "dickey" attached to the mummy by means of straps (figures 117 and 118). The dickey is usually decorated with several registers of traditional funerary scenes. The mask is of thick, gilded stucco.

While masks of Egyptian type were still quite popular at the beginning of the Roman Period, there was increasing use of masks of thick stucco; these were more realistic, and they were often entirely individualized (figure 119). The eyes were generally made of inlaid glass paste, and the faces were painted with lifelike colors. Like the cartonnage masks, they were held in place by bandages. This abundant production, which is especially well attested at Antinoe, continued down to the beginning of the fourth century C.E.

At the same time, from the beginning of the first century of our own era on, there appeared in Egypt funerary portraits painted on cloth or wood (figure 120), in tempera and especially encaustic; these are called "Faiyum portraits," because this region has yielded a great number of them. Thanks to them, we may contemplate a veritable gallery of portraits, sometimes stereotyped, but most often of a remarkable degree of realism and quality. This technique was Roman, quite close in style to the paintings at Pompeii, and it had nothing to do with Egyptian tradition. It is possible that some of these paintings were executed during the lifetime of their subjects, and that they were placed on view in the home before being put in

Fig. 117. Mask of a man, with "dickey" and back-piece. Stuccoed, painted, and gilded cartonnage. Meir. First century C.E. Cairo Museum.

place on the mummy. The example of a man from the beginning of the third century C.E., now in the J. P. Getty Museum, demonstrates this point well: it was found surrounded by a representation of Sarapis and another of Isis, forming a veritable triptych.[29] Another, discovered by W. M. F. Petrie in a tomb at Hawara, still had the frame and the thin cord that had been used to hang it.[30]

Painted shrouds, some examples of which go back to the New Kingdom, were rather widespread in the Roman Period (figure 121), no doubt substituting for cartonnages or coffins. They usually represent the deceased standing and flanked by Osiris and Anubis. Small "tableaux" surrounding the main scene depict traditional motifs: funerary deities, symbolic objects, and the like. A large group of these

Fig. 118. Mask of a woman, with "dickey." Stuccoed and painted cartonnage, gilded mask. Roman Period. Louvre.

shrouds comes from Antinoe. Datable to the third and fourth centuries of our own era, they mostly depict women wearing beautiful jewelry, including the ansate cross; this fact has sometimes led scholars to attribute a Christian origin to these women, though it seems this hypothesis is not to be maintained.[31]

Fig. 120. Portrait of a woman. Tempera on wood. Saqqara. Second century c.e. Louvre.

Fig. 119. Mask of a woman. Painted stucco. Antinoe or Akhmim (?). First half of the second century c.e. Louvre.

The latest painted mummy wrappings are probably those discovered at Deir el-Bahari in the temple complex of Hatshepsut: attached to the stucco mask is a painted cloth rectangle that is roughly stitched to the shroud and decorated with the ancient motif of the barque of Sokar (figure 122). These decorated shrouds, of a highly repetitive type, can scarcely antedate the fourth century of our own era.[32]

In tombs of the Graeco-Roman Period, we often find inscribed disks, called hypocephali (figure 123), made of stuccoed cloth, papyrus, or bronze, placed under the head of the deceased (hence their name). The motifs that decorate them usually include the heavenly cow, the Sons of Horus, Amun-Re in the form of an entity with four ram's heads, and various other

Fig. 121. Shroud of Amun, son of Antinoos. Stuccoed and painted cloth. Second century C.E. Louvre.

Fig. 122. Mask of a man, with "dickey." Stuccoed and painted cartonnage and linen cloth. Deir el-Bahari. End of the third to beginning of the fourth century C.E. Louvre.

Fig. 123. Hypocephali. Papyrus. Ptolemaic and Roman Periods. Louvre.

solar symbols. The text is that of chapter 162 of the Book of the Dead, an invocation, supposedly pronounced by the cow, that "the flame come under the head of the deceased," that is, that he maintain his body heat in the world to come.

THE TOMBS

The tombs themselves changed very little. Let us set aside the problem of the Ptolemaic royal tombs: they have yet to be found, not even that of Alexander, though we know that his body was brought to Alexandria and placed on view in a glass coffin.[33] This tradition implies that he had been embalmed. The many cemeteries of private persons, however, give us a good glimpse of the different categories of burials.

The Alexandrian cemeteries are distributed all along the coast, from east to west, and some of them have the appearance of veritable catacombs. The multiple funerary chambers contain either benches on which sarcophagi were placed or niches for the funerary urns, for often, in the Ptolemaic Period, Greek-style cremation was practiced.[34] Certain tombs are decorated in a mixed style, Greek and Egyptian, while others contain funerary stelae of purely Greek type. The tombs recently discovered by the excavations of Jean-Yves Empereur in the western sector of the city furnish a good example of this habitat of the dead, in which the periods of occupation succeeded one another from the beginning of the Ptolemaic Period to the Christianization of Alexandria.[35]

The catacomb of Kom el-Shuqafa (figure 124)

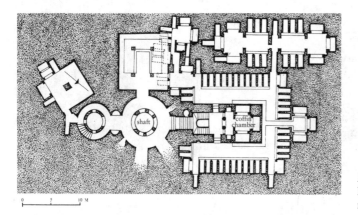

Fig. 124. Plan of the necropolis of Kom el-Shuqafa (Alexandria). Roman Period.

is the most interesting funerary ensemble on the architectural level: it is a vast tomb extending over three levels, constructed between the first and the fourth century of our own era. The superstructure consists of a portico, beneath which there opens up a broad spiral staircase leading to the principal tomb, which is located on the second level. Its layout is entirely comparable to that of a tomb of the pharaonic period, with a chapel containing the statues of a pair of deceased persons placed in two niches and a traditionally decorated burial chamber containing three coffins that are themselves typically Greek. All this is surrounded by a wide corridor in which there are niches, closed with slabs, containing no fewer than three hundred deceased persons. Adjacent galleries give access to other groups of tombs. In this vast ensemble, various types of burials coexisted: individual burials in sarcophagi, terra cotta jars, or pits dug into the ground itself, and collective burials in vaults.[36]

The necropolis of Terenuthis in the western delta includes a multitude of funerary chapels of various sizes and types distributed somewhat anarchically over a vast area. The principal interest of this necropolis is the presence of hundreds of funerary stelae (figure 125) on which the deceased are most often depicted in an attitude of prayer. Later, this pose would often be adopted in Christian iconography.[37]

In Middle Egypt, Tuna el-Gebel, the cemetery of Hermopolis, is a veritable city of the dead (figure 126). It was used from the Ptolemaic to the Roman Period. Certain tombs are of a highly particular type: they are brick constructions covered with a coating of stucco, often

with a columned portico, and including an elevated level that was reached via an external staircase. The deceased were placed in a funerary chamber inside this elevated portion. This is the case with the tomb of Isidora, who is identified by a long, poetic funerary inscription in Greek: her coffin was placed on a bench carved into a wall, on which was painted a bed in the form of a stylized lion of the traditional type.[38]

Leaving aside these examples, we may note that in the Graeco-Roman Period, funerary architecture was generally simple. It consisted of constructions of unbaked brick topped by "Nubian" vaults with oblique arches, or more often still, of shaft or pit tombs, or of vaults

Fig. 125. The deceased on her funerary bed. Limestone stela. Necropolis of Terenuthis. Roman Period.

Fig. 126. Funerary house. Tuna el-Gebel, cemetery of Hermopolis. Ptolemaic and Roman Periods.

dug into elevated ground (figures 127 and 128). A good example of such a necropolis is that of Dush, a small town in the south of the great Oasis. Shaft tombs are dug into a bed of sandstone at the top of a rather large mound, while tombs with superstructures and vaults are located on the periphery. In this sort of necropolis, we cannot discern any particular care with regard to the architecture, a fact that is undoubtedly explained by a modest economic level. The necropolis near the temple of Hibis in el-Kharga Oasis, however, furnishes examples of rather good tombs cut deeply into thick layers of sandstone (figures 129 and 130).

What otherwise characterizes this period is the overcrowding of tombs (figure 131) and the reuse of old tombs. This situation is explained, on the one hand, by the generalization of mummification, and on the other hand, by the lack of available ground to expand these immense cemeteries, wedged as they were between cultivable zones that needed to be preserved and the desert, into which it was not

Fig. 127. Coffins and mummies in place in their tomb. Necropolis of el-Baqawat, T LXVI (el-Kharga Oasis). Fourth century C.E. Archives of the Metropolitan Museum of Art, New York.

Fig. 128. Mummies in their tomb. Necropolis of Ain Labakha, T35 (el-Kharga Oasis). Ptolemaic and Roman Periods.

practical to penetrate too far. It is thus that certain tombs at Deir el-Medina, dating to the New Kingdom, were found filled with mummies of the Ptolemaic and Roman Periods, while those in the Valley of the Queens also sheltered mummies from the later stages of history.[39]

Tomb decoration was most often summary, or even absent. Even so, the principal tomb at Kom el-Shuqafa preserves a highly interesting decoration, with bas-reliefs depicting funerary scenes and deities. Another tomb in the same group is decorated with both Egyptian and Greek funerary scenes.

There are some beautiful examples of painted decoration at Hermopolis and at el-Muzawwaqa (figures 132 and 133) in el-Dakhla Oasis. At the latter site, some decades ago, A. Fakhry discovered two Roman Period tombs with almost purely Egyptian decora-

Fig. 129. Sarcophagi dug into the sandstone layer. Necropolis of Hibis (el-Kharga Oasis). Persian Period (?), reused in the Roman Period.

Fig. 130. Tomb with multiple burial chambers dug into the sandstone. Necropolis of Hibis (el-Kharga Oasis). Persian Period (?), reused in the Roman Period.

Fig. 131. An example of an over-crowded tomb: burial chamber V of tomb 20 of the necropolis of Dush (el-Kharga Oasis). Roman Period.

Fig. 132. The deceased conveyed to his tomb on a wheeled chariot. Painting from the tomb of Pedubaste. Muzawwaqa (el-Dakhla Oasis). First century C.E.

Fig. 133. A paradisiacal vision of the hereafter. Painting from the tomb of Petosiris. Muzawwaqa (el-Dakhla Oasis). Second century C.E.

Fig. 134. Plank cover of the coffin of Chelidona. Painted wood. Thebes (?). Roman Period. Louvre.

tion.[40] Similarly, the tomb of Siamun at Siwa, which dates to the third century B.C.E., has a high-quality decoration whose motifs are typically Egyptian, though certain elements of this decoration, as well as the clothing of the deceased and the members of his family, display a foreign, perhaps Libyan, influence.[41]

In the tomb on Tigranes Pasha Street in Alexandria, which probably dates to the second century of our own era, the paintings range in theme (and in a rather maladroit fashion) from Greek decorative elements to Egyptian motifs.

FUNERARY BELIEFS

The decoration of tombs, as well as that of cartonnages and coffins (figure 134), demonstrates the persistence of the traditional beliefs. We must, however, nuance this assertion. The arrival of a large number of Greeks in Egypt at the beginning of the third century B.C.E. was accompanied by a relative diffusion of Greek funerary customs and ideas regarding death. The practice of cremation was relatively widespread at Alexandria, and we know of cases, though they are rare, of persons who specifically refused to be mummified. Greek-language funerary inscriptions referring to traditional themes often express ideas quite different from the Egyptian ideal: regrets regarding the life the deceased is leaving behind, a vision of death as a sort of eternal night, and formulas of the type "no one is immortal."[42]

In fact, we are witness to a sort of progressive "funerary acculturation" of the Greeks, more and more of whom came to adopt Egyptian mortuary customs. This fact should cause no surprise, given the hopeful expectation of life to come expressed by Egyptian religion, as compared with the generally somber vision of the world beyond held by the Greeks. The juxtaposition of Greek and Egyptian ideas and images makes a striking appearance in the funerary inscription of a lady named Aphrodisia, wife of a high-ranking officer at Edfu, in the second century B.C.E.: while the Greek text evokes classic notions such as "Time, which

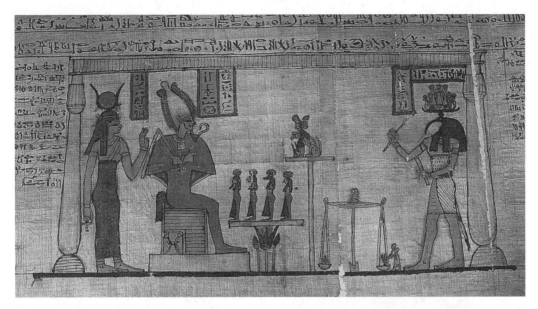

Fig. 135. Weighing of the heart in the presence of Osiris. Funerary papyrus. Roman Period. Louvre.

Fig. 136. Osiris. Painted wood. Late Period. Louvre.

Fig. 137. Isis making the gesture of mourning. Stuccoed and painted wood. Late Period or Ptolemaic Period. Louvre.

Fig. 138. "Doll." Molded and painted terra cotta. Necropolis of Dush, T80 (el-Kharga Oasis). First century C.E.

watches over all," "the spindles of the Fates," and "Hades," where the deceased bemoans her fate, the hieroglyphic text, which is far more optimistic, asks the gods of the world beyond to preserve her body and to praise her in the presence of Osiris.[43] The Osirian myth remained influential, as testified by the many representations of the god in the funerary material. This fact corresponds to the preeminence of the cult of Osiris in this period, of which we see evidence, at Dendara, in the chapel built on the roof of the temple, which was dedicated to the rites of the death and rebirth of this god celebrated during the festivals of Choiak. A recent discovery at Karnak confirms the robustness of Osirian ritual: numerous representations of the god excavated in a sort of "catacomb" attest to the penetration of Osiris into the domain of Amun.[44] This was probably a tomb created to shelter the figurines of Osiris that were made for the festivals of Choiak.

Mummification itself, however summary, was an imitation of Osiris. The Book of the Dead, which was still copied in the Ptolemaic Period, perpetuated the doctrine of the Judgment of the Dead (figure 135) and the "justification" of the deceased, which enabled him to enjoy a "second life." In the Roman Period, it was replaced by other funerary books, such as the Book of Breathings. Statuettes of Osiris and Isis (figures 136 and 137) and of other funerary deities, such as Anubis, all of them guarantors of this survival, have been found in tombs, as in the preceding periods.

Solar doctrines were also very much present in the funerary beliefs of these periods. We see evidence of these doctrines in the decoration of cartonnages and coffins, where the motifs of the solar barque and the winged scarab often appear.

Ushabtis progressively disappeared in the Roman Period, which might indicate that the concept according to which the deceased would have need of respondents or servants was fading away. In the tombs of the Graeco-Roman period, though, we often find nude female statuettes of the type called "concubine of the deceased" and phallic male statuettes, attesting no doubt to belief in the persistence of sexual activity in the world beyond for both genders. This practice continues the older one, attested since the Middle Kingdom, of placing figurines of nude women with exaggerated genital areas in the tombs. One female figure from a tomb in the necropolis of Dush, though, is obviously a doll and not a ritual figurine (figure 138).

There was a new custom that originated in the Graeco-Roman Period: that of placing a coin next to the deceased. This coin was a ritual offering to Charon, the ferryman who, according to Greek belief, conveyed the deceased across the river Styx to the realm of the dead. But this idea of a crossing in no way contradicted Egyptian belief, which had always included a sailing or a crossing to arrive at the world beyond. Chapter 99 of the Book of the Dead contains a dialogue of the deceased with the pilot who was to ferry him across the celestial river, that is, the Milky Way.

It seems, moreover, that the concept of punishments reserved for those who committed wrongs in this world was introduced into the

Egyptian vision of the world to come. The Demotic tale of Setne (preserved on a Roman Period papyrus but undoubtedly of earlier date) describes the visit of Setne and his son Si-Osiris to the realm of the dead, where they discover chambers in which criminals suffered various tortures, while the just were admitted to the realm of the blessed.[45] This moralizing vision of the world beyond appears already in certain texts from the tomb of Petosiris.

7   The Passage from This Life to the Next

Egyptian mummification techniques were perfected slowly and progressively; at the same time, from prehistory down to the period of Roman domination, funerary practices changed. Thanks to texts, and thanks to the mummies themselves, which continue to be studied scientifically, we can reconstruct the mummification process as it was practiced at its apogee, that is, during the first millennium B.C.E. We are also well informed regarding the rituals carried out after mummification to enable the deceased to enjoy a future life.

We have almost no Egyptian text describing the details of mummification; at most, we have texts regarding the bandaging ritual. Our best source is still Herodotus. This historian, who visited Egypt in the 450s B.C.E., left us a precise description of the practices of his time.[1] Often considered a scarcely reliable teller of tales, he nevertheless seems to be a trustworthy witness with regard to what concerns us here. Though his testimony is of relatively late date, the agreement between what he has to say and the information derived from the scientific study of mummies permits us to think that the techniques he describes are those already in use in the New Kingdom.

According to Herodotus, when the family brought the body of a deceased person to the embalmer, the latter would show them painted wooden models of mummies, allowing them to judge the results obtained by the different available treatments. In this way, the clients could knowledgeably choose the quality of the treatment the deceased would receive. There were in fact three classes of mummification, with, of course, corresponding prices.

The first-class treatment was the most elaborate, and it permits us today to contemplate perfectly preserved bodies that still display their facial expression during life. According to Herodotus, the embalmers began by removing the brain with the help of a "curved iron implement" (in reality, a sort of bronze rod ending in a hook, of which we have many examples). At the same time, they poured a liquid into the cranial cavity to dissolve the remaining brain tissue. Then, using an "Ethiopian stone" (i.e., obsidian), they made an incision in the side and removed the intestines, which they washed with date wine and aromatic substances. Next, they filled the abdomen with various balsamic products, in particular, myrrh and cinnamon, after which they restitched the incision. Then began the desiccation of the body with natron, which lasted seventy days. Finally, the body was washed, and then it was wrapped in bandages made of "byssos," the finest linen fabric; the bandages were held in place by means of a sort of gum.

There are few modifications to be made to this description. It can be complemented, however, thanks to information derived from archaeological exploration and, to a certain extent, from Egyptian texts. It seems that prior to mummification, in a place known as the *ibu*, the body was washed with water mixed with a little natron. The mummification itself occurred in the *per nefer*, the "beautiful house," or in the *uabet*, the "pure place." This place must originally have been a sort of tent or light structure set up near the cemetery.[2] In the later stages of history, use was made of brick constructions capable of holding many bodies at the same time.[3] Texts of the Roman Period in-

Fig. 139. Instruments used in mummification (goblet, funnel, knife). Louvre.

dicate that the embalmers were supposed to remain outside the city, whether to work or to dwell: this is shown by their designation *exopylitai,* literally "living outside the gates."[4] We can easily imagine that the disagreeable sights and odors of the embalming activities led their fellow citizens to avoid contact with this peculiar profession.

It is likely that the first operation performed on the body was the removal of the brain (figures 139 and 140), usually via the ethmoid sinus and the nostril, as described by Herodotus, but also, though much more rarely, via the occiput. The cranial cavity was more or less completely filled with a product rendered liquid by heating and introduced via the nostrils with the help of a sort of double-tubed funnel, examples of which have been found. In its solid state, this product, whose composition could vary, took on a vitreous, blackish appearance. Next came the abdominal evisceration. The place where the incision was made changed: prior to the time of Tuthmosis III, the incision was normally lateral and vertical, located at the level of the left side. Afterwards, the abdomen was often cut open at a lower spot, parallel to the fold of the groin. In certain cases, the opening could be made on the rear of the flank.[5] To be sure, the intestines were removed first, as Herodotus says. But these were not the only viscera involved: the liver, the stomach, and the lungs were also removed. The heart, however, was not removed, or, if it had been inadvertently extracted from the thorax along with the lungs, it was usually put back in place

after having been separately mummified, a practice that confirms the importance the Egyptians attached to this organ.[6] For the sake of security, a scarab known as the "heart scarab," on which a formula borrowed from chapter 30 of the Book of the Dead was inscribed, could replace this essential organ in case it was destroyed. On the heart scarab of King Sebekemzaf II of Dynasty 17, we read:

> O my heart of my mother, my heart of my different ages, do not testify against me, do not take sides against me in the Tribunal, do not let the Scale incline against me before the weigher (i.e., Thoth), for you are my force, which is in my body, the modeler who gave life to my limbs.[7]

As a general rule, the embalmers did not touch the kidneys, the spleen, the bladder, or

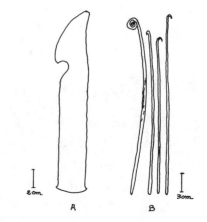

Fig. 140. Instruments used in mummification: special tool for detaching the viscera (A), hook used to extract the brain (B). After Dr. F. Jonckheere.

the female reproductive organs, all of them much less accessible to blind manual exploration and whose importance, in any event, does not seem to have been recognized by the Egyptians. The viscera that were removed were separately mummified with the aid of natron and then bandaged. These viscera packets were then placed in canopic vessels (figure 141), which were themselves stored in a wooden or stone box. In certain periods, the packets were placed near the mummy, or even inside the body. The case of Queen Hetepheres, the mother of Cheops, is the first known example of evisceration and preservation of the organs: the viscera were placed in the compartments of an alabaster box that, when it was discovered by Reisner, still held them bathed in the preserving liquid, which was a natron solution.[8] The unique character of this discovery unfortunately does not allow us to comment on the frequency of this procedure of preserving the viscera in a liquid.

After the viscera were removed, the body underwent a new external, and then an internal, cleansing, followed by a temporary packing of the abdominal cavity with cloth. It was then that the body was plunged in natron. The term "bath," which is often used, is inappropriate: Herodotus speaks of salting (*taricheuein*, ταριχευειν) and covering (*kryptein*, κρυπτειν) of the body, which is enough to prove that this stage did not involve a liquid. The experiments of A. Lucas, and later P. Garner, who succeeded in making rat mummies, confirmed that in order to be effective, the natron had to be used in crystal form.[9] Natron is a natural mixture of sodium chloride (ordinary salt), carbonate, and sodium sulfate found in a region on the western border of the delta, midway between Alexandria and Cairo; the area is today called the Wadi el-Natrun. We otherwise know of further sources of natron, in particular in the region of Darfur, from which natron was brought by caravans using the "Forty-Day Trail," the Darb el-Arbain. The "natron bath," however, was certainly not as long as stated by Herodotus. The seventy days he mentions included, rather, the entire length of time needed to make the mummy, with the bandaging probably taking the longest amount of time. This much seems confirmed by the text of Genesis describing the funeral of Jacob:

> Joseph commanded the physicians in his service to embalm his father. So the physicians embalmed Israel; they spent forty days in doing this, for that is the time required for embalming. And the Egyptians wept for him seventy days.[10]

Complementary information is furnished by the Demotic Story of Setne, which tells us that the thirty-fifth day was the day when the bandaging began, and the seventieth, the day when the mummy was placed in its coffin.[11] In fact, the duration of the various steps must have varied according to the class of mummification, the first class certainly needing more time than the others.

Dehydrated and completely rigid, the body was again washed and then covered with more or less oily and balsamic products intended to endow it with a certain suppleness and a "good smell." The washing of the body at this point seems to have had an exceptional ritual importance, for it evoked the myth of the rising

Fig. 141. Canopic vessels with the heads of the four Sons of Horus serving as covers. Late Period. Louvre.

Fig. 142. Flank plate of Queen Henuttawy. Gold. Dynasty 21. Cairo Museum.

Fig. 144. Sheaths for the toes of the right foot of Psusennes I. Dynasty 21. Cairo Museum.

of the sun from the primordial ocean and thus the regeneration of the deceased. Rarely, the evisceration incision was resewn. Sometimes it was covered with a plate of wax or metal, always gold for royalty (figure 142). The natural orifices—nostrils, mouth—were often stopped up with linen plugs (figure 143) or strips of resin. Pharaohs were even more richly provided, with, inter alia, sheaths of gold encasing the individual fingers and toes (figure 144).

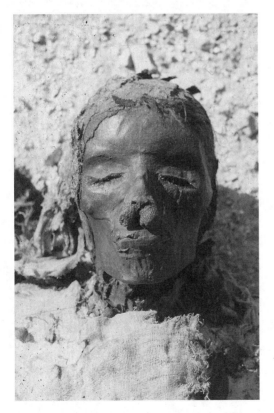

Fig. 143. Head of the mummy of a woman. Linen plugs fill the nostrils and the mouth. Necropolis of Dush, T56 (el-Kharga Oasis). Roman Period.

The appearance of the body could also be enhanced by placing various objects (such as onions) in the eye sockets to restore a normal volume to them, by applying makeup or paint to the face, or even by placing a wig on the head. In the later periods of history, leaves of precious metal could be placed on the tongue, the eyes, and the external female genitals. The nails could be attached to the fingertips to prevent their falling off.

It was now that the bandaging began. This procedure undoubtedly had a purely ritual character, but we must not lose sight of its beneficial aspect, for it served to insulate the body, at least relatively speaking, from the environment. After the Embalming Ritual, which has been preserved to us on two papyri from the Roman Period[12] (themselves copied from older texts), the embalmers began by placing a shroud directly on the body, and then they proceeded to a preliminary wrapping of the fingers and the toes with bands of fine linen. Next came the head, which was carefully bandaged beginning with the right shoulder. Next, the thorax, and the arms as well, were surrounded with bandages above the shroud (figure 145). Finally, the legs were bandaged. To be sure, the wealth of the deceased was a factor: the quality and the quantity of the fabric used could vary considerably. Amulets (figures 146 and 147) could be placed between the layers of wrappings, and upon the head of the mummy there was sometimes a crown of flowers and leaves, the "crown of justification" (figure 148). Many scholars have asserted that in the Roman Period, when bandaging often attained a remarkably aesthetic quality, the mummies to which it was applied were of extremely bad quality. We do not share this opinion be-

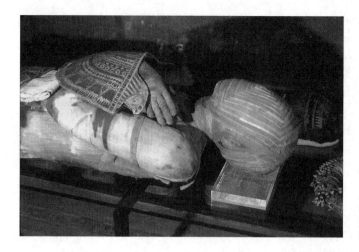

Fig. 145. Head and torso of a mummy. Meticulous bandaging and plaques of cartonnage cutouts. Ptolemaic Period. Louvre.

cause our own field experience has shown that there is no systematic discrepancy between the quality of the bandaging and that of the mummification.

During the bandaging, unguents and oils were spread on the pieces of fabric to assure their adhesion. At each step, a priest pronounced the prescribed prayers or invocations:

> For you comes the oil! It brings life to your mouth, sight to your eye . . . it gives you your ears to hear what you like . . . it gives you your nose to inhale the festal perfume . . . it give you your mouth after having provided it with its discernment, like the mouth of Thoth, which discerns what is just![13]

The Egyptians attached great importance to the preservation of the head, a concern that seems legitimate. In fact, study of mummies in cemeteries shows that breaking the neck, which led to the separation of head and body, was not a rare event. It sometimes occurred during the mummification process, as evi-

Fig. 146. Amulet in the form of a human-headed heart. Stone and glass paste. Dynasty 19. Louvre.

denced by mummies found with various devices in place to keep the head in place on the trunk. Yet, the fact that "reserve heads," so numerous in Old Kingdom tombs, disappeared at a point when there was decisive progress in the quality of mummification tends to show that these heads had indeed been intended to mitigate technological deficiencies.

The decoration of the tomb of Tjui at Thebes, dating to Dynasty 19, gives us a look at the various processes involved in the making of a mummy (figure 149).[14] One scene shows a stage in the wrapping, while another depicts the embalmers daubing the mummy with a product from a pot. In yet another scene, artisans seem to be making the coffin.

The decoration of the coffin of Djedbastetiufankh (figure 150) and that of Mutirdis, both from el-Hiba and now in Hildesheim, illustrate nearly all the mummification process.[15] Both have a type of decoration that is apparently quite rare. Scholars now agree that these coffins, which were long dated to Dynasty 26, belong to the Ptolemaic Period (second or first century B.C.E.). The decoration of the lids occurs in registers that are to be read from foot to head, six on the former coffin, and eight on the latter.

On the coffin of Djedbastetiufankh, we see the following:

> In the bottom register, the deceased is represented in the form of a fleshless being, black in color. He is washed in a basin by two personages

Fig. 147. Amulets: *djed*-pillar and Isis knot (*tit*). Late Period. Louvre.

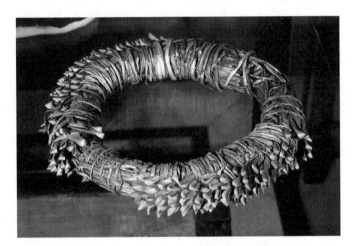

Fig. 148. "Crown of justification" made of flowers and leaves. Ptolemaic Period. Louvre.

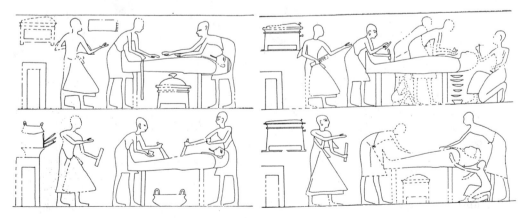

Fig. 149. The different stages in the making of a mummy. Decoration of the tomb of Tjui. Thebes. Dynasty 19. After A. J. Spencer, 1982.

Fig. 150. The phases in the making of a mummy. Coffin of Djedbastetiufankh. El-Hiba. Second to first century B.C.E. Hildesheim, Roemer- und Pelizaeus Museum.

(vignette on the left), and then, standing in a ditch, he is anointed with two liquids (the pots of the officiants are of different colors).

In the second register, the deceased is lying on a funerary bed in the form of a stylized lion. Walking toward the bed are four priests, the first of whom wears an Anubis mask and holds, in one of his hands, a hooked instrument and perhaps pliers, and in the other, bandages. This detail might show that the priest is readying himself to begin the bandaging. The body is lying on its back, the head resting on a headrest. The surface of the bed has the form of chevrons that seem to correspond to a view from above of a bed frame made of wickerwork, as is often the case with funerary beds found in tombs (figures 151, 152, and 153). Other interpretations view it as plants evoking the beds of greenery of the "grain Osiris" figures. The fact that the feet of this bed are doubled and that we see the bed frame seems to us to constitute an attempt at representation in perspective.

The third register represents two steps in the wrapping of the mummy:

On the right, the priest in the Anubis mask is bending over the mummy, which is almost entirely bandaged and lying on the lion bed, which is this time shown viewed from the side. Under the bed are two bags tied shut, each with a stick emerging from it: these could be the "leftovers"

Fig. 151. The deceased on his funerary bed, detail from the coffin of Djedbastetiufankh. El-Hiba. Second to first century B.C.E. Hildesheim, Roemer- und Pelizaeus Museum.

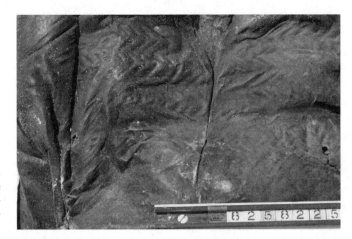

Fig. 152. Back of a mummy displaying, on its skin, the imprint of the wickerwork of its funerary bed. Necropolis of Dush, T58 (el-Kharga Oasis). Roman Period.

of the mummification process, which we know were buried near the tomb. Such leftovers have been found near several Theban tombs, the best known example being that of Tutankhamun.[16]

On the left, the mummy is completed. It is lying on the funerary bed, under which we see the four canopic jars whose covers are sculpted in the form of the heads of the four Sons of Horus.

In the fourth register, two priests are represented on the left. One of them is the lector priest, who is holding an inscribed tablet, while the other can be recognized from his leopard's skin. On the right, there are also two priests, one of them wearing the Anubis mask, and they are followed by three women. In the middle, separating the two groups, are ritual offerings.

The fifth register represents the funerary bar-

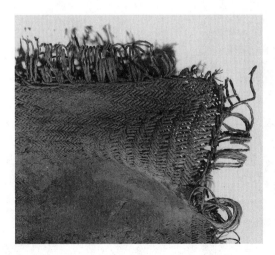

Fig. 153. Wickerwork mat from the frame of a funerary bed. Necropolis of Dush, T60 (el-Kharga Oasis). Roman Period.

que, preceded by three priests bearing standards. The deceased will cross the Nile in the barque to reach the necropolis.

Finally, in the upper register, the four Sons of Horus surround a *djed*-pillar, symbol of the resurrection of Osiris, while a winged Isis and Nephthys frame the scene.

The same motifs appear on the coffin of Mutirdis, with some supplementary scenes: priests surrounding offering tables laden with food, the deceased in a barque towed by four jackals, and so forth.

We easily see the interest of these coffins, with their details of different stages of the mummification process and their evocation of certain aspects of the funeral. In the same museum in Hildesheim, there is an extremely rare Anubis mask of painted terra cotta (figure 154), probably intended to be worn by a priest, either during the funeral or in the course of a procession.[17]

THE FUNERAL

The completed mummy, generally in the form of an oblong packet, was placed in its cartonnage or wooden containers and then returned to the family. At that point, the funeral could begin. This ritual was customarily entrusted to funerary priests, but the family of the deceased, in particular the eldest son, had its role to play. The first phase of the ceremony consisted of a procession that conducted the

Fig. 154. Anubis mask. Painted terra cotta. Sixth to fourth century B.C.E. Hildesheim, Roemer und Pelizaeus Museum.

deceased to the tomb. In the case of wealthy individuals, this procession could include any number of funerary priests, professional mourning women (figures 155, 156, 157), family members, friends, and servants. At the head of the procession were the priests, one of them carrying an incense burner. Oxen, or sometimes men, dragged a sledge that carried the barque bearing the "chapel" in which the mummy lay. This was a miniature barque, analogous to the processional barques of the gods, and not the actual boat that the participants must have used in reality to cross the Nile (when such a crossing was necessary). The miniature barque recalled the pilgrimage that the deceased were believed to make, via the Nile, to Abydos and Buto, the holy cities of Osirian legend. The crossing of the Nile by the deceased was the consequence of the location

Fig. 155. Bust of a wailing woman. Painted terra cotta. New Kingdom. Louvre.

Fig. 156. Mourning women. Detail from the coffin of the lady Madja. Deir el-Medina. New Kingdom. Louvre.

of cemeteries on the west bank, while the living often inhabited the east bank. We see this scheme clearly established in the New Kingdom, when the principal religious center was Thebes, whose topography corresponds to this east-west distribution. Naturally, there were

Fig. 157. Mourning women. Bas-relief from the Memphite tomb of Haremhab. Limestone. Saqqara. Dynasty 18. Louvre.

places in Egypt where the cemeteries and the town were on the same bank, making it unnecessary to cross the Nile, yet the image of the boat journey remained in force, for it referred to the myth of the Osirian pilgrimage. In the Ptolemaic Period, the sledge could be replaced by a wheeled chariot. We find this chariot, which already appears in a bas-relief from the funerary chapel of Petosiris at Tuna el-Gebel, represented on funerary papyri and in the paintings in the tomb of Pedubaste at el-Muzawwaqa, which dates to the first century of our own era. The sledge bearing the coffin was followed by a second one that carried the box containing the canopic jars. At the end of the procession came servants bearing offerings, along with the furnishings intended to be placed in the tomb: these consisted, in part, of certain objects of daily life that the deceased had used—bed, chair, headrest, chests containing clothes, toilet objects—and specifically funerary materials, such as *ushabti* boxes, statuettes, and a Book of the Dead. Naturally, the quantity of material placed in the tomb varied considerably according to the means of the owner.

Once the Nile was crossed, the procession proceeded to the tomb. There, the initial ceremony consisted of a ritual dance performed by professional dancers, as well as a reading of texts by the lector priest. Next, the "Opening the Mouth" ritual was performed over the mummy in its coffin, which was set upright in front of the entrance to the tomb. Prior to the

New Kingdom, this extremely ancient rite was carried out on a statue and not the deceased himself, but from the end of Dynasty 18 on, the mummy was the object of the ritual. The ritual is often represented in Theban tomb paintings and in the vignettes of the Book of the Dead. While the coffin was held upright by a priest wearing an Anubis mask, the *sem*-priest, called "the son he loves" (clearly, he played the role of the son par excellence, Horus, the son of Osiris) and dressed in a panther skin, assisted by one or more other priests, held various implements to the mouth of the mummy. These included a sort of adz and a sort of chisel, with which it was believed the *sem*-priest could restore breath, speech, and the use of the senses to the deceased. The mummy was then taken down into the burial chamber to enjoy its repose of "millions of years."[18] From that time on, the body would remain in the tomb, while the deceased's *ba* could come and go at will.[19] The Book of the Dead of Nebqed depicts the *ba*, already during the Opening of the Mouth ritual, flying down the shaft that led to the burial chamber (figure 158). Similarly, a painting in the tomb of Arinefer at Deir el-Medina depicts the mummified body inside the tomb, while the *ba* is fluttering outside it (figure 159). This belief in the ability of the *ba* to leave the tomb is expressed in many formulas in the Book of the Dead (literally, the "book of going forth by day"). It explains the widespread fear that the dead might return to settle scores with the living regarding wrongs that the latter might have committed toward them.

The family of the deceased—in particular, the eldest son—was in principle supposed to supply him with the nourishment intended to assure his subsistence in his "second" life. Food offerings were placed at the entrance to the tomb: these were traditional items, the loaves of bread, cakes, fruits and vegetables, fowl, and jugs of beer so often represented in the tombs (figure 160). We may imagine that these offerings were "redistributed" to the officiating priests and the necropolis personnel.

Other food offerings were placed in the tomb itself for the direct benefit of the deceased. In a tomb at Saqqara dating to Dynasty

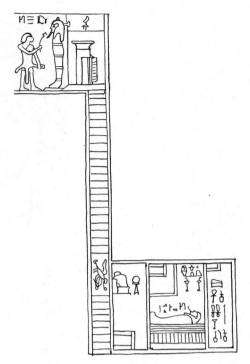

Fig. 158. Regeneration of the deceased: the *ba,* in the shaft of the tomb, goes to join the mummy in its burial chamber. Book of the Dead of Nebqed. New Kingdom. Louvre.

2, archaeologists found a whole funerary repast comprised of loaves of bread, fish, fowl, pieces of beef, fruits, cheeses, and cakes.[20] This custom lasted down to the latest periods of history. Many examples, though on a more mod-

Fig. 159. The deceased in his tomb, his *ba* hovering outside. Painting in the tomb of Arinefer (Theban tomb 290). Deir el-Medina. Dynasty 20.

Fig. 160. The deceased at his offering table, served by a funerary priest. Painting in the tomb of Petosiris. Muzawwaqa (el-Dakhla Oasis). Second century C.E.

est scale, have been found in the tombs of the Ptolemaic and Roman Period cemeteries of el-Kharga Oasis. In the New Kingdom, in certain cases, these offerings were carefully mummified and placed in wooden boxes shaped approximately like their contents. One such group of food offerings was found in the tomb of Yuya and Tuya, not to mention those in the tomb of Tutankhamun and other Theban tombs of the same period (figure 161). Besides these real offerings, offerings were painted or carved on the walls of the funerary chambers; from the Old Kingdom on, we see representations of the deceased seated in front of his offering table, which is laden with various foodstuffs. These representations were supposed to stand in magically for real offerings in case the latter were interrupted: thus, the deceased would never be deprived of food. The Egyptians had evidently observed that even in the case of pharaohs, the offering service would eventually be interrupted. It is in connection with the furnishing of the nourishment necessary for survival that we may also interpret the scenes of livestock raising, slaughter, and harvesting so often represented in the mastabas of the Old Kingdom, as well as the "models" of the same scenes in the tombs of the Middle Kingdom.

Otherwise, it seems that a funerary banquet could be celebrated near the tomb by the members of the family. Remains of such a meal, accompanied by the byproducts of the mummification process, were discovered in 1906 by Davis in a cache near the as-yet undiscovered tomb of Tutankhamun.[21] These remains included jars containing lamb and bird bones, jugs for wine and water, along with drinking cups, and even floral garlands that must have been worn by the participants.

Offerings had to be renewed at fixed times, probably on the anniversary of the burial and on the occasion of certain festivals, such as the "Beautiful Festival of the Valley" in the Theban region. In the case of pharaohs and highly placed personages, foundations were endowed to perpetuate their funerary cult. This offering cult, in theory carried out by the family, was in fact assured by specialized priests. In the Ptolemaic Period, these priests were called *choachytai* (water pourers), a term that evokes the rite of pouring out libations of water. It seems in fact that liquid offerings played an important role in the funerary cult.

Of course, we observe some variations in ritual according to the means of the deceased or

Fig. 161. Food offerings for a deceased person. Thebes. Dynasty 18. London, British Museum.

the period under consideration. Thus, in a number of tombs in the Roman Period necropolis of Dush, and in the older cemetery at el-Deir, excavators have noted the presence of deposits of locks of hair, a rite unattested elsewhere and whose meaning has yet to be clarified.[22]

The food offerings were supposed to assure the subsistence of the deceased. But food alone did not suffice to guarantee him survival, for it was believed that he had to travel in the world beyond, to make a journey strewn with pitfalls and dangers resulting from the presence of maleficent powers. To evade these traps along the way, and to be able to affirm his innocence before Osiris, the deceased needed to make use of the magical formulas written on the sides of coffins in the Middle Kingdom, and in the New Kingdom, on Book of the Dead papyri. From the New Kingdom on, near the mummy, either in the coffin or beside it, there was often a box, surmounted by a statuette of Osiris (figure 162), that contained the papyrus roll. This practice would continue in use down to the beginning of the Roman Period.

Fig. 163. Isis-Aphrodite. Molded terra cotta. Ptolemaic Period. Louvre.

Fig. 162. Ptah-Sokar-Osiris. Stuccoed wood. Necropolis of Dush, T53 (el-Kharga Oasis). End of the Ptolemaic Period or beginning of the Roman Period.

Fig. 164. Funerary stela of Osirwer. Painted limestone. Ptolemaic Period. Louvre.

Ushabtis, or "respondents," whose origin went back to the Middle Kingdom (when they were called *shawabtis*), were also protective presences. These were small statues of stone, Egyptian faïence, or wood, anepigraphic or inscribed with the name of the owner, on whose behalf they were supposed to do work in the afterlife. They often bear the text of chapter 6 of the Book of the Dead, which gives them the name "respondents," for these "servants" were believed to respond in case the deceased was called on to perform compulsory labor.[23] Their number, which was relatively small at the beginning, grew to such a point that in certain cases, there was one for each day of the year. They were then divided into groups of ten supervised by "foremen" who assured they would do their required tasks. The complete collection of Tutankhamun's *ushabtis* is the finest example of this type of figurine.[24]

Other statuettes (Anubis, *djed*-pillar, etc.) could also be placed in the tomb, especially in little niches dug into the four walls of the burial chamber. The tomb of Tutankhamun is a good example of this practice, as well.

In tombs from the Middle Kingdom on, we begin to find wood, stone, or even faïence representations of nude women, sometimes accompanied by a child. After nearly disappearing in the Third Intermediate Period, these figurines reappeared in somewhat different form in the Ptolemaic and Roman Periods. In this period, too, there was a custom of placing molded terra cotta statuettes depicting various deities, such as Isis (figure 163) and Harpokrates, in the tombs, and even profane images that were usually in a style more Greek than Egyptian.

Because of the double function of kings, both royal and sacerdotal, the funerary furnishings of the pharaohs assumed huge proportions. Even in the tombs of ordinary private persons, however, we can find relatively abundant and varied furnishings, often related to everyday life. The contents of the tomb of Kha and his wife Meryt, now in the Turin Museum, are representative of this phenomenon.

During the New Kingdom, there were changes in tomb furnishings, with objects of daily use tending to become less frequent.[25] Even so, in tombs down through the Roman Period, we continue to find a greater or lesser number of furnishings that reveal not only the religious beliefs of the deceased (figure 164) but also, in many cases, their daily activities.

8   Animal Mummies

I gave bread to the hungry, water to the thirsty, clothing to the one who was naked. I cared for the divine ibises, falcons, cats, and dogs, and I ritually buried them, anointed with oil and bandaged with cloth.[1]

In Egyptian thought, there was no difference, it seems, in the nature of men, animals, and gods: according to the creation stories, the god who created the world produced all species from the "humors" of his body, or brought them into existence by his thought and his speech. It is thus no surprise that gods often assumed the form of animals or of half-human, half-animal hybrids, or even chimerical, purely animal beings such as Amyt, the "Devouress," who was part crocodile, part hippopotamus, and part lion.[2] In the first dynasties, gods had human forms, but it is not excluded that the earliest cults were those of animals. The names of nomes (figure 165), which would persist down to the end of Egyptian civilization, are perhaps the most tangible trace of such cults: Black Bull (Heliopolis), Black Dog (Kynopolis), Oryx (Beni Hasan), Hare (Hermopolis), greyhound (Lykopolis), and so forth. Still, the only animal for which there is conclusive proof that its cult existed at this early date is the Apis bull, the "living soul" of the god Ptah at Memphis. Otherwise, there were several gods who could be represented in their sanctuary by a living animal, chosen from among others that were raised in the temple enclosure. Thus, a living falcon incarnated the god Horus at Edfu, a ram the god of Mendes (and, undoubtedly, the god Khnum at Elephantine), and a crocodile the god Sobek at Kom Ombo and in the sanctuaries of the Faiyum. In the Faiyum, though, the

incarnation of the god could be either the mummy of a crocodile or a living animal, as was the case at Kom Ombo, where there was a crocodile pool.

It was only natural to mummify animals who were the living image of a god, but there were others who also benefited from this treatment. In the later stages of history, we witness a considerable expansion of the "sacralization" of animals, that is to say, of the practice of deifying them through mummification. It seems, in fact, that most of these animals were raised in the temple enclosures and then killed and mummified for the purpose of being sold to pilgrims, who offered them as ex-votos to the deity with whom they were associated.[3] This practice involved a rather large assortment of animals, from the cats associated with Bastet to the ibises connected with Thoth, to cite only the best known of them. These animals, which were mummified and thus sacralized, had to be buried in specific places, which led to the establishment of gigantic catacombs containing hundreds of thousands of mummies, as at Saqqara (figure 166)[4] and Tuna el-Gebel.[5] They could also be placed in human tombs that had become disused, as in the case of the Bubasteion at Saqqara.[6]

Diodorus Siculus records interesting details about the raising and the funerals of these sacred animals:

> For each species of venerated animal they have consecrated a tract of land which produces a revenue sufficient to feed and care for its members. . . . Whenever any of these animals dies, they wrap its carcass in fine linen; and beating their breasts in lamentation, they take it to be embalmed. There they treat the body with oil of

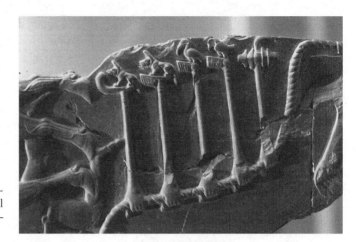

Fig. 165. Clan standards with animal figures. Detail from the "bull palette." Schist. Abydos. C. 3300–3200 B.C.E. Louvre.

cedar and sweet-smelling substances that can preserve it for a long time, then they bury it in a consecrated grave.[7]

Among the sacralized animals, we must count the dogs found in cemeteries dating back to the predynastic period. The dog was worshiped especially at Kynopolis (near Ashmunein) and at Lykopolis (Asyut). The animal is not always well identified: it could be a dog or a jackal.[8] Two rather similar gods could be represented by a canine, Anubis (figure 167) and Wepwawet, both of whom had the function of protecting the dead. Thousands of dog mummies, rather poorly prepared, have been found in a large Roman Period necropolis at Abydos. Recently, at the site of el-Deir, our Alpha-Necropolis team discovered a rather large number (around five hundred) of canine mummies in reused human tombs (figure 168).[9]

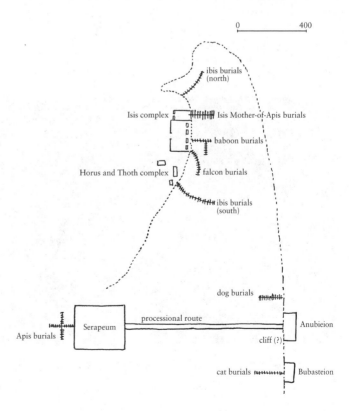

Fig. 166. Plan of the animal cemeteries of north Saqqara. After J. Ray.

Fig. 167. Head of a statue of Anubis. Wood with gold and obsidian inlays. Tomb of Tutankhamun. Dynasty 18. Cairo Museum.

Apes, essentially baboons (a representation of Thoth, as was also the ibis), were mummified and buried in cemeteries that were usually near a sanctuary of the god they incarnated. This was the case at Tuna el-Gebel, the cemetery of Hermopolis (figure 169), and Saqqara North. But the tombs in the Valley of the Monkeys (also called the West Valley), which is located near the Valley of the Kings in the Theban region, do not seem to have been linked to the presence of a sanctuary.

Certain fish were mummified (figure 170), in particular the Nile perch, the *lates,* which gave its name to the city of Latopolis (Esna) and which was associated with Neith, its goddess. A few miles west of the city, there is a large fish cemetery containing many of these mummies, of all sizes and often in an excellent state of preservation. But understandably, the mummy of a small fish in its wooden "coffin," four inches long, which was found in the midst of the cat mummies at the Bubasteion of Saqqara, is of problematic interpretation.

An extremely rare example of a mummified frog (figures 171 and 172) was found in a tomb in the necropolis of Dush, placed between the legs of a mummified and emasculated adult male.[10] This custom no doubt refers to the myth of Osiris, one version of which recounts that the sexual organ of the god, thrown into the Nile, had been devoured by an oxyrhychus fish; as for the frog (figures 173 and 174), it no doubt alluded to the rebirth of the deceased. From at least the Middle Kingdom on, the frog was a symbol of the goddess Heket; she was associated with Khnum, the creator god, and she was often represented in the birth scenes of the Ptolemaic and Roman *mammisis*. In Egypt, the frog became such a popular symbol of the rebirth of the dead that it even appears on

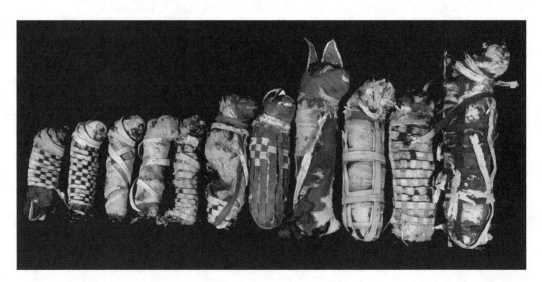

Fig. 168. Eleven canine mummies, carefully bandaged. Necropolis of el-Deir, T E9 (el-Kharga Oasis). Roman Period.

Fig. 169. The god Thoth in the form of a baboon. Hermopolis. Second Intermediate Period.

Fig. 171. Frog mummy. Necropolis of Dush, T54 (el-Kharga Oasis). Ptolemaic Period (?).

Christian lamps, accompanied by the word *anastasis,* "resurrection."

Other animals with attested religious significance could also be mummified. Such is the case, for example, with serpents, mongooses, scarab beetles, a number of birds, gazelles, and shrews. Scattered among the falcon mummies in North Saqqara were rather numerous mummified shrews, most often wrapped collectively in a single packet and sometimes placed in small, rectangular limestone coffins. The association of this animal with the falcon seems logical, for we know that the shrew was associated with Horus Mekhenty-Irty.

A final category of mummified animals is that of pets: the baboon of Princess Maatkare, or the cat of Prince Tuthmosis, whose stone coffin has been found. In the case of private persons, but apparently rarely, the aim of mummification was probably to assure the immortality of an especially beloved animal. The story of Maatkare's baboon is surprising: it was long believed that this small mummy, which was buried with the body of the princess in her coffin, was that of a newborn infant. X-ray examination corrected the error, revealing that it was in fact a hamadryas baboon.[11]

Some species, however, seem never to have been mummified. The reasons might have been religious in the case of animals deemed maleficent because they were linked to the god Seth, such as the donkey, the hippopotamus, and the pig.[12] We may note, though, that burials of donkeys and horses are attested in Nubia.[13]

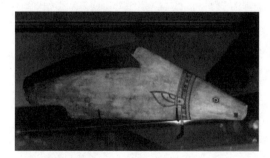

Fig. 170. Coffin in the form of a fish containing a mummy. Painted wood. Date uncertain (Late Period–Roman). Louvre.

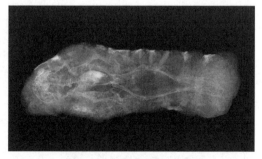

Fig. 172. X-ray of the mummy of a frog, identified as *Rana mascareniensis.* Necropolis of Dush, T54. Ptolemaic Period (?).

Fig. 173. Two frogs. Egyptian faïence. Late Period. Louvre.

THE SPECIAL CASE OF SACRED BULLS

The Apis bulls were an entirely special category about which we are extremely well informed. Unlike other animals linked to a divine power, Apis was unique. It was chosen according to extremely precise criteria: it was exceptional for an Apis to be succeeded by a calf it had engendered. At the death of an Apis, priests went out in search of a replacement who met the established criteria. According to the Roman writer Aelian, there were no fewer than twenty-nine criteria, leaving us to think that the selection was extremely rigorous.[14] The most salient markings were a white triangle on the forehead and crescent-shaped patches on the flanks. Other sacred bulls also had their distinctive markings: the bull who would incarnate Mnevis had to be entirely black, with tufts of hair on its body and its tail. As for the Buchis bull, it had to be of a species with short horns and a hump on its withers, and white in color, with a black head.

Once selected, the new Apis, according to Diodorus, made a stay of forty days in a place called Nilopolis (whose location remains uncertain), and then he was taken to Memphis at the time of the full moon.[15] At Memphis, where he had his own "residence" near the temple of Ptah, there was a clergy specially attached to him. According to certain authors, he also had a "harem" of selected cows, while according to others, he had only one "wife." One thing is certain: the sacred character of the Apis was reflected on his mother. She was the object of special care, and she was even buried in a cemetery reserved for her, the "Cemetery of the Mothers of Apis," which is currently being explored at Saqqara North. The mother of Apis was, moreover, the object of a cult and identified with Isis-Hathor.

At the end of his life, the bull was buried in the Serapeum (figure 175), a vast catacomb dis-

Fig. 174. Mummy label with a Demotic inscription and a drawing of a frog. Wood. Date uncertain (Late Period–Roman). Louvre.

Fig. 175. The catacombs of the Serapeum of Memphis. After Perrot and Chipiez.

covered by Mariette in 1850. Down to Dynasty 26 (700–525 B.C.E.), it seems that he was not satisfactorily mummified, though canopic jars of Dynasties 18 and 19 attest to the practice of evisceration. Some of these jars, which are relatively large, are now in the Louvre. The oldest coffins, however, which were discovered intact, contained nothing more than fragments of broken bones. We thus see the repetition of a scenario we already observed in the Old Kingdom with regard to human mummification: the viscera were removed and preserved, though there was as yet no use of procedures that would enable the preservation of the entire body. We may thus hazard the conclusion that the practice of evisceration made its appearance earlier than the natron bath.

We may easily imagine, moreover, that the mummification of such huge animals posed problems that long remained insurmountable. From Dynasty 26 on, the bulls were properly mummified. A papyrus in Vienna, written partly in hieratic (a cursive form of hieroglyphs) and partly in Demotic (a cursive script that appeared in Egypt at the end of the seventh century B.C.E.), and dated to the end of the Ptolemaic Period, contains precise information regarding the procedure that was followed:[16] the body had to be washed with water and "properly packed with cloth," after which it was anointed with oils and wrapped in bandages. The evisceration could be done either by abdominal incision or by anal extraction. The eyes were replaced by artificial eyes of cloth. Two teeth were extracted and replaced by artificial teeth, undoubtedly to imitate the loss of the milk teeth and to symbolize the regeneration of the Apis.

The magnificent Apis embalming tables, made of a single block of alabaster, are still at Memphis. The sides, decorated with lion's feet and heads, recall the funerary beds that are often represented and have sometimes been found in human tombs. Other, smaller tables, probably intended for the treatment of the viscera, have also been found. The mummification of an Apis was undoubtedly more difficult than that of a human being, for the quantity of water to be extracted from the body of the an-

Fig. 176. Votive stela: person worshiping before Apis. Painted limestone. Serapeum of Memphis. Late Period. Louvre.

imal was evidently far larger, entailing a much longer natron bath.

Thanks to stelae from the Serapeum (figures 176 and 177), we are well informed regarding the chronology of the Apis bulls (they could live as long as twenty-six years, in the case of one Apis that died during Dynasty 22) and the circumstances of their burial. There has been no recent scientific study of the remains of the Apis bulls. We have only the excavation reports of Mariette, who describes their miser-

Fig. 177. Votive stela: person worshiping before the mummified Apis lying on a pedestal. Serapeum of Memphis. C. 650 B.C.E. Louvre.

able state of preservation.[17] Moreover, except for two Apis tombs dating to Ramesses II, all the others known to date were pillaged: in fact, these bulls had been richly endowed with jewels and amulets.

Once prepared, the mummy was wrapped in shrouds and bandaged. A sort of gilded stucco mask covered its head, with artificial eyes of glass paste and a gilded wooden disk between its horns. Then the funeral could begin. There was a close analogy with human ritual, for the Opening of the Mouth ritual also occurred before placing the body in the tomb. We also know that mourning women participated in the funeral. On one stela, Prince Psammetichus, son of Amasis, reports that he mourned at the death of Apis and consumed nothing but bread, water, and vegetables during the seventy days that elapsed between the beginning of the mummification process and the burial of Apis.[18] Carved on another, perhaps contemporary stela from the Serapeum is a text concerning a bull that died in year 23 of Amasis (Dynasty 26, 547 B.C.E.):

> [A]ll the ceremonies were carried out for him in the house of purification . . . a large granite sarcophagus was prepared . . . a shroud was made for him of "secret" fabric coming from the sacred city of Sais to assure his protection. His jewels were made of gold and all sorts of precious stones. . . . The Majesty of this god (i.e., Apis) ascended to the sky in year 23, day 6 of month 7 . . . the lifetime of this god was eighteen years and six months.

The burial of an Apis was costly in the extreme. The king often made a contribution, as mentioned in the inscriptions; in the later periods of history, various temples could be required to share in these expenses.[19]

There is more than one Apis bull cemetery at Saqqara. During a period from Amenhotep III to year 30 of Ramesses II (c. 1250 B.C.E.), the burials were individual. Then, and down to year 52 of Psammetichus I (612 B.C.E.), the burials were grouped in a small subterranean gallery (these tombs are now inaccessible). From that time on, a larger subterranean gallery was laid out perpendicular to the preceding one, and it was used down to the end of the Ptolemaic Period and even beyond. Most of the bulls buried in this last gallery received magnificent monolithic sarcophagi (figure 178) weighing up to seventy tons, in contrast to the earlier coffins, which were wooden and much smaller in size. The stone sarcophagi were placed on either side of large galleries, in vaults whose walls were lined with polished limestone. Once the bull had been placed in its tomb, these vaults were closed and sealed, and by order of the king, a stela was placed at the entrance to commemorate the death and burial of the animal. Other stelae, offered by private citizens, were placed on the walls of the entrance gallery. Today, all the vaults lie open, their walls despoiled of their lining, and the sarcophagi are pillaged. The stelae, for their part, are now in various museums. They depict Apis in various ways, most often as a striding bull, but sometimes lying on the sledge that served to convey him to the necropolis, and sometimes as a standing man with a bull's head.

Fig. 178. Sarcophagus of Apis in place in its vault. Serapeum of Memphis. Late Period.

While the Apis burials were largely pillaged and the mummies much damaged, the same is not true of those of Buchis (figure 179), the sacred bull that was the image of the god Montu at Hermonthis south of Thebes. The necropolis discovered in 1926 dates back to Dynasty 30 (378–341 B.C.E.); it contains thirty-five tombs arranged on either side of a subterranean gallery, as at the Serapeum.[20] These burials convey a great deal of information regarding the mummification of the bull: the viscera were removed via the anus, not through an abdominal incision. The needed instruments—bronze retractors and containers outfitted with tubes—were found among the funerary material. The bull was positioned lying down, with its hooves folded under its body, and it was attached to a sturdy plank by means of bands of cloth strung through metal hooks. The head of the animal was covered by a gilded mask with inlaid eyes. A headdress made of a disk surmounted by two large feathers was attached between the horns. This is exactly the image we find on the stelae from the

Fig. 180. Cartonnage of a cow, Mother of Apis. Saqqara. Date uncertain (Late Period–Roman). Cairo Museum.

necropolis. One of them, dating to 288 C.E., depicts the emperor Diocletian making an offering to Buchis, and it enables us to affirm the exceptional longevity of this cult. As in the case of the Mothers of Apis at Saqqara (figure 180), scholars have identified tombs of the Mothers of Buchis (figure 181).

The cult of the Mnevis bull is well attested at Heliopolis, but with the exception of two tombs, his cemetery has not been found. It seems that the mummification and bandaging procedures were similar to those of Apis.

Fig. 179. Buchis bull. Bas-relief. Date uncertain (Late Period–Roman). Louvre.

Fig. 181. Skeleton of a cow, Mother of Buchis, still in place on its wooden plank. Necropolis of Armant, tomb 14.

Normally, bovines were butchered, either to feed the living or as offerings to the gods (though the latter came eventually into the hands of the priests). Nevertheless, archaeologists have found mummified remains of bulls and cows that were not necessarily sacred animals, such as the bulls discovered at Abusir. Among the latter, mummies of beautiful appearance contained, in reality, the disparate remains of several animals.

SACRED CROCODILES

There were a number of cult places dedicated to Sobek, the crocodile god (figure 182). Among the animals inhabiting Egypt in the historical period, the crocodile was certainly the most redoubtable. But the Egyptians did not approach them univocally: in certain cases, the crocodile was regarded as a beneficent power linked to the sun and the fecundating waters (this was the case with the crocodile gods of the Faiyum), while in others, it was a terrifying being more or less identified with Seth, enemy of the gods and power of chaos. In cult hymns, the crocodile could be invoked as a god "amiable of face, sweet of love, beautiful of appearance, brilliant of colors," and in the Faiyum, one of its names in the Graeco-Roman Period was Πνεφερως (Pneferos), "beautiful of face." In one hymn at Kom Ombo, he is, at one and the same time, a luminous being, a creator, and a violent god, a ferocious animal that "shatters bones, breaks limbs, and drinks the blood of the one who crosses his path."[21]

In the Middle Kingdom, the cult places of Sobek were in the delta and in the Faiyum. In the New Kingdom, an important cult place was dedicated to him at Sumenu, near Hermonthis.[22] In the Ptolemaic Period, the god's principal sanctuary, besides that at Krokodilopolis, capital of the Faiyum, which bore his name, was that of Kom Ombo, whose construction began in the second century B.C.E. and continued down to the third century of our own era. It is probable that in each sanctuary of Sobek, a crocodile was the "living image" of the god. At Theadelphia, Graeco-Roman Period stelae depict the animal lying on a small

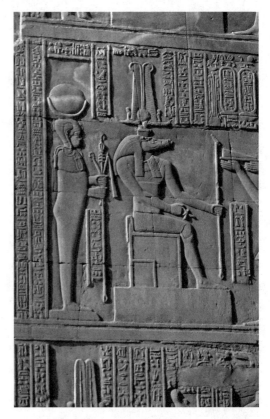

Fig. 182. The crocodile god Sobek enthroned. Sandstone bas-relief. Kom Ombo, temple of Sobek and Haroeris. Ptolemaic Period.

naos, with a priest before him making an offering or a gesture of prayer.[23] Another of these stelae depicts him swimming in his pool.[24] The Greek inscription on a granite statue of the crocodile god Petesuchos, stemming from Krokodilopolis and dating to April 16, 58 B.C.E., evokes the day when the god "manifested himself," which was on June 21, 60 B.C.E., quite probably the day when the living animal was "recognized" among his congeners as the incarnation of the god.[25] Moreover, it seems that in certain temples of the Faiyum, the image of the god was a crocodile mummy. In the north temple at Karanis, we can see deep niches that served to hold the mummy resting on its stretcher (figure 183). At Theadelphia, archaeologists found the stretcher used to carry it in procession (figure 184). A fresco from this temple represents the procession itself: the crocodile is wrapped in a white shroud that leaves his head, which

Fig. 183. Niche intended to receive the mummy of the sacred crocodile. Karanis, temple of Pneferos and Petesuchos (Faiyum). Roman Period.

Fig. 184. Niche intended to receive the sacred mummy, with its processional stretcher in place. Theadelphia, temple of Pneferos (Faiyum). Ptolemaic Period. Alexandria, Graeco-Roman Museum.

bears the crown of Osiris, uncovered. Moreover, certain temples of Sobek had facilities for raising crocodiles, such as the one at Narmuthis, recently excavated by an Italian mission, where unhatched eggs were found.[26] There is no doubt about the sacred character of these animals: it was from among them that the "living image" of the god had to be chosen. These nearly domesticated crocodiles constituted, in any case, a veritable curiosity for foreign travelers as they passed through. A text of Strabo informs us that they brought offerings of cakes and mead, which the priests proceeded to stuff down the animal's gullet.[27] Herodotus claims that the priests "adorned" their sacred crocodiles with bracelets and earrings.[28]

In some temples in the Faiyum, there was a cult of a pair of crocodiles, each of whom represented one aspect of the god. This was the case at Karanis, and also at Tebtunis, where there coexisted a Sobek-Geb and a Sobek-Re-Harakhty.[29]

Numerous crocodile cemeteries have been found throughout the valley, at Kom Ombo, Esna, Gebelein, Tihna, el-Hiba, Letopolis, and so forth. Some mummies are of extremely high quality, with the animal preserving its characteristic appearance (figure 185). The mummies could be entirely complete, and they could include eggs or even young in great number in the same container. Others, though, are quite mediocre; sometimes, they turn out to be false mummies or packets containing nothing but a few bones scattered in some straw, reinforced by palm stalks. On the outside, these mummies often seem to be of good quality, with bandages and cartonnages. Many of these cartonnages, however, particularly those of the crocodile necropolis of Tebtunis, have been destroyed so as to recover the Greek papyri used to make them.

CATS

Egypt has been considered the cradle of the domestic cat.[30] There seem to have been two kinds of cat in the historical period: a breed domesticated rather early and related to modern

Fig. 185. Mummy of a little crocodile. Date uncertain (Late Period–
Roman). Louvre.

cats, *Felis sylvestris libyca,* and a wild breed, the large marsh cat, *Felis chaus.*[31] With regard to the domestic cat, it must be noted that in a way, it is more aloof from man than the dog can be. We know of many cases of cats who have returned to a life that, if not wild, is at least independent. Perhaps this is why dogs are much more frequently represented in Egyptian art during the earlier dynasties, with the cat scarcely appearing before the Middle Kingdom and becoming more frequent especially in the New Kingdom.

In the art, we see the cat as a pet seated under the chair of its mistress, or accompanying the man of the house during a hunt (see the painting from the tomb of Nebamun at Thebes, figure 186),[32] or even as a household "helper" hunting rodents. But it also had a religious significance. In solar myths, the cat is a companion or even a form of the sun god Re. In this capacity, it is depicted defeating the serpent Apopis, a hostile force who threatened to prevent the sun from rising. This combat is represented in the vignettes illustrating chapter 17 of the Book of the Dead, as well as in tombs of the Ramesside Period.[33] The cat is also depicted receiving a cult on stelae from Deir el-Medina.

The relationship of this animal to Bastet, the cat goddess, was the source of its importance. Bastet is known from the Old Kingdom on, but it was in the Bubastite Dynasty 22 (945–773 B.C.E.) that the city of Bubastis (Tell Basta) in the delta and its goddess first attained preeminence. It was at this time that the local temple of Bastet was considerably enlarged and saw its influence extend beyond the merely local level. The goddess was represented as a lion-headed woman, which led to her connection with another feline goddess, the lion Sakhmet (figure 187). The two goddesses came to be considered as two opposite but complementary forces: Sakhmet represented force, violence, and even war, while Bastet represented tenderness, gentleness, and maternity. In the representations, it is sometimes difficult to distinguish the lion's head from that of a cat. It seems that it was in Dynasty 22 that the cat came to be viewed as a manifestation of Bastet. It is also in this period that we see the appearance of large numbers of bronze or faïence images of seated or recumbent cats, often accompanied by kittens. Given the number of examples still in existence, there must have been a considerable production of these images. A vast cat cemetery has been found at Bubastis.[34] The mummies were laid to rest in ditches with walls of brick or hardened clay, and sometimes placed in terra cotta receptacles.

Another lion or cat goddess, Pakhet, had her temple at the Speos Artemidos, near Beni Hasan, where a large cat cemetery was also discovered. The mummies were often placed in

Fig. 186. Nebamun's cat hunting birds. Painting from the tomb of Nebamun. Dynasty 18. London, British Museum.

Fig. 187. The goddess Sakhmet. Gilded wood. Dynasty 18. Cairo Museum.

small, animal-shaped coffins of wood or bronze. In the nineteenth century, it was from this cemetery that tons of mummies departed for England, where they were used as fertilizer. It is reported that a single cargo of about nineteen tons would have contained some 180,000 mummies. Many other cat cemeteries have been found, especially in the Theban region, where a "resting place of cats" is mentioned in the text of a Demotic papyrus of the second century of our own era.[35]

The study of cat mummies, which had been done in the past on a relatively restricted number of individual examples (fifty-three mummies in the British Museum),[36] has recently been carried out on a greater scale in the framework of the exploration of the Bubasteion of Saqqara (more than three hundred examples).[37] The latter study has confirmed that most often, these animals did not die of natural causes. On the one hand, most of them were young or subadult, while on the other, they presented cervical disjunctions or skull fractures, leading us to think that they had been de-

liberately killed (figure 188). We may infer that the mummies had been made to be sold to pilgrims who no doubt offered them in the sanctuary as witness to their gratitude or piety. The existence of breeding facilities near the temples, at least in the later stages of history, is well attested and must have responded to this demand. Many papyri mention the existence of cat breeders (*ailouroboskoi*).

The external appearance of the mummy varies: in some cases, it looks like an elongated packet (figure 189), with the head left visible by the bandaging and the legs folded along the body, as shown by X-rays. Examples of this type are on view at the British Museum. In other cases, the legs are separately bandaged (figure 190), yielding a more lifelike appearance, as we can see with the mummies in the Louvre. The wrappings could be quite sophisticated, with the head modeled in stuccoed cloth and painted; most often, however, the bandaging is rather crude. Often buried without a protective covering, the cat could sometimes be enclosed in a wooden coffin that itself had the appearance of a seated animal (figure 191). The size of these wooden coffins varied, sometimes enabling the coffin to contain a complete mummy, and sometimes only some bones. More rarely, it was a stone or wooden

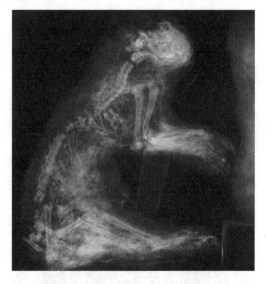

Fig. 188. X-ray of a cat displaying fracture of the cervical spine and the rear of the skull. Saqqara, Bubasteion. Date uncertain (Late Period–Roman).

Fig. 191. Cat coffin. Wood. Date uncertain (Late Period–Roman). Louvre.

Fig. 189. Mummy of a cat nicknamed "skittle mummy." Date uncertain (Late Period–Roman). Louvre.

coffin in the form of a box. A wooden example in the Turin Museum is decorated on one of its ends with two seated cats face to face, flanking the hieroglyphic sign *nefer*.[38] Another type is constituted by a bronze box surmounted by a statuette of a cat. As in the case of humans or of other animal mummies, false or incomplete mummies are not lacking. These could be individuals damaged before or during the embalming process. If we admit the votive function of these mummies, false mummies could be explained not only by a lack of conscience on the part of the personnel charged with making them, but also by too high a de-

mand. The presence of numerous false mummies (as many as 25 percent at Saqqara) argues in favor of their mass production.

BIRDS

Forty species of birds were mummified. This fact, however, does not mean that all of them were sacralized; indeed, far from it. The birds associated with a deity were principally the falcon, image of Horus, god of kingship; the ibis, sacred to Thoth; and the vulture, which was sacred to Nekhbet. As for the ibis, it was the white ibis with a black head, *Ibis religiosa sive aethiopica*, which has today disappeared from Egypt. It has been hypothesized that this fact is related to the large number of birds that were mummified, but this does not seem convincing: rather, it was the major artificial drainage projects in the delta during the nineteenth century that led to the disappearance of the ibis, which had survived to that time, through considerable alteration of its biotope. There were many breeding facilities for ibises in the later stages of Egyptian history, and vast cemeteries have been found in diverse localities. The largest

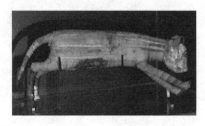

Fig. 190. Mummy of a cat with legs separately bandaged. Date uncertain (Late Period–Roman). Louvre.

was probably that of Tuna el-Gebel, the cemetery of Hermopolis, whose principal temple was dedicated to Thoth.[39] Inside a huge enclosure, in three subterranean galleries (one of them entirely empty), were packed thousands of conical terra cotta jars, each of them containing one or more birds. Others were placed in small stone coffins deposited in niches dug into the walls of the galleries. Like all the other birds, the ibises were dried but not eviscerated. The wrapping, though, was generally extremely painstaking. Sometimes, the mummy was completed by a false head with a beak, and the head bore the characteristic crown of Thoth. A small room next to the entrance of the oldest gallery must have served as the workshop where the mummification took place. In it was found an embalming table with a channel for the runoff of liquids, and which still bore traces of resinous products. Jars set into the floor contained natron, salt, and turpentine. Other large ibis cemeteries have been found at Abydos, where large jars contained as many as a hundred birds, also bandaged, as well as eggs. There was also a cemetery in North Saqqara.[40] At this same site, immense galleries sheltered thousands of falcon mummies (figure 192) in terra cotta jars, as well as vulture mummies in large jars.

RAMS

The ram was the sacred animal of more than one god: Amun, Khnum, Harsaphes. It also re-

Fig. 192. Falcon mummy. Necropolis of the falcons. North Saqqara. Date uncertain (Late Period–Roman).

ceived a cult at Mendes, under the name Banebdjedet, "the ram lord of Mendes." Two species were known in ancient Egypt: *Ovis longipes palaeoaegyptiaca*, with long, spiral, horizontal horns, and a species that appeared later, *Ovis platyura*, whose curled horns were similar to those of European rams today. There

Fig. 193. Ram mummies with their cartonnages inside a tomb. Muzawwaqa (el-Dakhla Oasis). Roman Period.

Fig. 194. Mummy of a ram in its painted and gilded cartonnage. Elephantine. Date uncertain (Late Period–Roman). Louvre.

is no trace of the breeding of sacred rams around the temples, but we have information regarding the coronation of the animal as the living image of the god of Mendes during the reign of Ptolemy II. This animal had a "residence" called "mansion of the rams," evidently a sheep barn with a pen.[41] Ram cemeteries have been found at Mendes, Tebtunis, Tihna, Elephantine, and el-Muzawwaqa in el-Dakhla Oasis (figure 193). The rams of the Roman Period cemetery at Elephantine were enclosed in cartonnages (figure 194) that were often of excellent quality and placed in sand-stone coffins.[42] The room where these animals were embalmed has also been found. It is quite likely that in the temple of Amun, and in that of Khnum, a living ram was believed to incarnate the god.

Being linked to the traditional religion, animal mummification would persist to the end of the fourth century of our own era, when there was again the question of a search for a new Apis bull in the year 362 C.E.; after that, the practice disappeared with the spread of Christianity and the interdiction of the pagan cults. The same was not true of human mummification, which would last much longer. Most animal mummies are late in date, Ptolemaic and Roman, and this increase in the mummification of animals and the rendering of honors to them is often considered a sign of a certain regression in Egyptian religion. In our opinion, this was not at all the case. In all periods, from the beginning of Egyptian history on, the gods were either linked to animal figures or could take on animal form. What was new in the later periods of history was that mummification techniques became more accessible, and probably less costly, making it possible to apply them not only to many more humans but also to animals. In older periods, when human mummies had been relatively limited in number, animal mummies could only have been rare. When it comes to the customs of ancient Egypt, we too often tend to privilege interpretations based on religion and symbolism, to the detriment of concrete motivations and economic constraints.

9 The Last Mummies

The rising influence of Christianity did not bring about a sudden end to mummification. In fact, we must not think of Christianity as a religion that was, from the outset, powerful and capable of battling traditional religious practices. We know almost nothing of the beginnings of Christianity in Egypt; legend attributes its introduction to the apostle Mark, but there is no historical proof of this. It is only at the end of the second century C.E. that we have some evidence for the establishment of Christianity at Alexandria, with a highly regarded catechetical school. In the course of the first three centuries, Christianity seems not to have spread in Egypt in the same ways as in Palestine or Asia. Proof of this point is afforded by the texts of Nag Hammadi: written in Coptic, they probably constituted the library of a Christian community in Upper Egypt in the fourth century C.E.. A number of these texts have a Gnostic character reflecting currents of thought quite different, on certain points, from what would become "official" doctrine, and they are much influenced by Egyptian and even Iranian ideas. These texts include gospels describing Christ and the apostles (gospels of Thomas, Philip, and Mary Magdalene) that were not retained in the canon of New Testament texts. The heterodox nature of these Christian communities of Egypt can explain how it was that silence was imposed on them and that we know so little about the beginnings of Egyptian Christianity.[1] In the third century, however, and especially in the fourth century, ecclesiastical structures were progressively set in place, and we bear witness to the appearance of a movement that would spread far and wide, both within and outside Egypt: monachism. The last great "ordeal" for the Christians of Egypt, as for all Christians in the empire, was the persecution under Diocletian at the turn of the fourth century.

Afterwards, once it had acquired legitimacy, Christianity spread gradually throughout the cities and the *chora* (the countryside). At the same time, we observe a progressive disaffection with regard to the traditional religion, which had clearly suffered from the economic difficulties of the third century. This disaffection, though, was unequal from one region to another. It was only at the end of the fourth century (391–392 C.E.) that imperial edicts ordaining the closing of the "pagan" temples put an end, at least theoretically, to the practice of the traditional cults.

The religious difference between Christians and the rest of the population entailed scarcely any changes in their daily lives. They lived in the same villages as their "pagan" compatriots, and they were buried in the same cemeteries. In fact, during at least the first three centuries, and even beyond, it seems that Christian tombs were intermingled with the others. This point can be affirmed in the necropolis of Hawara, in that of Karara near el-Hiba (figure 195), where pagan tombs were included in the Christian cemetery, and at el-Baqawat in el-Kharga Oasis (figures 196, 197, and 198), where pagan tombs of the fourth century C.E. were found in the proximity of the much more numerous Christian tombs.[2]

Not content just to use common burial places, the Christians also had themselves mummified. Unfortunately, we have as yet no systematic study of mummies identified as Christian.

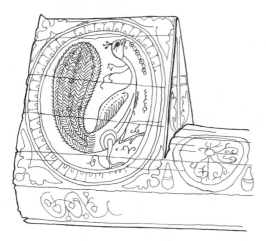

Fig. 195. Detail of a Christian coffin decorated with a peacock, symbol of resurrection. Necropolis of Karara (el-Hiba). Fifth to seventh century C.E.

A study by G. Castel of the burials of the monks of the Monastery of Saint Mark in the Theban region has shown that the bodies were covered with blocks of salt and with "greasy" products that have not been formally identified. The bodies presented no trace of evisceration, which of course does not preclude some

other type of treatment. Clothed in their used monastic habits, the bodies were wrapped in ten superimposed shrouds covered by a leather apron, all held in place by a network of bandages.[3]

The study carried out by E. Prominska on three monks from the same monastery confirmed that bodies were still preserved with care.[4] The type of mummification employed consisted essentially of the use of blocks of natron, with no traces of abdominal evisceration. According to Prominska, one of the monks seemed to have been bandaged rather hastily, perhaps while he was still alive. This mummy displayed traces of blows to the occiput and the face, as well as traces of blood. Another had a damaged thorax, making it possible to see the lungs, the diaphragm, and the esophagus. On the whole, these three mummies were rather well preserved. The hair, beard, and body hair were abundant, and the nails were long. The skin seemed as a whole dry, but in places, it was covered with a sort of grease that seemed to the investigator to have been se-

Fig. 196. Painted decoration of the small dome of the "chapel of peace": the conversation between Paul and Thekla, the Virgin of the Annunciation (right). Necropolis of el-Baqawat (el-Kharga Oasis). Sixth to seventh century C.E.

Fig. 197. General view of the necropolis of el-Baqawat (el-Kharga Oasis). Sixth to seventh century C.E.

creted by the cadaver: it might have been adipocere, a phenomenon well known to forensic medicine. In any case, "classical" Egyptian mummies never display such an "emission" of

Fig. 198. Interior of a funerary chapel with a shaft leading to the burial chamber. Necropolis of el-Baqawat (el-Kharga Oasis). Sixth to seventh century C.E.

fatty substance. These observations permit an affirmation that the natron was not used in the same manner as in traditional treatment. The odor of the cadavers was, for the investigator, "characteristic." At Dush, we were able to observe a highly disagreeable odor coming from mummies that were clearly late in date and comparable to those of the monks examined by Prominska.

In the burials found near the Monastery of Epiphanius at Thebes, archaeologists found bodies swaddled in layers of cloth. Between the layers were juniper berries and blocks of salt.[5]

In the Christian cemetery of el-Hiba, the bodies displayed thick layers of salt between the shrouds. Certain of them, which were mummified, had been placed in wooden or terra cotta coffins; others, which were simply swaddled, had been placed on wooden frames.[6]

At Dush, in the so-called dovecote cemetery located around 875 yards from the principal necropolis, some bodies were uncovered in a funerary enclosure that contained seven individual ditches. This group was the object of a survey in 1990. The bodies were of an appearance similar to that of the mummies described by Castel and Prominska, and their preservation seemed quite good (figures 199, 200, and 201), though they gave off a strong odor of putrefaction, which is not, as a general rule, the case with classical mummies. Their color was grayish, similar to parchment, and clearly different from that of the "black" mummies or that of the light (chamois) color found in the

Fig. 199. Mummy in place in an individual pit. Christian necropolis of Dush, T P1 (el-Kharga Oasis). C. 380 C.E.

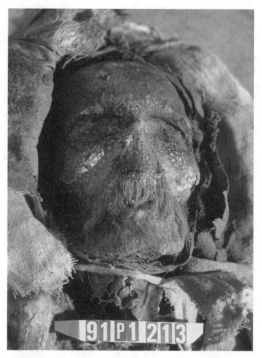

Fig. 201. Well preserved head of an elderly man. Christian necropolis of Dush, T P1 (el-Kharga Oasis). C. 380 C.E.

neighboring cemetery. The bodies were not bandaged in the strictest sense but rather wrapped in a shroud large enough to contain the entire body. The shroud was held in place by thin cords (figure 202). Two of the mummies (that of a man and that of a little girl) had the mandible fastened by a chin strap that was knotted at the top of the head, something that had never before been observed on the many mummies exhumed at Dush (E. Prominska also signaled this practice). Like the Christian mummies of the Theban region, the mummies of Dush were literally covered with blocks of salt that formed a veritable coating. They presented no evisceration incision. X-rays showed, however, that the quality of mummification was not low, even if its nature was different. Often enough, certain habitual characteristics were found, such as the condensation of the vertebral disks and epiphysial cartilage. These mummies, which are undoubtedly Christian, given the style of burial and the type of tomb (in which a coin datable to the years 375–378 C.E. was found), seem to have coexisted in time with mummies "manufactured" according to the strictly traditional technique and found in a non-Christian context.[7]

Between 1987 and 1990, the monastery of Abu Fano, south of Minya, was explored by a

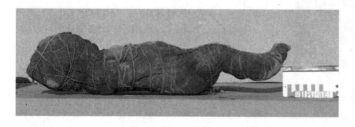

Fig. 200. Bandaged mummy of a baby. Christian necropolis of Dush, T P1 (el-Kharga Oasis). C. 380 C.E.

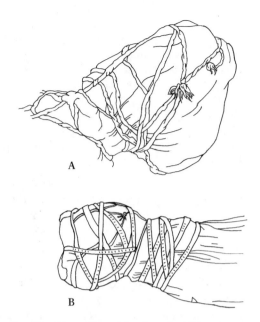

A

B

Fig. 202. Disposition of the shrouds and bandages on Christian mummies. Head of the mummy of a child (A), Christian necropolis of Dush, T P1. Feet of the mummy of a monk (B), Monastery of St. Mark, Thebes (after E. Prominska).

team led by H. Buschhausen. This was probably one of the first monasteries in Egypt, dating to the fourth century of our own era. A number of monks' tombs were found under the pavement of the church; a complete study of some of the mummies was made—in particular, that of Apa Bane, the patron saint of the monastery.[8]

During the fall 2004 excavation season, our own team discovered a Christian cemetery at the site of el-Deir. We found some subjects that had been spontaneously mummified, while others had benefited from intentional mummification; the latter differed slightly from that used for "traditional" mummies, but it was comparable to what was observed at the monastic sites mentioned above. Here were buried the population of a village, including men, women, and a number of children. Most often, they were buried in individual ditches, but sometimes, they were interred in small, vaulted subterranean tombs that contained several individuals. The bodies were not bandaged, but rather wrapped in superimposed shrouds (as many as ten for a single subject)

that were often decorated with geometrical motifs, including crosses. These shrouds were held in place by thin cords or by bandages with hems that were knotted in a rough-and-ready fashion. In at least one case, a man was dressed in a decorated tunic that covered yet another, simpler tunic that served as a shirt. These were clearly clothes intended for everyday use. There was an indisputably Christian sign: the right hand of two men had been positioned by the embalmers in such a way that they were making the sign of benediction.[9]

These various examples show that mummification continued to be practiced in Christian Egypt, even in a monastic milieu. As late as around 600 c.e., Bishop Abraham of Hermonthis would give instructions to assure his burial "according to traditional customs."

The "finery" of the mummies changed, however: instead of being bandaged, the body was most often wrapped in a simple shroud, as we were able to verify in the Christian tomb at Dush and in some of the Christian tombs at el-Deir. The deceased could also be dressed in clothing he must have worn in everyday life (we found an example at el-Deir). The monks of the Monastery of Saint Mark retained their monastic habits, which were covered by the shrouds. But there is no trace of shrouds in several burials at Antinoe, which must date to the third century at the earliest. Thus, two mummies from Antinoe now in the Grenoble Museum are dressed in woolen robes with woven decoration, and they wear a crown of leaves. The same is true of the female mummy called the "embroiderer," now in the Brussels Museum,[10] which is dated to the first half of the fourth century. While the mummification has seemed mediocre, or even nonexistent, to those who have studied the body, her clothing is of high quality and richly decorated. The woman is dressed in at least two superimposed tunics with woven decoration and two sashes decorated with bands and with medallions depicting birds, fish, flowers, and bunches of grapes, all in extremely fresh colors. On her head is a bonnet surmounted by a sort of thick garland made of tufts of polychrome wool. Her head and feet rest on cushions that are also decorated with woven medallions. Also at Antinoe, archaeologists have found a series of painted shrouds dating to the same period (fourth century) and depicting women wearing sumptuous clothing: purple tunics with a medallion, embroidered shawls, and jewels in quantity, all of which seems to indicate that, in a manner that was not rare, deceased persons were buried in their finery rather than in modest shrouds. Some of these women have the ansate cross that became a Christian symbol, though it is uncertain whether they were Christians.[11]

Christians did not reject mummification, which was never forbidden by canonical texts: belief in resurrection at the end of time (an end of time that was often believed to be at hand) could accord well with a care to preserve the body. Moreover, any attempt to contravene so ancient and deeply rooted a tradition would undoubtedly have been doomed to failure. A recollection of the ancient techniques of traditional mummification appears clearly in a Coptic text of the life of Pachomius, the founder of monasticism:

> When a sinner is on the point of death, two pitiless angels stand near him . . . they place a curved object like a hook in his mouth, and they extract the miserable soul from his body; it is claimed that it is black and shadowy.[12]

This text preserves, of course, a distorted memory of the technique of extracting the brain.

A bandage fragment from Oxyrhynchos bore a Christian inscription manifestly intended to protect the corpse, at the same time testifying to belief in resurrection: "Jesus said, 'Nothing is buried that is not to rise again.'"[13] This inscription can be compared to those on funerary cloths with invocations to various pagan deities.

When they spoke of burying the dead, Christians as well as pagans said, "going to the mountain." A text regarding the nuns of the first convent established in Egypt, that of Tabennesis, states:

> If anyone of the sisters passed away, the mothers would make a shroud for the body to be wrapped in. Then the appointed brothers would stand in solemn gathering there under a portico, while the sisters stood far from them on the other side, chanting, until the burial took place. They would go to the mountain even more solemnly, while the sisters themselves chanted behind the hearse.[14]

The well known Graeco-Roman Period practice of keeping the mummified body at home for a certain time, without burying it, was kept up in the Christian community: this practice can be explained by the fact that the family did not always have a tomb ready at the time of death. According to Diodorus, it could even happen that the body of a deceased person was offered as security for a loan. These strange practices are confirmed by the existence of "mummy cupboards," which have been found in particular at Abusir el-Meleq, as well as by the label on the mummy of a certain Senbesis, which tells us that 261 days passed between his death and his burial. The *Life of Saint Anthony* written by Bishop Athanasius in the second half of the fourth century informs us that

> [t]he Egyptians were in the habit of taking the dead bodies of righteous men, and especially those of the blessed martyrs, and of embalming them and placing them not in graves, but on biers in their houses, for they thought that by so doing they were doing them honour.[15]

This usage clearly differed somewhat from traditional custom, for it had to do with preserving the body of "holy men" so as to venerate them. In any event, Anthony opposed a custom he considered "neither legitimate nor holy," and he asked his disciples not to allow anyone to "take his body into Egypt," but rather, to bury it on the spot.

It is clear that despite the pressure of tradition, the Christian authorities attempted to distance themselves from certain pagan practices, even if they were unable to forbid them directly.[16] In addition, the debate concerning resurrection with or without the body must also have influenced the positions taken by church leaders. It was probably the arrival of

Islam that brought a definitive end to the practice of mummification by imposing burial directly in the ground, with the corpse wrapped only in a shroud.

Christian tombs differed little from those of pagans, at least at first, when Christians and pagans shared the same cemetery, as at Hawara and at el-Hiba. We can observe a change, however, especially at el-Baqawat. The tombs that are apparently the oldest are collective, and they are veritable mud brick constructions, with a façade either in the form of a temple gate flanked by columns or consisting of rounded archways. They include a chapel surmounted by a cupola. A shaft dug into the ground gives access to the burial chamber. At the periphery of the cemetery, there are individual tombs (figure 203), many of them grouped around the "great church." These are simple, shallow ditches lined with brick, topped either by a low rectangular superstructure or by a heap of rubble covered with a coating of lime.[17] In Egypt as elsewhere, this custom of burying the dead in individual

tombs around the churches would last for centuries in the Christian communities.

The practice of funerary offerings is well attested among the Christians. In the tombs at el-Hiba, archaeologists have found coins, tools, ceramic vases, jewels, and musical instruments. At Antinoe as well, they have discovered vases of ceramic, faïence, or alabaster, as well as glass objects, lamps, and terra cotta statuettes. These objects could indicate either belief in the continuation of life or the idea that the deceased might have need of these objects at the time of the Resurrection. In any event, lamps were placed in the tombs, as had already been done in pharaonic times, and as before, the anniversary of the funeral was commemorated. Certain tombs display a juxtaposition of pagan and Christian beliefs: thus, in a tomb at Ballana in Nubia, archaeologists found a gold cross, a scarab, and coiled strips of lead. Another strip, this one of gold, bore a magical formula, written in Greek, with an invocation to Isis.

But while Christians and pagans were long

Fig. 203. The sector of individual tombs in the necropolis of el-Baqawat (el-Kharga Oasis). Sixth to seventh century c.e. Archives of the Metropolitan Museum of Art, New York.

able to coexist peacefully in the same villages and cemeteries, there came a time when traditional funerary practices were abandoned, and the tombs thus came to be neglected: people undoubtedly no longer dared to bring the customary offerings to the deceased. We see Christian "holy men" choosing tombs for their retreats; located at the edge of the desert, these burial places assured the isolation they sought. Thus, when Anthony decided to withdraw from the world, he retired into a tomb and "closed the door on himself." In his youth, Pachomius had the habit of "going into tombs filled with dead persons and spending the entire night, from dusk to dawn, praying before God." While ascetics dwelling in a tomb no doubt found there the "social death" they sought and were thus able to "repudiate their life," it seems they had scarcely any respect for the dead whose rest they disturbed. In fact, according to a curious dialogue between the holy man Makarios and a dead pagan whose skull he found lying in the desert, those who "did not know God" were condemned to dwell after death in a subterranean place in the midst of torments, the worst of which was never again "to see anyone face to face," for "the face of one is fixed to the back of another. Yet when you pray for us, each of us can see the other's face a little."[18] Such was the strange and terrifying afterlife that Christians would ascribe to those who for centuries had considered death a passage leading to a blessed life.

Part Two

Mummification and Science

10   Historical Background

The scientific study of mummies began with Egyptology. Mummies had, of course, been an object of curiosity and interest since the first European travelers set sail for Egypt. At the beginning of the seventeenth century, these travelers acquired the habit of bringing back this particular type of "object" to grace collectors' "cabinets of curiosities." Superintendent M. Fouquet had such a cabinet, along with two coffins that La Fontaine admired, imagining them to be those of Chephren and Cheops! The collector F. de Peiresc of Aix-en-Provence also had a mummy,[1] as did the painter Peter Paul Rubens, who made several drawings of it. In the eighteenth century, there was an increasing interest in archaeological objects, including coffins, which often arrived in Europe with their contents intact. It was thus that many mummies made their way into private collections, and most of them eventually entered the collections of museums, a fact that in large part assured their survival. This history of acquisition meant, however, that quite often it was no longer possible to specify just where in Egypt the mummy had come from.

Many of the mummies remaining in Egypt were destroyed. Pillaging was the most common cause: mummies were deliberately destroyed to recover jewelry, amulets, and other items that adorned them. The pillage of tombs had begun early in antiquity. During the First Intermediate Period, which was marked by a series of political, social, and especially economic upheavals, all the royal pyramids were opened and plundered. It goes without saying that the tombs of the nobles experienced the same fate. It has been shown that some of them had been pillaged even before the burial chamber was sealed.[2]

This activity continued, reaching an unequaled scale under the Ramessides. A major legal proceeding under Ramesses IX brought to light scandalous violations of tombs in the Valley of the Kings.[3] During Dynasty 21, in the wake of these robberies, the high priests of Amun felt obliged to regroup the royal mummies in the tomb of Amenhotep II (KV 35) and in the cache at Deir el-Bahari (DB 320) in order to protect them. In the same way, many mummies of priests and priestesses of Amun were assembled in the hypogeum of Bab el-Gusus, which was also located at Deir el-Bahari. Pillaging did not stop, however, as testified by the depredations committed in the royal tombs of Tanis, whose condition was duly recorded by P. Montet when he discovered them in 1939. Down to the end of antiquity, even the most modest tombs fell victim to pillaging. We ourselves found an example of this phenomenon in the necropolis of Dush: a tomb with a vaulted chamber (T69) was superimposed on an older shaft tomb whose burial chamber had been entirely despoiled before it was eventually reclosed, its entrance hidden under a layer of *muna* that covered the back wall of the new tomb. The two tombs, which date to the Roman era, were not far apart in time, to judge from the surviving artifacts.[4]

In the Middle Ages, an Arabic-language manual for the "perfect plunderer of tombs," *The Book of Buried Pearls,* circulated far and wide and would be copied for centuries. It described precisely how to locate and plunder tombs, and it even contained magical formulas to protect the thieves.[5] Another important cause of destruction at that time was the quest for *mumia,* a product with supposedly therapeutic properties, which was prepared using mummies that had been reduced to powder. It is possible that this property was attributed to mummies because bitumen (*mumia* in the Persian language) was believed to heal wounds and mend broken bones.[6] In the fifteenth and sixteenth centuries, the practice of reducing mummies to powder, which had already been mentioned by an Arab physician in the twelfth century, touched off a veritable wreaking of havoc in the cemeteries. Thus, in 1551–52, Cordelier André Thévet, who would later become the chaplain of Catherine de Medici, traveled to Egypt and tried the product on himself, thus scandalizing Ambroise Paré.[7] In principle, *mumia* was used in powdered form, but the body could also be boiled to produce a brew, an example of what is called, in German, "pharmacopoeia of filth" (*Dreckapotheke*). Demand was such that some began to produce fake *mumia*: the French physician Guy de la Fontaine, who visited Alexandria in the sixteenth century, discovered a shop where this "remedy" was concocted.[8] These abuses eventually led to a ban on the marketing of the product, but the discontinuance of its use barely postdates the beginning of the nineteenth century.

The use of *mumia* was not limited to therapeutic ends; in the nineteenth century, it was also used to produce "mummy brown," a pigment used in paint. Funerary wrappings were also used to make paper.[9] Animal mummies, in particular those of cats, were exported in vast numbers to England, where they were used as fertilizer. Finally, according to Mark Twain, mummies were even burned to fuel the engines of steam locomotives.

Napoleon's expedition to Egypt inaugurated the scientific investigation of that land. The archaeological aspect of this investigation centered essentially on the monuments, to be sure, but in the process, many mummies were discovered, especially in the Theban region. Many plates in the *Description de l'Égypte* produced by that expedition depict whole or fragmentary mummies, drawn with considerable care, though not always accurately. Animal mummies were not omitted (figure 204).[10] These discoveries did not, however, lead to a truly scientific study of mummies. An exception was the approach taken by the brothers Champollion in Grenoble, who unwrapped and studied a Ptolemaic mummy, now in the museum of that city.

Throughout Europe, the publication of the *Description de l'Égypte* touched off an extraordinary infatuation with the antiquities of Egypt, a veritable Egyptomania. The pillaging of antiquities continued on a grand scale. And thus began many of the major collections, which were put together by the official representatives of European governments, such as H. Salt and B. Drovetti, who would enrich the Louvre, the British Museum, the Turin Museum, and others. At that time, there was no control over the export of antiquities. The search for jewels and amulets continued, leading to the more or less precipitous removal of the bandages from mummies.

During the first half of the nineteenth century, this practice of unwrapping mummies assumed a pseudoscientific veneer. G. Belzoni, who had worked in the Valley of the Kings, described tombs filled with mummies (figure 205), some of which he brought to London. Unwrapping sessions were conducted before a "select" audience. T. Pettigrew, a London surgeon and professor of anatomy, was among the first to give lectures on mummification followed by public unwrappings, to which tickets were sold. The knowledge Pettigrew acquired enabled him to write the first serious work on mummification.[11] Scientific excavations began in the middle of the century, but they did not put a stop to clandestine digs, which they sometimes even indirectly inspired.

A. Mariette, who departed for Egypt in 1850 with the mission of searching for Coptic manuscripts, "forgot" this objective and was seized by a passion for pharaonic Egypt. He took up residence there, and with the support of the Khedive, he founded the Direction des Fouilles, which later became the Service des Antiquités. He devoted all his energy and authority to an attempt to save the antiquities from pillaging. It was his inspiration that in one way or another led to a change in attitudes: it is said that he obliged his wife to give up a

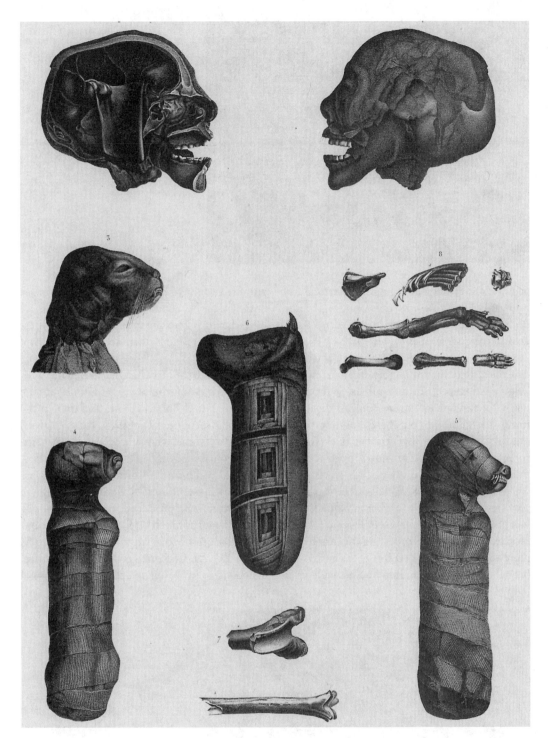

Fig. 204. Human and animal mummies. *Description de l'Égypte*, vol. 2, pl. 51.

Fig. 205. Woman in a tomb filled with mummies. Watercolor by J. G. Wilkinson.

genuine scarab she had bought! A particularly important initiative was the founding of the Boulaq Museum to shelter the objects discovered in the course of excavations.

Still, it was only gradually, and at a relatively late date, that mummies benefited from this heightened respect for antiquities, and particularly for sarcophagi (figure 206). At this time, it was still possible to purchase mummies without difficulty and to bring them back to Europe, where they were unwrapped during private "soirées." Too often, they were afterwards destroyed. In 1889, G. Le Breton, the director of the Ceramic Museum in Rouen, who had gone to Egypt in search of Coptic fabrics, recruited a team of clandestine diggers to explore the tombs in the region of Akhmim. He brought back three mummies, as well as a number of fabrics he had removed from other bodies that he abandoned where they lay.[12] Even during licit excavations in the cemeteries, mummies were most often not studied or even preserved.

This state of affairs changed somewhat with the discovery of the royal mummies in the cache at Deir el-Bahari (1881) and then in the tomb of Amenhotep II (1898), yet even then, there were some who would not stop themselves from destroying such prestigious remains. A special room in the Cairo Museum was assigned to these mummies. Soon, a descriptive monograph was produced, consisting mostly of photographs taken by E. Brugsch accompanied by a brief text written by G. Maspero.[13]

In 1895, W. C. Röntgen discovered X-rays, which led to his being awarded the first Nobel

Fig. 206. Sarcophagi assembled in a temple. Print from G. Ebers.

Prize in physics in 1901. In 1896, W. F. Petrie wondered whether mummies should not be X-rayed, notwithstanding the fact that the relative weakness of the devices of the period meant that only the extremities of the arms and legs could be investigated. We can only admire Petrie's scientific clarity: he understood the importance of studying human remains, and he realized that for the first time, scholars had at their disposal a nondestructive means of investigating mummies.

In the years that followed, radiology and other technologies for investigating the human body were put to use. In 1897, a Dr. Bloch of Vienna took the first X-ray of the entirety of a mummy.[14]

On March 26, 1903, Tuthmosis IV was solemnly unwrapped in a room of the Cairo Museum by G. Maspero, assisted by E. Brugsch and G. Daressy, in the presence of a select group of Egyptologists and physicians. In the same year, G. E. Smith asked Dr. H. Milton to X-ray the mummy of this pharaoh. The results made it possible to determine the king's age at death and to show that he was much younger than had been thought on the basis of historical documents. In fact, the immature character of the skeleton made it possible to affirm that the king was at most twenty-five years of age when he died.[15] And yet, in 1912, when G. Elliot Smith published the first complete description of the royal mummies, he did not make use of radiography, doubtless because of excessive concern that the X-rays might damage the bodies. The thick layers of resinous unguents made a precise study of the mummies almost impossible, and only a clinical evaluation made it possible to determine their approximate age.[16]

Between 1903 and 1909, L. Lortet and C. Gaillard published an exhaustive study of many animal mummies from various sites, most of them dating to the later stages of Egyptian history. Their survey included dogs, cats, rodents, cattle, sheep and goats, birds, reptiles, fish, mollusks, and other species as well. X-rays played a role in their work.[17]

In 1907, in Manchester, the Egyptologist M. Murray undertook the first scientific study

(with autopsy) of the mummies of "two brothers" from the Middle Kingdom. Well in advance of her time, she had brought together an interdisciplinary team that included anatomists, chemists, and textile specialists.[18] A later study by A. R. David and her team showed that these two individuals were indubitably unrelated, notwithstanding the fact that the inscriptions on their coffins indicated they had the same mother.[19]

In 1910, M. A. Ruffer developed a technique for rehydrating mummified tissues, enabling the histological, anatomopathological, and parasitological study of mummified remains (figure 207). He identified the eggs of *Schistosoma haematobium* (the cause of schistosomiasis) in the kidneys of two mummies dating to Dynasty 20.[20] In the same year, G. E. Smith and D. E. Derry discovered a case of leprosy in a Coptic mummy at el-Bigha in Nubia.[21]

In 1913, Dr. Bertoletti described the first transitional lumbosacral vertebral anomaly, which was observed on X-rays of a Dynasty 11 mummy.[22]

In 1926, a mummy was X-rayed for the first time in France at the Musée Guimet in Paris (figure 208).[23] Some journalists, astonished at the fact that the recently discovered mummy of Tutankhamun had not been X-rayed, were desirous of demonstrating the feasibility of the procedure. From the Musée Guimet, they obtained the loan of a mummy, that of a female musician, probably from the later stages of Egyptian history. The equipment used was a low-powered, portable device. The procedure, which was rendered somewhat difficult by the absence of electricity at the museum (a power

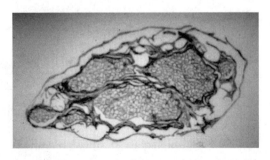

Fig. 207. Cross-section of a nerve, after M. A. Ruffer, 1911.

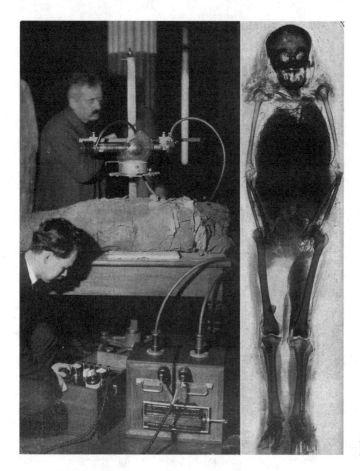

Fig. 208. X-raying a mummy in the Musée Guimet, Paris, 1926.

line had to be hooked up for the occasion), was carried out, not without trial and error, thanks to the ingenuity of the technician, M. Bonin. The interpretation was entrusted to Professor G. Lardennois and to A. Moret, who was at that time Professor of Egyptology at the Collège de France. While it proved possible to investigate the arms and legs satisfactorily, the same was not true of the trunk, which was filled with resin and packing, causing it to appear as an opaque area on the negatives.

In 1931, R. L. Moodie X-rayed a group of seventeen Egyptian and Amerindian (Peruvian) mummies, seven of them children (figure 209), as well as a number of animal mummies, most of them Egyptian.[24] Among the human mummies from Egypt, which were from various periods (one belonged to the predynastic era: it was undoubtedly a "natural" mummy), he found signs of osteoarthritis, arteriosclerosis, and dental pyorrhea. His X-rays were of

extremely good quality for the period.[25] One of the mummies had been "shortened" by the embalmers, who broke and removed a part of the femurs in order to fit it into a sarcophagus that was too small for it.[26]

In 1933, W. B. Boyd, with L. G. Boyd and then with L. C. Wyman, perfected the first technique for determining the blood group of mummies from the remains of the muscles of a group of 131 Egyptian mummies (and 226 Indian mummies).[27] In 1936, P. B. Candela proposed another technique using pulverized osseous tissue. He studied 30 mummies of Egyptian women from Dynasty 21.[28] This type of investigation is still done today.

In 1942, Dr. F. Jonckheere published a thorough study of a mummy in Brussels believed at the time to be that of the royal scribe Butehamun. Jonckheere's work included X-ray study of the mummy, followed by its unwrapping and description, and finally, its autopsy.[29]

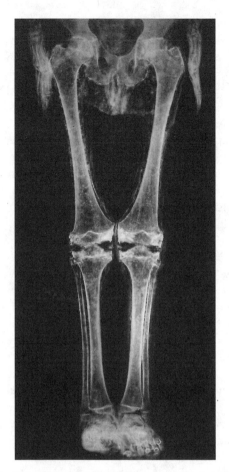

Fig. 209. X-ray of the legs of the mummy of a child. There seem to be calcifications of the pelvis (schistosomiasis?). There are growth arrest lines on the lower ends of the tibias. After R. L. Moodie, 1931.

In 1955, A. T. Sandison definitively perfected the technique of rehydrating tissues, which has changed but little since that time.[30]

In 1966, Dr. P. H. K. Gray published X-rays of the mummies in the Leiden Museum,[31] and then, in 1968, those in the British Museum and the Liverpool Museum.[32] At the time, this was the largest group of mummies, 133 in number, ever X-rayed. This investigation remains of considerable importance, not only because of the number of subjects but also because of the quantity of data collected. Unfortunately, though, these were extremely heterogeneous groups that included mummies from a number of periods (from predynastic "natural" mummies to mummies of the Roman Period), many with uncertain provenance and even date.

Dr. J. E. Harris, a stomatologist, participated in excavations at Gebel Adda during the Nubian salvage campaign; he X-rayed nearly one thousand skulls with the aid of special equipment that required no source of electricity: a unit containing a radioactive element (Ytterbium 169). In this study, unfortunately, the postcranial skeleton was not systematically taken into account. In association with E. F. Wente, Harris then turned to the royal mummies of the Cairo Museum, in the framework of a vast stomatological study of the ancient and modern populations of Egypt.[33] This work included an attempt to determine the family relationships between the pharaohs on the basis of their anthropological characteristics. The study brought to light incompatibilities between the classic identifications of the mummies and their probable genetic filiations. Moreover, their evaluations of the mummies' age at death did not always coincide with the historical information.

In 1974, a mummy in the Royal Ontario Museum (ROM) in Toronto was studied by a team of Canadians and Americans.[34] This was the mummy of a weaver named Nakht, dating to the Ramesside Period, which was discovered at Deir el-Bahari in a reused Middle Kingdom tomb.

In 1976, Ramesses II was taken to Paris for restoration work. The team directed by L. Balout and C. Roubet took advantage of his arrival to undertake a large number of noninvasive examinations that included, besides radiology, a study of the fungi responsible for the observed deterioration and a study of the vegetal remains in and around the mummy. It was confirmed that the pharaoh had lived to a ripe old age and that he had suffered from lesions resulting from arthritis and ankylosing spondylitis, in particular on the hips and the cervical spine. In this same area of the body, the investigators discovered a postmortem fracture that occurred during the mummification process. Afterwards, the mummy was sterilized with gamma rays and placed in a Plexiglas coffin filled with sterile air.[35]

In 1979, A. R. David and her team published their study of seventeen mummies in the Manchester Museum ranging in date from the New Kingdom to the Roman Period, along with other, fragmentary human remains.[36] This study included the "two brothers" examined by M. Murray in 1907. Thirty-one animal mummies in the museum were also studied. The investigators made use of all modern scientific means. The project was facilitated by the proximity of a particularly well-equipped hospital. A team of highly specialized researchers was able to study the bodies using all possible scientific approaches: histology and anatamopathology, radiology, study of the insects found on the mummies, textile analysis, radiocarbon (C_{14}) dating, and facial reconstruction on the basis of cranial characteristics. Only one of the mummies was the object of a genuine autopsy, a limitation that was imposed for the sake of maximal respect for this irreplaceable material.

In 1979, E. Strouhal, assisted by Dr. L. Vyhnánek, reviewed all the mummies preserved in Czech museums and private collections.[37] These collections included twenty-four entire bodies and many incomplete remains, as well as sixty-nine animal mummies. Their study centered on physical anthropology and paleopathology. Many of these mummies belonged to old collections and were of indeterminate provenance. Some, however, came from the excavations of B. Bruyère at Deir el-Medina and had been acquired with the help of J. Černý.

Since the early 1980s, there has been a considerable increase in the scientific study of mummies in museums. In 1980, A. Cockburn and his team from Detroit published four mummies in the museum of the University of Pennsylvania, which were X-rayed and thoroughly examined (PUM I–IV).[38] In 1981, R. Grilletto published the initial results of his anthropological study of mummies discovered during excavations in the cemetery of Antinoe. More recently, with E. Delorenzi, he published a study of the mummies in the Turin Museum.[39] In 1991, a multidisciplinary team made an exhaustive study of a mummy in the Kestner Museum in Hannover, including such items as the textiles, the balms, and the wooden coffin.[40] A complete study of the

mummies, including some animal mummies, in the Musées Royaux in Brussels was published in 1999.[41] In 2001, a multidisciplinary team published their examination of a mummy in the Narodowe Museum in Cracow.[42] On the occasion of an exhibition in the British Museum in 2004, the mummy of a priest from Dynasty 22–23, Nesperennub (British Museum inventory number 30720) was scanned and re-examined by J. H. Taylor.[43] More recently still, the mummies in the Leiden Museum were the object of yet another complete study, principally by CAT scan.[44]

Meanwhile, thanks to a portable scanner placed at the disposal of Egyptian researchers,[45] Dr. Z. Hawass initiated a vast project intended to investigate a large number of mummies, not only those in museums such as the ones in Cairo and Luxor, but also those at sites where excavations are being conducted. The royal mummies and the mummies of Bab el-Gusus in the Cairo Museum are part of this project, as are those from the tombs of Thebes and mummies recently discovered in Bahriya Oasis.[46] Insofar as it concerns the study of mummies in the field, this undertaking ties in with that initiated in 1982 by C. Roubet and R. Lichtenberg.[47] Rather than study mummies in museums, whose provenance and date are often uncertain or even impossible to determine, these researchers chose to devote themselves to mummies from a known and precisely dated site, and to conduct this study in the field. The site was the necropolis of Dush (el-Kharga Oasis), which was in use from the end of Ptolemaic Period to the end of the Roman Period. Many analytical techniques could not be used, to be sure, given conditions in the field, but a statistical and paleodemographic approach proved possible, largely compensating for the limitations imposed by their choice. This first effort was concentrated on seventeen mummies.

Since 1984, this work has been continued by F. Dunand and R. Lichtenberg, complemented by the study of skeletal remains in collaboration with J. L. Heim. At present, a group of sixty-five complete mummies have been X-rayed, and more than two hundred skeletons have been examined. It must be noted that most of the skeletons show signs of having once been mummies that deteriorated due to conditions unfavorable to preservation, for the cemetery was located near irrigated fields.

In 1986–88, a Japanese team studied mummies from Qurna. The human material consisted of the often fragmentary remains of 166 mummies from two tombs. The dating ranged between Dynasty 18 and the Graeco-Roman Period, with the latter principally represented. To date, their published works bear mainly on methods of cranial evisceration.[48]

The study of the Roman Period mummies discovered by C. Leblanc's team in several tombs in the Valley of the Queens has been completed by Drs. A. Macke and C. Macke-Ribet.[49] The work carried out by these investigators consists of the anthropology and paleopathology of 142 mummies (and 164 fragments), with a detailed analysis of mummification techniques. Radiology is not being used.

In 1994–97, and then in 2003, following on the work done at Dush, F. Dunand, J. L. Heim, and R. and M. Lichtenberg conducted a study of the same type on the human remains in the necropolis of Ain Labakha (el-Kharga Oasis). This necropolis, which was excavated by the Egyptian Antiquities Organization between 1992 and 1994, is contemporary with that at Dush. Thus, a new group of sixty-four Roman Period mummies, whose state of preservation is much better than that of the mummies of Dush, have been X-rayed.[50]

Since 1998, similar work by the same team at the site of el-Deir has to date enabled the X-ray study of thirty-seven complete mummies and forty detached heads. Additionally, about three hundred skeletons have been studied anthropologically. The mummies at this site, many of them damaged by pillaging, date to the Graeco-Roman Period, like those of Dush and Ain Labakha, but certain older ones might date back to the fifth century B.C.E. In 2004, the team discovered a Christian necropolis and uncovered some scores of mummies.

The mummies X-rayed by the team at these sites in el-Kharga Oasis now total 170 complete individuals and 59 mummified heads.

In 2003–4, R. Lichtenberg studied and X-rayed the human remains from the site of Tebtunis.[51] These are essentially skeletal remains of about sixty individuals. To the extent that bodies were mummified, it seems to have been done hastily. In 2005, Lichtenberg studied and X-rayed twenty mummies from the tomb of Pashed (DEM 323) at Deir el-Medina. These mummies proved to be from the Ptolemaic Period.[52] Also in 2005, at Saqqara, M. and R. Lichtenberg X-rayed in situ nine Dynasty 25 mummies in tombs nearly twenty-three feet below the surface of the ground.[53]

At Adaima, the human remains from predynastic cemeteries were studied by E. Crubézy and his collaborators in the framework of the excavation directed by B. Midant-Reynes.[54] These skeletons were the object of a thorough anthropological and paleopathological study. The same type of study is currently being pursued by an Australian and Canadian team in the necropolis of Kellis (el-Dakhla Oasis), whose tombs are of Ptolemaic and Coptic date.[55]

The study of mummies is not confined to human remains, as we have seen in our survey of the examination of mummies in museums.[56] Between the years 1992 and 2002, R. Lichtenberg was able to apply his technique of examination in the field to more than three hundred cat mummies from the Bubasteion of Saqqara.[57]

Quite recently (campaign of 2004), after the discovery of many canine mummies in some of the tombs in the necropolis of el-Deir (el-Kharga Oasis), fifty-four mummies were X-rayed and studied by R. Lichtenberg.[58]

Mummies have benefited from ongoing technological progress in imaging and medical analysis. Computerized axial tomography (CAT scanning) is the most interesting technique because, like classical tomography, it enables close analysis of images by eliminating the superposition of different structures and also by compensating for the considerable differences in contrast furnished by mummified bodies. Unfortunately, for a long time, scanning could be done only in a well-equipped radiological facility, and its use could scarcely be envisaged in the desert (at least, with the financial means usually available to archaeological missions). Today, with the possibility of placing a scanner on a truck, this handicap has in large part disappeared.

Another approach, the study of DNA (deoxyribonucleic acid) has been undertaken in certain cases, notably by S. Pääbo.[59] Theoretically, it is rich in promises, but to date, its application to Egyptian mummies still poses major problems.

We can thus say that mummies have never been more studied than they are today. Whenever new technology for medical analysis or imagery makes its appearance, even in the domain of forensic medicine, efforts are made to apply it. Such study leads to an ever more precise understanding of the conditions of life in ancient Egypt and of the illnesses from which populations suffered, making it possible to reinforce and even clarify other archaeological and textual data. Moreover, it remains imperative that this irreplaceable and indeed nearly unique material be investigated by nondestructive means.

11 Methods of Studying Mummies

The scientific study of mummies long remained in its infancy. It is not until the beginning of the twentieth century that it merits consideration here.

At present, researchers have a large number of techniques, more or less simple to implement, at their disposal. In fact, the choice depends essentially on where the mummies are, for certain sophisticated methods can be envisaged only in the framework of a well-equipped laboratory. It is thus the mummies kept in museums that are likely to be subject to complete investigation. Nevertheless, until now, there have been limitations linked to the invasive nature of certain types of examination. Only exceptionally, for example, has it been possible for researchers to remove samples from the royal mummies in the Cairo Museum. And it was strictly forbidden to take even the smallest sample from the mummy of Ramesses II when it was studied in Paris in 1976 (where it was taken essentially to be restored). It has thus been almost impossible to carry out the DNA studies on these mummies that alone would put an end to the uncertainties regarding their identification and filiation, especially those of Dynasty 18.

The protocol for studying a mummy is related to what would be followed by a practitioner of forensic medicine doubling as a historian. It is necessary to use all available techniques while bearing in mind that mummies are objects of limited number and irreplaceable, and that each one can bear information unique to it. The investigator must always maintain the greatest possible respect for their integrity.

Every study of a mummy must be preceded by the most thorough cleaning possible (figure 210), and this is especially true of mummies that have lost their bandages and are thus most often encrusted with sand. This procedure, which must be done with meticulous care, can take a long time because of the fragile nature of the mummified body. It goes without saying that this detail has mainly to do with mummies in the field.

CLINICAL OBSERVATION

Clinical observation remains fundamental, and it often supplies precious details.[1] General appearance, state of preservation, and color are details that can yield information on the technique of mummification that was used and the period when the mummy was made, not to mention all the details related to pathological conditions, which sometimes lead to a diagnosis of the cause of death. The appearance of the body also furnishes an indication of its age. Naturally, if the mummy is "complete"—that is, if its bandages are preserved, or even its cartonnage or coffin—we are better able to know when it was made, and often even the identity of the subject. Such identifications are often possible in the case of mummies in museums, for they ended up where they are because of their beautiful appearance and the well-preserved condition of their containers. We must, however, recall the frequency with which coffins were reused and thus remain cautious regarding these identifications.[2]

PHOTOGRAPHY

Photography is indispensable, of course, because it furnishes an objective record of all the

Fig. 210. The workman Abdullah cleaning a mummy at the excavation site of the necropolis of Dush (el-Kharga Oasis), 1982.

aspects described above. It must be done rigorously and for anthropometric rather than aesthetic purposes, notwithstanding the fact that some faces that are still rather beautiful might invite an attempt to create a "portrait." Mummies are relatively difficult to photograph because their generally dark color contrasts with their surroundings; the use of a dark background makes it possible to remedy the problem. Drawings are often of great help in recording certain details, as is also the case with the copying of decoration or texts that are difficult to photograph because of the shape of a cartonnage or coffin, or because of their state of preservation.

If an unwrapping is undertaken (which is to be avoided to the extent possible), it will always be photographically recorded so as to enable an analysis of the method of bandaging employed by the embalmers and to document the stages of the procedure.

ENDOSCOPY

Endoscopy is the use of medical fibroscopes whose suppleness enables the exploration of the natural and artificial cavities of mummified bodies. Thus, endoscopy of the abdominal cavity of Ramesses II revealed that the thorax was not accessible, because it contained a packing of cloth made of threads of linen and gold. This discovery supported the hypothesis that the heart was still in the thoracic cavity, as seemed indicated by X-ray examination, which had revealed a median opacity in the thorax.[3] Easily,

and without danger to the mummy, endoscopy can reveal canopic packets or make it possible to specify the type of packing that was used. It can also identify the remains of abdominal organs that were not removed by the embalmers. It has even been used to explore the spinal column of a mummy in the San Lazzaro di Armeni monastery in Venice.

RADIOGRAPHY (AND MEDICAL IMAGING TECHNIQUES)

Radiography (figure 211) has become practically the rule for mummies in museums, and for more than twenty years now, it has regularly been used by the Alpha Necropolis team in studying mummies in the field in el-Kharga Oasis. In the past, when radiological material was not widely available and practically untransportable, there was the extremely difficult problem of arranging the famous "rendezvous" of mummy, radiologist, and equipment. This problem imposed itself especially when it came to on-the-spot radiography of "mummified populations" that could scarcely be transported over large distances to a hospital or a properly equipped museum. We ourselves resolved the problem by using portable equipment and setting up a radiology lab at the site itself or in its vicinity. Radiology is a technology that supplies a great deal of morphological information while remaining entirely noninvasive. It enables the making of a high-quality evaluation of the condition of the skeleton and in principle a valid evaluation of lesions either of the bone or of certain internal organs in the many cases where abdominal evisceration was not carried out. When radiography is done by placing the subject at a distance of at least ten feet, it is called "teleradiogaphy," and, with a small (16 cm long) ruler made of lead placed beside the mummy, it is easy to obtain negatives that permit anthropometric study. This X-ray anthropometry was used on the skulls of Gebel Adda during the salvage campaign in Nubia by J. E. Harris and K. R. Weeks, and then by J. L. Heim and R. Lichtenberg at Dush, Ain Labakha, and el-Deir, three sites in el-Kharga Oasis, where about 170 mummies have been X-rayed by this method. Comparison between classic, osteometric anthropology and radiological osteometry has shown that with regard to the points of reference measurable by both methods, it is possible, without problem, to combine the series of classic osteological measurements with those furnished by X-rays. Only some details escape radiological osteometry (for example, certain measurements of the facial skeleton), but radiological osteometry supplies knowledge inaccessible without it—for example, the study of growth arrest lines.

Tomodensitometry (CAT scanning) is a highly interesting development in radiology, for it enables close cross-section analysis and three-dimensional reconstruction of mummies. For a long time, CAT scanning entailed a major handicap, in that it could be done only in a hospital because the equipment was heavy, bulky, costly, and not easily transportable. It was thus necessary for the mummy to come to the equipment. The situation is now changing with the Egyptian Mummy Project initiated by Dr. Z. Hawass, which involves the use of a traveling scanner that minimizes the need to move the mummies.

For the record, we shall cite classical tomography, or cross-section radiology. It yields information similar to that of CAT scans, which have replaced it.

Another modern medical imagery technology, magnetic resonance imagery (MRI), cannot be applied to mummies, which are, of course, desiccated corpses: this procedure depends on the presence of hydrogen atoms (or protons) in the body in the form of water. For the same reasons, ultrasound tomography applied to mummies would scarcely yield pertinent results.

THE STUDY OF HAIR

The study of hair (figures 212 and 213) can be rich in information, for it supplements the results of anthropological study. It is based on microscopic examination and on chemical analysis of dyes. Thus, it has proven possible to determine that, aside from some traces of henna dye, Ramesses II's hair was red, rendering it improbable that he belonged to a dark-skinned ethnic group, a hypothesis advanced with no scientific basis by certain writers.[4] Their hair is among the best-preserved structures of mummies, and it is almost always possible to analyze it and determine the presence of dyes. Let us recall that study of the hair of the "elder lady" found in one of the caches in the tomb of Amenhotep II revealed a similarity to that of the lock of hair deposited in a miniature coffin in the tomb of Tutankhamun, and which was reputed to have belonged to Queen Teye. This identification agrees with that advanced by J. E. Harris and K. R. Weeks

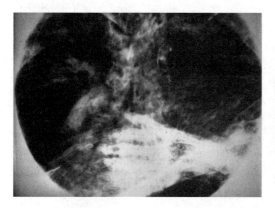

Fig. 211. Frontal X-ray of the thorax of the mummy of Ramesses II, confirming the presence of the heart, which was separately mummified and then set back in place, to the right.

Fig. 212. Head of the mummy of a woman with abundant hair. Necropolis of Ain Labakha, T25 (el-Kharga Oasis). Roman Period.

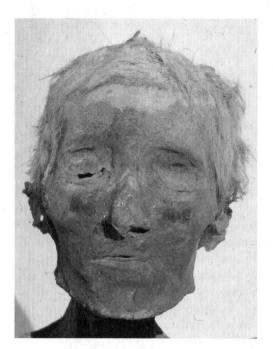

Fig. 213. Head of the mummy of an elderly woman whose white hair was dyed yellow. Necropolis of Dush, T58 (el-Kharga Oasis). Roman Period.

on the basis of their anthropological and stomatological study of the mummy.[5]

HISTOLOGY AND ANATOMOPATHOLOGY, BACTERIOLOGY

The possibility of rehydrating mummified tissues has led to the histological investigation of mummies and, consequently, to anatomopathology, that is, the study of pathological tissues. This study is a precious resource that, at the expense of the removal of relatively minimal samples from the mummy, makes it possible to detect certain pathological conditions. Similarly, infectious diseases can be identified by means of bacteriological techniques. The only drawback to these methods is that they necessitate the removal of samples from the mummies.

THE STUDY OF BLOOD GROUPS

The study of blood groups, a technique that is already old, assists greatly in studying the fil-

iations of ancient populations, just as it does for those today. In some rare cases, it has been used on royal mummies. It has thus been established that Tutankhamun's blood group is the same as that of the mummy, as yet not conclusively identified, from tomb 55 of the Valley of the Kings.[6] The problem of the identity of this mummy has yet to be resolved. As in the case of the methods just described, the determination of blood group necessitates taking samples from the mummies, which is not always possible. It must also be noted that the method is not absolutely reliable, for certain groups do not remain well preserved: a subject of type AO can be taken for a type O, because the antigen A, which is fragile, can break down over time. This risk is of less concern nowadays, however, because the tests are more sensitive.

THE STUDY OF DNA (DEOXYRIBONUCLEIC ACID)

The study of DNA is not yet common in the study of mummies, but it is rich in potential. It could, in particular, make it possible to eliminate the remaining uncertainties regarding the identification of the kings of the complicated Dynasty 18: more than twenty mummies from the cachette at Deir el-Bahari and from the tomb of Amenhotep II have yet to be identified. In the same way, it could aid in determining the family relationships of the occupants of collective tombs, whose identity is often unknown. It could also, for example, make it possible to determine the genetic relationships between populations settled in the Nile valley and those of the oases.[7] The obstacle, again, is the need to take samples from the bodies. Moreover, it requires samples that do not risk having been contaminated by foreign contact with the mummy, whatever the reason: embalming products, handling by the embalmers, or by excavators (whether clandestine or official). For DNA analysis of a mummy to be reliable, it is thus necessary to remove teeth or bony fragments that cannot have come into contact with the outside world, for such contact would obviously have entailed contamination.[8] The indispensable conditions for DNA study are thus difficult to bring together. It is, however, a particularly interesting technology, and more and more teams are endeavoring to apply it.

ELECTRON MICROSCOPY

Electron microscopy, a modern technology, makes it possible to push back the bounds of traditional optical microscopy and thus to study extremely small structures. Researchers have already applied it to mummies, using it to study human tissues and pathogenic agents.

The use of electronic microscopy is based on the fact that the equivalent wavelength of an electron beam is much shorter than the shortest wavelengths used in optical microscopy, resulting in a much higher resolving power. This is the case with transmission electronic microscopy. In another technique, analytic electronic microscopy, the electrons react on the constituent elements of the material analyzed: the investigator studies the X-rays produced by this reaction. A third technique, scanning with an electron beam, makes it possible to study the surface of the specimens analyzed: scanning electron microscopy.

CARBON 14 (C_{14}) DATING

Carbon 14 dating is a highly imprecise method, due to the overly large range of the dates it is capable of furnishing. It can be put to use, however, in particular for mummies of the later periods of Egyptian history, because the range becomes ever narrower as we approach our own time. This method can thus complement the "classic" methods of dating, which include the mummification technique itself, and above all the objects that accompany the mummies, especially ceramics. Moreover, it requires the removal of samples from the body. Because of this imprecision and the need for samples, C_{14} dating is relatively seldom used.

12   Mummies in Museums

Thanks to the favorable conditions in which they were kept, mummies in museums became the object of scientific study at a relatively early date. In fact, museums are generally located in cities with major hospitals and well-equipped laboratories capable of carrying out the most sophisticated forms of examination. By now, most mummies in European museums have been thoroughly examined, resulting in in-depth knowledge of their internal anatomy and of the techniques with which they were mummified. Nevertheless, it must be noted that their study has been hampered by a significant disadvantage: the frequent absence of precise information regarding the provenance of the individuals, their date, or their identity.

The mummies in museums most often arrived there after complex wanderings. Purchased either officially or on the "unofficial" antiquities market (when they were not stolen), they were often once in private collections before eventually being bequeathed to a public collection. These circumstances explain why their provenance is often unknown.

It is not possible to summarize all the studies carried out on individual mummies in museums. Here we limit our inventory to the largest groups, along with isolated individual mummies that have been studied using all the techniques available for investigation.

THE MUMMIES FROM THE ROYAL CACHES

The discovery of the cache of royal mummies at Deir el-Bahari, that in the tomb of Amenhotep II, and that in the tomb of Tutankhamun brought to light most of the pharaohs of the New Kingdom. Certain scholars, though, feel that yet another royal cache remains to be discovered. In 2004, a royal mummy found in the Michael C. Carlos Museum at Emory University in Atlanta was identified as probably that of Ramesses I; it is now in the Luxor Museum. This group of mummies, unique in the world, has naturally been of great interest to scientists, not to speak of its sensational impact on the general public.

The first studies of these mummies were essentially descriptive. In 1912, G. E. Smith published an initial description of all the known royal mummies as a volume of the Catalogue général of the Cairo Museum (since 1902, the museum had been located in the premises it occupies to this day). In 1920, in collaboration with W. R. Dawson, he published *Egyptian Mummies;* in Smith's opinion, scholars disposed of sufficient human remains to study "the origin and development of this singular practice" of mummification.[1]

Room 52, where the royal mummies were on display, rapidly became a major center of attraction for visitors to the Cairo Museum. In the 1930s, the mummies were moved to the Mausoleum of Zaghlul, but by World War II, they were returned to room 52 of the museum, where they could be viewed only with special permission. After the war, the room was again opened to the public. Later, President Sadat barred visitors because of the respect due to these illustrious dead. He had planned a mausoleum to shelter all the mummies, but his death interrupted this project.

Today, eleven royal mummies, including the most prestigious and the best preserved, are accessible to the public in a new room that assures them a beautiful setting as well as an environment favorable to their preservation. In fact, we invoke the term "royal mummies" somewhat loosely, for some of the group have not been identified, while others, even if they were once members of the palace entourage, were not of royal blood. Moreover, two of these mummies are on display in Luxor: Ramesses I in the Luxor Museum and Masaharta in the Museum of Mummification. Not all these mummies have been thoroughly studied. While some, such as the mummy of Ramesses II (figure 214), have been almost completely investigated, others have been rather more cursorily examined. The mummy of Masaharta, that of King Pinudjem II, and that of his wife, Queen Nesikhons, all from the cachette of Deir el-Bahari, have not even been X-rayed.

In point of fact, investigation of these royal mummies has furnished most of our information regarding mummification in the New Kingdom. As a group, however, the pharaohs are not representative of the Egyptian population as a whole, for obvious reasons of social level. It is infinitely more likely that they were better fed and cared for than their subjects. The physical condition of the respective groups and the maladies from which they suffered cannot have been identical, and certain conditions from which commoners suffered would have been nearly absent among the pharaohs: for example, peasants would have been far more at risk for contracting schistosomiasis.

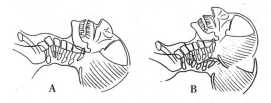

Fig. 214. Diagram showing that the neck of Ramesses II was fractured during the embalming process, when the resin was introduced into the skull. A: The sketch shows a dislocation between C5 and C6 and the abnormal orientation of the upper surface of the intracranial resin. B: If the cervical column is restored to its normal appearance, the surface of the resin becomes horizontal. The fracture thus occurred after the resin was introduced.

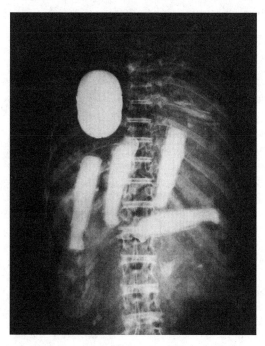

Fig. 215. X-ray of the thorax of Queen Nedjmet, showing the amulets of the four Sons of Horus and the heart scarab. After J. E. Harris, 1980.

The royal mummies have been systematically studied by J. E. Harris (figure 215).[2] This work makes it possible to address the question of their age at time of death, though with a considerable margin of error. Importantly, through study of cranial morphology, he showed that certain mummies had been incorrectly identified—for example, that of Amenhotep I, who could not have been the son of Ahmose. He also discovered certain pathological conditions, such as arthritis, ankylosing spondylitis,[3] arterial atheroma, and poliomyelitis.[4] At a later date, E. Strouhal demonstrated that the smallpox from which Ramesses V died must have originated in an epidemic that had spread in the palace.[5] To the present day, however, compared with other studies, those involving the royal mummies have been incomplete, due to the numerous restrictions stemming from their exceptional character. Only noninvasive methods (essentially radiology) have been allowed, with the exception of cases where it proved possible to authorize some small samples, such as those of the hair of Ramesses II found at the bottom of the coffin when his mummy arrived in Paris in 1975. Thus, to date, it has not been possible to conduct the DNA studies that would probably make it possible to determine the filiations that remain uncertain, especially in the case of Dynasty 18. The Egytian Mummy Project initiated by Dr. Z. Hawass should enable significant advances in the study of these mummies.

THE MUMMIES STUDIED BY P. H. K. GRAY

In the 1960s, P. H. K. Gray studied a total of 133 mummies, in collaboration with W. R. Dawson for the mummies in the British Museum, E. Slow for those in the Liverpool Museum, and P. Vijlbrief for those in the Leiden Museum.[6] His work was based on radiology, and he expressed astonishment that it had rarely been used prior to the time of his own work. He particularly stressed the drawbacks of many methods that damage mummies by the unwrapping they entail, and especially by the need to remove samples from them. Gray's approach was a double one: as an Egyptologist, and as a physician interested in paleopathology.

Archaeological Approach

According to Gray, when a researcher is confronted with a "packet" called a mummy, the first question to arise is that of the presence or absence of human remains inside the bandages. In fact, in the nineteenth century, many false mummies were made in response to the demand for this sort of object. Moreover, certain small mummies thought to be the bodies of children have turned out to be those of animals, or even just material, such as wood![7]

Determination of age and sex is another important question, for mummies are often in reused coffins inscribed with information regarding their original owner and not the present occupant.[8]

The contribution of X-rays can be valuable in determining the mummification technique that was used. The presence of canopic packets in the abdominal or thoracic cavity brings to mind the mummies of Dynasty 21, while their presence between the legs is an indication of a later date. The presence of solidified resin in the abdominal cavity or the skull is characteristic, according to Gray, of mummies of the Ptolemaic Period. To us, his last assertion seems debatable, if only in light of the study of royal mummies. He prudently concludes, though, that radiography does not in fact make it possible to date a mummy solely on the basis of mummification technique.

The presence of amulets is easily detected by X-rays, enabling their removal with only limited incisions in the bandaging.

Paleopathology

Paleopathology turned out to be the most important aspect of Gray's work. He began his study thinking that radiography would contribute no more than information regarding skeletons, but later he realized this was not at all the case. Still, it remains clear that it is the skeleton that is richest in detectable pathological details, especially if the mummy was eviscerated and many of its internal organs thus removed. Gray's findings include the following:

- Osteoarthritis was widespread and mostly attacked the spine: out of eighty-eight adults studied, fifty-seven (65 percent) bore lesions.
- Growth arrest lines, or Harris lines, were observed in about 30 percent of the cases, indicating that from the point of view of the state of health, conditions were rather deficient (by modern standards).
- Dislocations and fractures, some of them set, were frequent. Gray cites the case of a man from the Ptolemaic Period who had his forearm severed above the wrist, and whose mummy had a prosthesis replacing the missing hand. This might have been a postmortem reconstruction.[9]
- Most often, the appearance of the feet gave the impression that shoes had not been worn.
- Congenital anomalies of the type spina bifida occulta were often noted. Others, such as enchondromas (benign cartilaginous tumors that appear inside bones) and osteogenesis imperfecta, were observed.

- Dental condition was bad, with mostly apical cysts resulting from opening of the pulp chamber due to considerable abrasion of the crowns.
- Maladies of the soft tissues were confirmed: calcified atheroma of the arteries of the legs (rare), gallstones (one case), kidney stone (one case).
- Opacity of the intervertebral disks has often been considered a consequence of ochronosis. This is a condition of genetic origin, still called alkaptonuria, that entails metabolic problems. Gray, however, attributed this opacity to the mummification process, given the frequency of this type of image.[10]

Other significant conditions he expected to encounter did not come to light, such as tuberculosis, cancer, leprosy, rickets, and syphilis (whose existence in the ancient world well before the discovery of America is now proved).

THE WORK OF A. COCKBURN AND HIS TEAM

The selection made by Cockburn[11] was the opposite of Gray's. While the latter, by dint of much effort, put together the largest group of Egyptian mummies yet X-rayed, Cockburn's group consisted of only five mummies. His methodology was entirely different: instead of limiting himself primarily to X-rays, he used all feasible methods of study available at the time, sometimes even at the price of significant damage to certain specimens that were subjected to a veritable autopsy.[12]

PUM II (Pennsylvania University Museum)

This mummy was studied in Detroit.[13] It is of unknown provenance, and, though the coffin is richly decorated, it bears no inscription giving the name of its occupant. The mummy was unwrapped and an autopsy performed on February 1, 1973 (figure 216), one week after X-ray examination, which had revealed, inter alia, the presence of six lumbar vertebrae (a transitional anomaly). The subject, a man thirty-five to forty years of age, had been excerebrated, as demonstrated by the presence of

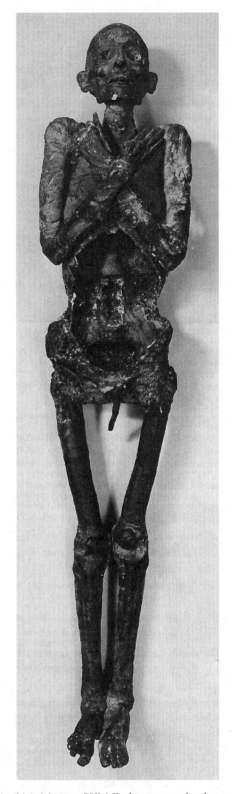

Fig. 216. Mummy PUM II after autopsy by the team of A. Cockburn, 1980.

resin in the cranium and by the discovery, thanks to tomographs, of a hole in the lamina cribriformis of the ethmoid bone. Four canopic packets were observed inside the abdominothoracic cavity, where they had been inserted via the incision that had been made for the abdominal evisceration. The bandages were difficult to remove because of the hardness of the layers of linen, which had been stuck together by an abundant quantity of resin. The fingers and the toes were found to have been bandaged separately. Twenty-four hours after the unwrapping, the color of the mummy had changed from light brown to a dark brown that was almost black.

A ball of cotton had been placed between two layers of bandages, an exceptional instance, for cotton was not used in Egypt until the Roman Period. This cotton might have served as an amulet, according to M. Johnson.

When the mummy was opened up, samples were taken from the interior of the trunk at some distance from the evisceration incision. These samples were used to start cultures, but these proved to be sterile.

The front of the lumbar column was removed to expose the marrow.[14] The investigators found only some "resin," which upon analysis turned out to be a polymerized vitreous product, somewhat like amber and made of juniper oil. Small quantities of camphor and myrrh were also present.

Study of the canopic packets revealed that one of them contained the spleen and some intestinal fragments, while the other three contained only lung tissue, showing that the embalmers took some liberty with what tradition ordained. Anatomopathological study of the lungs revealed silicosis and anthracosis. The intestine contained an *Ascaris lumbricoides* egg.

Radiology revealed arteriosclerosis (atheroma) lesions. There was also an abnormal appearance of the right fibula and tibula, indicating a lesion whose exact nature could not be specified: periostitis?

Protein research enabled R. A. Barraco, a member of Cockburn's team, to detect proteins with a molecular weight of 150,000, but biologically inactive. The study of heavy metals showed that their weight was much less than in present-day men, by a ratio of 1 to 10.

The mummy contained insect chrysalises that had been killed by the introduction (in abundance) of hot resin into its cavities. These were *dermestids,* probably *frischii, piophila casei, atheta* sp., and *chrysomia* sp.

Carbon 14 dating yielded 170 B.C.E. ± 70 years. The coffin seems to have been "mass produced" rather than made especially for the subject. Its late style accords well with the dating. Taken together, the indications permit a dating of this mummy to the Ptolemaic Period.

PUM III

PUM III is an entirely bandaged female mummy; its head was separated from the body by way of a postmortem accident. Her age at death was estimated as between thirty and forty years, taking dental abrasion into account. Her height is just over 5'2".

The mummy was wrapped in many layers of linen; the arms and legs were separately bandaged, but not the fingers and toes. Inscriptions on certain pieces of cloth bore the name of the priest Imyhap, son of Wahibre, showing they had been reused; C_{14} dating yielded a result of 835 B.C.E. ± 70 years.[15]

Radiological examination showed a healed fracture of the second left rib, as well as Harris lines. The heart, the lungs, the diaphragm, and the liver were all identifiable.

Histological examination of the left breast revealed the existence of a common adenofibroma.

The autopsy could not be conducted in a rigorous fashion because of the extremely poor state of preservation. The thoracic organs were still in place, while the abdominal cavity was packed with resin-impregnated linen; this cloth had been inserted via the anus.

PUM IV

PUM IV is the mummy of a boy around eight years of age, about whom we have no precise information. According to the investigators, he might be from the Roman Period (first or second century C.E.).

The unwrapping revealed that the body was inside a fisherman's net, which was itself covered by a painted but rather crude, worn linen shroud. Inside these coverings, the bandaging was slipshod, with each layer of bandages only partially covering the next one, giving the impression of a job that was not carried out methodically. What seems exceptional is that the body was dressed in a short tunic that went down to the waist; it was decorated with two vertical strips that had been separately woven and then attached. This tunic covered three other, crude tunics that reached down to the feet.[16] Moreover, the body was resting on a plank, to which it had been fastened.

The skin of the mummy was dark brown in color, and it was perforated by numerous insect holes. Many little scarab beetles and larvae were also found. A considerable amount of matter had been lost via the perineum, which according to the investigators was a sign of anal evisceration. When opened, the cavity of the trunk turned out to contain a granular material, probably sawdust. Opening the skull made it possible to see the cerebral hemispheres, which were reduced in volume.

The American-Canadian Project: ROM I (Royal Ontario Museum)

ROM I was unwrapped and autopsied in Toronto in August 1974.[17] Like PUM II, it was first X-rayed, and tomography and CAT-scanning (for the head) were also used.[18] The mummy, that of a man named Nakht, came from Deir el-Bahari and had been acquired by Dr. C. T. Curelly, founder of the Royal Ontario Museum. The inscriptions on the coffin showed that its owner, a weaver, was attached to the funerary temple of Sethnakhte, the first king of Dynasty 20. This mummy is thus a good representative of the "middle class"; moreover, it is relatively well dated (reign of Ramesses III?), something rather rare among the mummies in museums.

The mummification was confined to the basics (probably the "third class" described by Herodotus), which was in contrast with the quality of the coffin. According to the investigators, the choice of an inexpensive mummifi-

cation might have made it possible to furnish the deceased with this well-made coffin. The bandaging was much less thick than that of many mummies of the same period, but the bandages were in good condition because of the absence of unguents. In the packing were found two large, sleeveless tunics that seemed to be Nakht's size. The subject seemed to be about fifteen years of age. These tunics used as packing material recall the adult tunic found in the bandaging of the mummy of a little girl from the necropolis of Dush.[19] The skin was the color of café au lait, and it was leathery to the touch. The teeth displayed incipient wear. The cerebral hemispheres, brown in color, were observable thanks to a postmortem cranial fracture. The penis was not circumcised.

Radiological study revealed the presence of Harris lines. The right side of the thorax contained a mass that was interpreted as the liver and the heart adhering to one another. The tomographies revealed the diaphragm.

Anatomopathological study revealed particles of granite in the lungs. The intestines contained a number of schistosome and tapeworm eggs. The liver was cirrhotic, and the spleen was enlarged. The probable cause of death was thus schistosomiasis. The investigators also found a subcutaneous cyst containing a *Trichinella spiralis* larva, which implied pork consumption.

Red blood cells of type B were identified. Study of proteins and fatty tissues seemed to indicate that Nakht had not been treated with natron (the fatty tissues were not saponified).

THE MANCHESTER GROUP

A. R. David and her team made a complete study of the seventeen mummies in the Manchester Museum.[20] The group included three individuals dating to the Middle Kingdom, three from the New Kingdom, three from the later periods of pharaonic history, and eight from the Graeco-Roman Period.

Several approaches were used in the investigation of this group: radiology, histology, anatomopathology, and parasitology. Not only the mummies but also their wrappings were studied.

The radiology was done in the Department of Neuro-Radiology and Anatomy at Manchester Royal Infirmary using the most sophisticated techniques, that is, besides standard radiology, tomography (figure 217) and CAT scanning. This last technique was implemented in the Department of Diagnostic Radiology at the University of Manchester.

Radiology yielded the following information:

• The age of the mummies. Though Egyptian mummies do not belong to the same ethnic group as the populations on which the tables used in Europe and the United States of America are based, these same tables were used to evaluate bone age. The same was true of the determination of age based on the dental formula, though this method is open to the same criticism: there is no assurance that the growth rate was the same among the ancient Egyptians as in modern European populations. In any event, this determination of age is valid only while the individual is still growing, until about twenty years of age. For older subjects, the determination of age is more difficult and somewhat subjective, being based on the development of osteoarthritis, on the state of dental abrasion, or on the presence of arterial calcification.

• The determination of sex, when not possible by direct examination, is often made possible by radiology of the pelvis and the skull.

• It proved possible to trace the evolution of mummification techniques, thanks to the chronological range of the Manchester mummies. The opinion expounded by the researchers was the "classic" one: When the first attempts at mummification were made, bodies were preserved solely by the use of sand. Over the centuries, there was an improvement in technique, with quality reaching a peak in Dynasty 21. After that, there was a gradual decline down to the Roman Period, when quality suffered as mummification became more widespread.[21]

• The investigators noted restorations intended to improve the appearance of the mummy: the placing of material under the skin to restore a lifelike appearance to the face, the placing of spherical objects (or onions) in the orbits, or the presence of an artificial phallus.

• The presence of resin in the cranial cavity was proof of excerebration (seven out of seventeen complete mummies). Cerebral remains were revealed, however, in five cases, undermining the "classic" opinion that the brain decomposed rapidly after death.

• Opacification of the intervertebral disks (figure 218) has been the subject of debate. The frequency of its occurrence (ten out of seventeen subjects) made it possible to reject the diagnosis of ochronosis, which had sometimes been advanced. The frequency of this condition, however, was greater than had been expected in two 1978 studies bearing on present-day populations, a fact that, according to the investigators, called for further biochemical studies.[22]

• Osteoarthritis, whether of the spine, the arms, or the legs, was quite frequent, affecting nearly all the adult subjects. A Schmorl node was discovered, and sagittal tomographs of the lumbar spine revealed calcified herniated intervertebral disks. Rheumatoid polyarthritis was not identified in this group of seventeen mummies, leading the investigators to conclude that in the past, when this condition was supposedly noted on mummies, it had most often been confused with osteoarthritis.

• Postmortem traumas were quite frequent and easily identifiable. Certain typical antemortem fractures were recognized in the study, such as a fracture of the iliopubic and ischio-

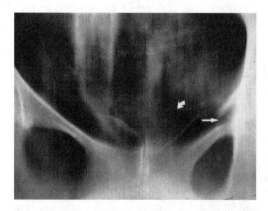

Fig. 217. Tomography of the pelvis of a mummy displaying a fracture (long arrow) of the left iliopublic branch and vesical calcifications (short arrow) caused by schistosomiasis. After A. R. David, 1979.

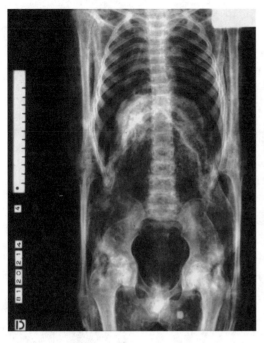

Fig. 218. X-ray of the thorax and the abdomen of the mummy of a man, revealing opacification of intervertebral disks by the embalming process. Necropolis of Dush, T20 (el-Kharga Oasis).

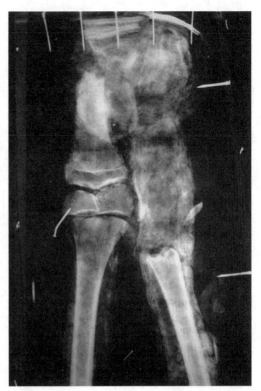

Fig. 219. X-ray of the lower extremities of an adolescent, showing the reconstruction of the missing legs (bitten off by a crocodile?). After A. R. David, 1979.

pubic rami that might have been the cause of death (absence of healing). One mummy (no. 1770) displayed amputation of both legs with what seemed to be bone regeneration, though in fact, this was due to the presence of mud in the bones, which had been severed by bites, perhaps from a hippopotamus or a crocodile (figure 219).

• Generalized conditions, such as decalcification of the spine with compressed vertebrae, were observed, which suggests that the person concerned was menopausal or that it was common senile osteoporosis. Growth arrest (or Harris) lines were noted in three out of the seventeen subjects. Vascular calcification was observed three times.

• Thinning of the parietal bones was observed once. This phenomenon, which is found in older subjects, has been well studied in other groups of Egyptian skulls and ascribed to the wearing of heavy wigs, or more likely, the carrying of heavy loads on the head.[23]

• Infectious or parasitic conditions were well represented. An ankylosis of the proximal interphalangian joint of the third finger was probably linked to a healed osteoarthritis. A *Filaria medinensis* (*Dracunculus medinensis*) was observed once. Schistosomiasis was diagnosed twice.

The Study of Teeth

Given that the subjects in this group were mostly preserved in mummified state, direct examination of their teeth was rarely possible. X-ray investigation thus assumed a great importance. Though the group was relatively small, it seemed representative. The condition of the teeth was like that of other groups studied in the past: rarity of dental caries down to the Ptolemaic Period, contrasting with the extreme wear of the crowns observed from the earliest periods. This condition reflects a diet containing hard particles capable of wearing the enamel. Bread made with wheat containing quartz particles coming from millstones or from wind-blown desert sand seems to have been the principal abrasive agent. At adult age, the wear led to opening of the pulp chamber, followed by pulpitis and secondarily by apical abscesses. Lowered dental articulation caused by the wear of the crowns led to temporomandibular joint disorders, which in their turn had an impact on the teeth and led to pathology, such as periodontitis.

The observed lesions included caries (four subjects), loss of teeth prior to death (eight), dental attrition (seven), dislocation of the mandible (one), dental abscesses (five), and periodontitis (five).

The Study of Fingerprints

The interest in fingerprints for purposes of identification has been fully demonstrated, in the area of forensic medicine, both for the living and for cadavers. On mummies, photographs and casts have been used. In fact, in certain cases, the folded position of the fingers prevented photography. Rather than using the traditional method, which consists of inking the fingertips and then transferring the prints to a sheet of paper, the investigators chose to collect the prints with a dental paste. The casts obtained were then painted with acrylic paint, inked, and used to obtain fingerprints like those obtained from living subjects. Naturally, because of cutaneous damage observable on the mummified material, the prints were not perfect. Still, they could be read, and they were of sufficient quality to catch a thief! Moreover, we know that careful study of the appearance of fingerprints enables an estimate of the age of an individual. In the case of Asru, a woman who lived during Dynasty 25, the fingerprints suggested an age of forty years, which agreed with the information obtained by other methods. The good condition of her hands and feet led A. H. Fletcher to advance the hypothesis that she might well have been a lady of polite society, and, given that her body came undoubtedly from Luxor, even a songstress of Amun.

Anatomopathology

Anatomopathology of mummified tissues has been available ever since the studies of M. A. Ruffer and the improvements made by A. T.

Sandison. Analysis of the soft tissues of the mummy of Nakhtankh, which had already been investigated sixty years earlier by M. Murray, focused on the remains that had in the meanwhile been kept preserved in jars and on the mummified viscera still in their canopic vessels. Lung tissue still adhered to a rib fragment; the tissue was affected by fibrosis and by the presence of fine particles. These pneumoconiosis lesions were confirmed by study of the mummified remains in the canopic vessel with the head of Hapy (the protective god of the lungs). To be sure, the inscriptions from the coffins of Nakhtankh did not indicate that the subject had been a stonecutter, but it is evident that living conditions in Egypt themselves sufficed to explain the occurrence of this sort of pulmonary lesion, as is still the case today.

As for Asru (figures 220 and 221), canopic packets were found between her legs. They proved to contain intestines whose study revealed the presence of parasitic worms of the *Strongyloides* family, but it was confirmed that these were not the cause of death. Nothing further could be said pending the pathology of Asru because at the time, no other tissues were available for analysis.

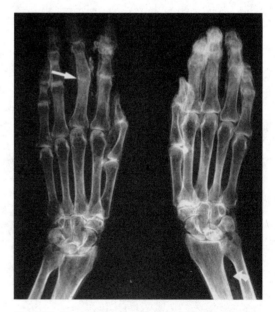

Fig. 220. X-ray of the hands of the lady Asru displaying ankylosis of joint P1–P2 (arrow), the result of interphalangian arthritis. After A. R. David, 1979.

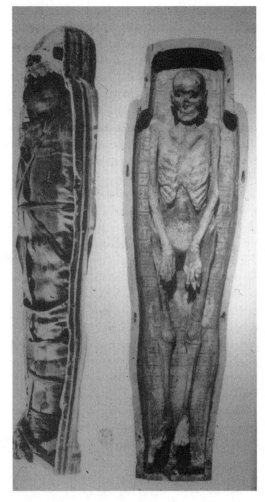

Fig. 221. Mummy of Asru in its coffin. After A. R. David, 1979.

Mummy no. 1770 presented a male *Filaria medinensis* (*Dracunculus medinensis*), which was found calcified in the anterior abdominal wall.

Electron Microscopy

Transmission electronic microscopy revealed the ultramicroscopic structure of the liver of one of the "Two Brothers." In the same way, it was possible to reveal the muscle fibers. Non-human structures, such as *Strongyloides* remains, could also be analyzed. One remark can be made with regard to all the examinations that were carried out: the cellular structures had for the most part disappeared because of the decomposition that spread rapidly after death.

Analytic electronic microscopy enabled the discovery of grains of quartz (SiO_2) in the lungs. A search for heavy metals, however, proved negative.

Scanning electron microscopy was used principally to study the insects found in the mummies. The investigators also attempted to utilize it to determine the ethnic affiliation of the Two Brothers. The two men seemed to have the same type of hair and should thus at least have been of the same ethnic group, though morphologically, their skulls were rather different.

THE MUMMIES IN CZECH COLLECTIONS

From 1971 to 1973, E. Strouhal, assisted by L. Vyhnánek and a team of researchers from various disciplines, studied all the Egyptian mummified remains in Czechoslovakia.[24] The human material included twenty-four complete mummies and twenty-nine isolated heads, to which must be added forty-four fragments of mummified members. Seventy-three animal mummies were also studied.

The methodology combined clinical description and X-ray examination. The latter included, in principle, overlapping frontal and profile positioning of all the subjects. As a general rule, the focal length was one meter (39.37"). The radiological technique was classic: use was made of film exposed between screens with the aid of mobile antiscatter (Potter Bucky) grids. Though the investigators were concerned to obtain precise anthropometric measurements, the radiographic protocols they used greatly limited their ambitions.

In the light of their studies, the investigators proposed a scheme permitting the dating of the mummies by mummification technique. The results were in accord with those of other researchers. Strouhal noted, however, that observations of this sort are not entirely reliable. Unlike Dawson and Gray, who noted that skeletal dislocations occurred most often in Roman Period mummies, Strouhal specified that he had noted no correlation between the dates and the condition of the skeletons.

The demographic data were based first of all on a determination of the age of the individuals, drawing on modern growth tables. These tables can be used, however, only prior to the end of growth. At adult age, the study of teeth, and the appearance of osteoarthritis and osteoporosis lesions were the elements taken into account. The appearance of the bones of the pelvis and the skull were used to determine the sex when the latter was not obvious from clinical observation. The sex ratio was not normal, about two males for each female, an observation already made by Gray and Dawson with regard to the mummies in the British Museum. In the age category of twenty to thirty years, however, there were clearly more females than males, due to death in childbirth, which is observable in all the statistics. The average age at death was 43.7 for the males and 41.3 for the women.

In regard to paleopathology, a single case of fracture was observed, of the trochanteric massif of the left femur of an older man; this fracture was probably the cause of death. Osteoarthritis, however, was frequent, mostly in the spine. Osteoporosis was also noted. Harris lines were observed only four times. Arteriosclerosis was noted in three older subjects. There was little in the way of dental caries, though caries was difficult to determine because of the amount of wear, which was quite frequent. The rare cases of caries (0.32 percent of the remaining teeth) occurred only in male subjects.

THE MUMMY IN THE LYON MUSEUM OF NATURAL HISTORY

In 1988, J. C. Goyon and P. Josset published the results of their complete investigation of a mummy in the Musée Guimet d'Histoire Naturelle in Lyon.[25] With the assistance of an interdisciplinary team, they examined, as completely as possible, an anonymous mummy that probably dates to the later stages of Egyptian history.

The work began with imagery consisting essentially of scanning the mummy (June 1986).

This was an eviscerated mummy, lacking the heart and the other viscera. The thoracoabdominal cavity, however, contained five canopic packets (figure 222), three in the right side of the thorax and two in the iliac fossae. One of the packets was in fact found to contain the mummified heart. The skull presented an ethmoidal breach and resin in the occipital region. The appearance of the bone trabeculae was compatible with an age of around thirty to forty years.

The procedures continued with the unwrapping, which was done methodically, attempting to compare the arrangement of the bandages with what is prescribed in the texts of the Embalming Ritual. These steps were, of course, photographically recorded. Superposed shrouds enclosed nearly the entire mummy, covering smaller pieces of cloth as well as bandages. The arms and legs were not bandaged separately. Among the torn-up and crumpled packing materials, the investigators found bits of a large piece of cloth that could have come from a boat sail.

Removal of the bandages revealed the mummy, which was black in color. The investigation continued with a veritable autopsy including, in particular, the opening of the cranium, revealing that "resin" covered the entirety of the internal surface of the skull. In the trunk, the evisceration incision was identified; it had been left open, with no plaque covering

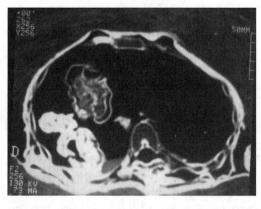

Fig. 222. CAT scan of the lower part of the thorax of the mummy of a man. Lyon, Muséum d'Histoire Naturelle. Image courtesy of P. Josset.

it. The thoracoabdominal cavity was opened in such a way as to permit the removal of the canopic packets for purposes of analysis.

Complementary examinations were carried out, in particular on the anatomopathological level. Study of the contents of the canopic packets seemed to show that natron had not been used to dry them; they might have been immersed in a liquid highly saturated with spices and resin. Lung disease, perhaps chronic bronchitis or tuberculosis, might have been the cause of death. Analyses were also made of the vegetal remains (pollens) and the textiles.

THE MUMMY IN HANNOVER

A German team including R. Germer investigated the Ptolemaic Period mummy of an adult female in the Kestner Museum in Hannover.[26] The study, done in Hamburg, was conducted thoroughly, with scans, a 3D reconstruction of the face, and complementary studies of the embalming products, the vegetal matter, the textiles, and the wood of the coffin. It was not possible to determine the cause of death, which occurred between twenty and thirty years of age. The mummy, whose arms were in the Osirian position, had been excerebrated, and canopic packets were identified in the thoracoabdominal cavity. The head seemed to be held in place by a stick, without doubt a stalk of *gerid* attaching the head to the thorax.[27]

THE MUMMY IN THE LEEDS MUSEUM

The mummy of a priest of Amun, discovered in 1823 by J. Passalacqua at Deir el Bahari, arrived in the Leeds Museum in 1828.[28] That very year, it was unwrapped and autopsied. In the early 1990s, the mummy was the object of a new and thorough study that included classic radiology, CAT scanning, histological examination, endoscopy, determination of blood group, and so forth. The mummy was of rather good quality, with canopic packets in the thoracic cavity. The man, a priest of Amun who

lived in the reign of Ramesses XI, had been in anything but perfect health: he suffered from osteoarthritis, atherosclerosis, and filariasis.

THE MUMMY IN THE BRISTOL MUSEUM

The mummy in Bristol is that of a certain Horemkenesi, scribe and *wab*-priest of Amun of Karnak.[29] It is from Deir el-Bahari, and it dates to the end of the New Kingdom. The mummy was X-rayed for the first time in 1978, and then, in 1981, after further X-rays, a scientific team at Bristol University unwrapped and autopsied it. In 1994, samples taken from the mummy at the time of the autopsy were the object of thorough investigation.

This was the mummy of a somewhat older man whose head was shaved, as befitted a priest. During the unwrapping, the investigators were able to determine, under the shrouds, the presence of packets of chalky mud and pieces of cloth intended to enhance the volume of the mummy. The arms had been bandaged separately and attached to the body. The skin, which had a leathery consistency, was brown and saturated with resin. The man had undergone an abdominal evisceration oriented parallel to the groin. Most of the organs, including the heart, were removed. Besides common osteoarthritis lesions, the skeleton had hyperostotic lesions, a much rarer condition. The presence of schistosomiasis was confirmed by antigenic methods. The subject also suffered from malaria, as proved by antigenic tests performed on small skin samples. These two maladies, in our opinion, were sufficient in themselves to have caused his death. A facial reconstruction was made.

THE MUMMIES IN THE BRUSSELS MUSEUMS

The Musées Royaux d'Art et d'Histoire contain eleven human and fifteen animal mummies, all of which were X-rayed, with the single exception of a Middle Kingdom mummy in extremely bad condition.[30] One of them was also CAT scanned. The mummies range in date from Dynasty 21 to the late Roman Period, the latest probably being a Christian mummy, the well-known "embroideress of Antinoe." With the exception of this mummy and two others, their provenance is unknown. The group includes seven adults and four children, none of the latter dating earlier than the Ptolemaic Period.[31]

THE MUMMIES OF LEIDEN

The mummies in the Leiden Museum were X-rayed by Gray in the 1960s.[32] In the meantime, they were studied again using conventional radiology and CAT scanning. The collection includes, besides thirty-one complete mummies, sixteen heads and seventy-two animal mummies.[33] The human mummies range in date from the Third Intermediate Period to the Roman Period. They stem in large part from the region of Thebes, and they are mostly persons of sacerdotal or parasacerdotal professions.

Twenty-nine mummies and eight heads were the object of a complete study focused essentially on anthropology and paleopathology.

The sex of the mummies was determined by study of the skull and the pelvis. Out of thirty-five subjects, the sex ratio was twenty-four men and eleven women, the predominance of males occurring in nearly all the groups that have been studied, including mummies investigated in the field. Height was evaluated using the American tables of Trotter and Gleser. The age at time of death could be estimated with limited precision, especially in the case of the adults. Out of twenty-seven subjects, seven died before the age of twenty (four of them before the age of ten), sixteen between twenty and fifty years of age, and four after the age of fifty. The youngest were all from the Roman Period.[34]

Paleopathological study bore mostly on the skeletons, for most of the mummies had been eviscerated. Again, the Harris lines were studied, taking into account only the lines longer than half the diameter of the bones. This criterion was chosen to eliminate images that might

have been produced by bandages and other artifacts. Thirteen cases of Harris lines were detected on twenty-seven subjects.[35] Studies of present-day populations seem to indicate that the lines appear especially between the ages of ten and fifteen.[36] Cases of scoliosis were seldom observed: three out of twenty-nine, in contrast to cases of osteoporosis and osteoarthritis. Four cases of calcified atheroma were noted. Bone resorption of the skull in biparietal bands was discovered in two cases, one man and one woman, both over fifty years of age.[37]

Exhaustive study of mummification technique revealed that on the whole, it was of high quality. Cranial evisceration was practically systematic, carried out by breaking through the ethmoid, seventeen times via the left nostril and thirteen times via the right. Abdominal evisceration was carried out in twenty-one cases out of twenty-seven, a high proportion considering that in the later periods of Egyptian history, it tended to be less often practiced.

The investigators found a great deal of resin and wadded cloth in the abdominal cavities. They observed, however, few canopic packets (perhaps because of the superposition of pieces of cloth, which made it difficult to read the X-rays), and only in some mummies dating to the Ptolemaic and Roman Periods. The menisci were observed only rarely. As the authors rightly noted, the condensations of the intervertebral disks that appeared on the X-rays stemmed from the mummification technique and not from ochronosis.

The arms were crossed over the breast in only three cases, all from the Ptolemaic Period. The remaining mummies had their arms extended, with the hands over the pubis in those from the later stages of pharaonic history, and the hands on the outer surfaces of the thighs in those from the Roman Period.

The funerary wrappings were studied. They seemed to have been quite carefully positioned, and the outer shroud was often covered with a net of faïence beads, while the Ptolemaic mummies were covered with pieces of cutout cartonnage. A rather large number of amulets and jewels were observed inside the funerary wrappings.

OTHER STUDIES

Other studies of mummies have been conducted, including those listed here.

A team directed by Dr. D. N. H. Notman investigated four mummies in Minneapolis (University of Minnesota Mummy Project). The mummy of an adolescent, the Lady Teshat, "possesses" two heads: one of them is her own, and the other, apparently the head of an adult, is placed between her legs. The meaning of this unusual presence remains unexplained.

A team in Munich directed by F. Parsche and G. Ziegelmayer studied the mummified remains (animals and humans) in the Egyptian collection in that city.[38]

J. Bourriau and J. Bashford studied two Roman Period mummies in Cambridge (one of whom is Hermione, famous for her beautiful portrait) in order to compare their faces, such as their portraits evoke them, with images furnished by radiography. The concordance seemed good.[39]

Beginning in 1983, M. Marx and S. H. D'Auria examined, using all the noninvasive techniques, the collection of human and animal remains in the Museum of Fine Arts in Boston.[40]

Five mummies and one skull in the Lille Museum of Natural History were X-rayed and CAT scanned by A. Macke in 1991.[41]

ANIMAL MUMMIES

From the middle of the first millennium B.C.E. on, and especially in the Ptolemaic and Roman Periods, mummification was extended to an ever-greater number of animals. The term "animal mummy" covers quite a range of quality, from perfectly preserved specimens to jumbles of bone fragments and even packets empty of any animal remains.

L. Lortet and C. Gaillard were among the first to interest themselves in animal mummies. In the early 1900s, they published their monumental catalog "La Faune momifiée de l'ancienne Égypte."[42] This was essentially a descriptive work that included only a few X-rays. Around the same time, Gaillard and G. Daressy published the catalog of animal mummies in the Cairo Museum.[43]

The catalog of Lortet and Gaillard, with its many identifications of mummified species, remains a reference work to this day. With regard to rams, we know that of the two species that existed in ancient Egypt, only *Ovis platyura aegptiaca,* with its curled horns, the sacred animal of Amun and Khnum, has been found mummified. Lortet and Gaillard studied a group of sacred rams of Khnum from the necropolis of Elephantine. One of these animals displayed signs of advanced vertebral osteoarthritis, suggesting to the investigators that it must have been kept in a dark, narrow space. A number of monkey mummies from the West Valley at Luxor displayed osseous anomalies that led to a diagnosis of Paget's disease in one of them. The dogs from the necropolis of Asyut (Lykopolis), which were generally well mummified, with even their fur preserved, quite often bore traces of strangulation.[44] These mummies, like those of cats that also bear marks of strangulation or cranial fractures, were probably made for the purpose of being offered to the gods as ex-votos. Another result of the work of Lortet and Gaillard was the highlighting of a particular technique regarding the calves from Asyut. It seems that the bodies had first been buried long enough for the flesh to decay and then buried a second time, with their bones wrapped in cloths and the head realistically reconstructed with the aid of cloth and the addition of false horns. Snakes were also studied, especially by radiography. Cobras were identified in one of the packets that were X-rayed. Packets found among falcon mummies contained numerous specimens, including mummified shrews.[45] A great many crocodile mummies (figure 223) were found at Kom Ombo. According to the investigators, the mummies were immersed in a bath of boiling "bitumen," for the mummies seemed to be covered with a thick layer of some sort of black product. Many heads had their snouts cut off. Glass eyes had been placed

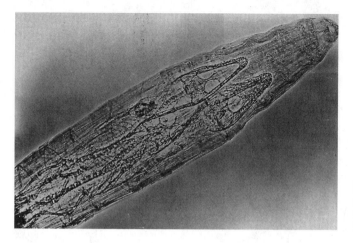

Fig. 223. X-ray of a crocodile mummy, showing the presence of three young animals. After S. Fleming, 1980.

in the orbits, with the iris painted yellow and the pupil black.

In 1931, when R. L. Moodie published a work on the human mummies from Egypt and Peru in the Field Museum in Chicago, he appended a study of the mummified animal remains.[46] On the whole, the quality of the mummification of these animals was relatively satisfying, resulting from techniques rather similar to those used on human bodies, including evisceration. A simplified technique had been used on small animals. The collection included a number of false mummies, especially those of cats. Not all the species mummified in Egypt were represented in this collection; notably, fish were missing. The species studied were cats, birds, a small crocodile, and a gazelle (?).

In 1979, E. Strouhal and his collaborators devoted several chapters to animal mummies in their study of the Egyptian mummies in Czech collections. A total of seventy-three subjects were studied and X-rayed. Some mummified fish were found, though they were difficult to identify, along with eighteen "packets" containing crocodile mummies (as many as fifteen in a single packet), an unidentified snake, and especially, a large collection of birds (thirty-two), including ibises and ten kinds of birds of prey. A stork was also purportedly identified. There were also twelve cats, two dogs, and a calf. Certain mummies were elaborately bandaged, with polychrome decoration. Several were false mummies.

The seventy-two animal mummies in the Leiden Museum were studied by Raven and Taconis. They included twenty-five cats, eleven falcons, thirteen ibises, six crocodiles, and seven packets containing one or more snakes. Most of the cat mummies and the two dog mummies were those of young animals; for the most part, they had been put to death deliberately, adding to what has often been noted regarding young animals of this sort.[47] Of the eleven falcon mummies, several larger ones had been labeled false, but X-rays revealed that in reality, they contained small birds. Among the thirteen mummies that seemed to be ibises, six were actually falcons. One huge crocodile mummy (nearly ten feet long), which had been the pride and joy of the museum, turned out to contain nothing more than two small animals; such examples of mummies "doctored" by ancient embalmers are not rare. The collection also contained some false mummies.

Until recently, most of our knowledge regarding mummies has come from the study of subjects in museums or in private collections. These studies have yielded information about the techniques of mummification and about the state of the health of the inhabitants of ancient Egypt, at least as regards a relatively privileged fraction of the population. The study of animal mummies has afforded us a better knowledge of the fauna of ancient Egypt, and it has also shed light on some rather unusual religious practices in that ancient land.

13 Mummies at Excavation Sites

Mummies at home . . . As we have seen, the study of mummies in museums suffers from the fact that we often do not know their places of origin, and that in any case, those places are extremely diverse, making it impossible to consider them as a population in the statistical sense of that term. A different orientation has thus made its appearance: the study of mummies at the sites where they are found. This practice guarantees their provenance, though at the price of limiting the number of techniques available to study them.

Archaeologists have been excavating the cemeteries of Egypt since the middle of the nineteenth century, but only much more recently have specialists begun to give human remains the same systematic study as other kinds of artifacts. We may well be amazed that in the cemeteries, more attention has been paid to tomb furnishings than to the occupants themselves!

THE WORK AT GEBEL ADDA

In 1965, during the salvage excavations carried out in Nubia because of the construction of the High Dam at Aswan (1960–70), J. E. Harris and K. R. Weeks studied a part of the human remains exhumed at Gebel Adda, near the temples of Abu Simbel.[1] More than five thousand bodies were found, some of them in skeletal state and others naturally desiccated. The two began by studying a group of complete skeletons and desiccated bodies, a study that included 149 measurements on each individual. Next, their investigation turned more specifically to the teeth in order to verify certain hypotheses of their own concerning tooth

growth, genetic or familial factors, and so forth.

Their methodology consisted of X-ray study of nearly one thousand skulls, enabling the observation of the major impact of dental abrasion, which was linked to the consumption of hard foods mixed with sand. This dental abrasion led to opening of the pulp chamber, with its usual complications. The researchers continued their work with a study of subjects from Giza and Luxor, that is, individuals considered to have belonged to the ruling class.

Their X-ray technique was a bit unusual: the device they used consisted of a unit containing Ytterbium 169 (Yt169), a radioactive material that permitted the taking of X-rays with no need for a source of electricity, but at the price of an exposure time that could take several minutes. In X-raying dry skulls, the time was obviously a matter of only relative importance. The radioactive period (i.e., half-life) of Ytterbium 169 being relatively brief, however, during the course of a season's campaign, the exposure time had to be increased due to the decrease in radioactive emission.

The basic goal of Harris and Weeks's study was to compare the development of the teeth in the two groups they studied (Nubia and Giza/Luxor), and then to compare these results with those obtained from studies of present-day populations, both Egyptian (two thousand schoolchildren in Aswan) and American.

THE MUMMIES IN THE VALLEY OF THE QUEENS

From 1986 to 1993, A. Macke and C. Macke-Ribet worked in the Valley of the Queens, on the west bank of Thebes, as part of the team directed by C. Leblanc.[2] They studied a large quantity of human material: 1,070 individuals (865 adults and 205 children) exhumed from twenty-one tombs. The mummies, dated by carbon 14 tests of the funerary wrappings, stem from a number of periods, from the New Kingdom down to the Roman era, with the largest group belonging to the latter period. It was, in fact, in the later periods of ancient history that the tombs on the Theban west bank were reused in response both to demographic growth and to the increase in the number of persons who were mummified. The reuse of older tombs became widespread. Moreover, the *nekrotaphoi* (undertakers) enlarged the existing burial places, creating veritable networks of galleries leading from one tomb to another. In nearly all cases, the deceased who filled these rock-cut tombs were of humble status.[3] It seems that this cemetery in the Valley of the Queens was at this time divided into "sectors," with the old tombs assigned to specific villages; there came a time, though, when this system could no longer be applied, due to overpopulation.

The Mackes conducted a demographic study whose results are roughly comparable to the information furnished by ancient texts. Child mortality was extremely high: fewer than one out of two reached adult age. Also noted was a high mortality rate among women of childbearing age, an observation made at most sites. Notwithstanding the overpopulation of the tombs, the investigators ascertained a population decline during the Roman Period, when the number of children per woman was insufficient to sustain the size of the population.[4]

A large part of their work was dedicated to a study of mummification technique, which was carried out on thirty-one mummies. Out of fifty skulls that were examined, only two had been excerebrated. Abdominal evisceration was observed in nineteen out of twenty-six cases, however, and six mummies still had their canopic packets in place.[5] In some cases, bags of natron left behind by the embalmers

were found in the abdomen. The skin, like the interior of the abdominal cavity, was often daubed with a reddish balm consisting of a mixture of bitumen, resin, and beeswax.[6] Nearly half the mummies had their arms crossed in the so-called Osirian position, but the investigators judiciously noted that we cannot draw any chronological conclusions from the position of the arms.

Major effort was devoted to an anthropological study in which the population of the Valley of the Queens was compared with several other population groups in Egypt and Nubia. Analysis revealed a population with little experience of outside influences, and which was clearly related to human groups of the same period inhabiting the region of Hu, Dendara, and Thebes.

Though they were radiologists, A. and C. Macke were unable to X-ray the mummified remains on site. Their paleopathological study therefore bore essentially on marks on the skeleton, that is to say, the many osteoarthritis lesions and some cases of ankylosing spondylarthritis, scoliosis, and osteoporosis. Trauma lesions were relatively rare. Benign tumors of the bones, in particular the skull, were observed, along with some cases of thinning of the parietal bones. There was a great deal of dental pathology, with parodontosis and considerable abrasion of the dental crowns.

THE CEMETERIES OF KELLIS (EL-DAKHLA OASIS)

C. A. Hope has directed an international team studying the ancient site of Kellis (Ismant el-Kharab) as part of a vast project, initiated by A. J. Mills, of identifying and investigating the sites of el-Dakhla Oasis.[7] Kellis is a huge site, essentially of the Ptolemaic, Roman, and Coptic Periods. It includes a temple dedicated to the sphinx-god Tutu, some churches, an urban settlement with houses and thermal baths, potters' kilns, hydraulic works, and, of course, cemeteries. This site has yielded a great deal of information regarding oasis life in the late Roman Period, revealing changes that took place over a long period of time, including climate change, human exploitation of the land, lifestyles, and religious beliefs and practices.

Several cemeteries were identified and studied. The graves of the west cemetery were dug into Nubian clay, some of them under a bed of sandstone. Some graves contained well-preserved mummified bodies provided with cartonnages and masks, while others contained remains in more or less disarticulated skeletal state. Several of these mummies were examined and autopsied; some had been subjected to cranial evisceration and insertion of resin, and some displayed abdominal evisceration and packing of the cavity with resin-soaked pieces of cloth. In several cases, the bodies and the bandages were themselves daubed with resin. Other mummies were not eviscerated, and autopsy revealed the desiccated organs still in place. Two mummies displayed traces of gilding on the skin (face, hands, arms). Remains of stalks of *gerid* were found in the tombs, and in one case, a mummy was still attached to its stalk. Examination of the cartonnages and the ceramics enabled the dating of these burials to the Ptolemaic Period and the beginning of the Roman Period.[8] Also in the western sector, a large tomb with a superstructure and a vaulted burial chamber contained twelve subjects, including seven children, well bandaged and probably mummified. This was apparently a family tomb, but it seems that the bodies were interred after the building of the tomb, which could date to the second century, while the mummies themselves seem to date to the end of the third and the beginning of the fourth century.[9]

The east cemetery is of an entirely different type. Established on a large plateau, it consists of two funerary enclosures surrounded by walls of unbaked brick; arranged within them are several individual pit burials with traces of brick superstructures. The general orientation is east-west, the deceased being placed with the head toward the west. Few artifacts were found in these graves, with the exception of some pieces of pottery that sometimes covered the body.[10] As of 2002, 378 individual graves have been investigated, permitting a valid statistical study.[11] Demographic study revealed a slightly higher number of women than men, a very high proportion of children who died at a young age (34.4 percent less than one year old), with a correlatively very low life expectancy, on the order of 16.7 years at birth.

The bodies were most often reduced to skeletal state because of the dampness of the soil, with the result that paleopathology was limited to conditions of the bone. Osteoarthritis was frequent, and tumors, either benign or malignant, could be observed (there was one case of a malignant bone tumor on a child). One case of spondylarthritis was visible on a man about fifty years of age. Certain conditions linked to metabolic disorders were noted. Common anomalies such as spina bifida occulta were often noted. Observed fractures differed in men and women, undoubtedly because of their different activities. Older women also presented fractures resulting from osteoporosis. Men presented fractures that were probably due to brawling. Two young adult men had suffered from leprosy, and two other subjects seemed to present signs of a leprosy that affected the facial skeleton. Three individuals seemed to bear tuberculous bone lesions.[12]

Moreover, a DNA study was undertaken on the basis of the skeletal remains from cemetery Kellis 2.[13] The objective of this research was to determine the genetic relationships among the members of this human group and to detect possible exogenous contributions.

THE MUMMIES OF ANTINOE

From 1896 to 1914, the cemeteries of Antinoe were investigated by A. Gayet, who was financed by the industrialist E. Guimet.[14] In these vast cemeteries, it was possible to excavate a huge number of mummies: in 1903, the count reached 47,000. Fortunately, most of them were reburied. A goodly number, though, those considered the most interesting, were dispersed among various museums, where they have been to a greater or lesser degree studied. Clearly, these mummies belonged to several different periods. While most of them were of late (Coptic) date, there are among them mummies "covered with gold leaf" and "sometimes entirely gilded from head to foot," which are certainly from the Roman Period. The type of mummy most represented, though, is the "white mummy," probably treated with salt and aromatics, according to Gayet, which also points to the existence of numerous outcrops of salt in the cemetery. Many bodies were neither excerebrated nor eviscerated, and they seemed desiccated and not very well preserved.[15]

In 1978, an Italian mission directed by S. Donadoni resumed excavation in this cemetery. The 120 bodies found were studied by R. Grilletto.[16] They were often covered with a thick layer of salt, confirming Gayet's observations. As in other cemeteries of the same period, a large number of children (51) were found. Age at death was forty-four for the men and thirty-two for the women. Paleopathological study showed that the teeth, which displayed little abrasion or caries, were affected by parodontosis with perialveolar abscesses. One case of ankylosing spondylarthritis was observed. It emerged from Grilletto's comparison with other groups of mummies from the pharaonic period (Asyut and Gebelein) that the inhabitants of Antinoe displayed somewhat different characteristics, possibly indicating the presence of contributions from exogenous populations.

THE CEMETERIES OF EL-KHARGA OASIS

The Sites Investigated

From 1976 to 1994, the French Institute of Oriental Archaeology in Cairo worked at the site of Dush.[17] Excavations at this site, which is located in the south of el-Kharga Oasis, were begun at the initiative of S. Sauneron, director of the Institute, and the work was continued by his successors. The site includes two temples, one of stone surrounded by a vast brick enclosure wall, and the other of unbaked brick; the remains of a town; ancient fields crisscrossed

by a complex irrigation system; and several cemeteries that were excavated beginning in 1978. From the ceramics discovered in the temple, the settlement seems to have been occupied from the Ptolemaic Period to the beginning of the fifth century of our own era.[18]

In 1981, Professor C. Roubet of the Museum of Natural History in Paris joined the team of archaeologists working in the cemeteries, initiating a program of study of the many human remains that were exhumed. In 1982, in the framework of this program, R. Lichtenberg conducted a radiological and photographic study of seventeen mummies.

From 1983 on, the investigation of the cemetery continued under the direction of F. Dunand. From 1984 to 1991, within this new framework, R. Lichtenberg, who was later joined by J. L. Heim, examined forty-eight complete mummies and sixteen isolated heads. A precise methodology for studying the mummies was put into practice, enabling study of mummification technique, paleopathology, and physical anthropology by means of teleradiography. The preserved skeletal remains (more than four hundred skeletons in more or less complete state) were studied by Heim using classical osteometric method. Since the individuals all came from the same ancient village, it was possible to make a paleodemographic study.

While the exhumed bodies were found in either mummified or skeletal condition, close study of the skeletons revealed that in most cases, they preserved remains of human tissues—cutaneous vestiges and often abundant hair—and also artifacts such as bandages, resin, and the like. It became clear that mummification had been widespread at Dush, and that conditions unfavorable to preservation were in large part responsible for the damage to the mummies. Tombs located near cultivated fields had been infiltrated by water from irrigation canals, and we must also bear in mind the devastating effect of repeated pillaging. One conclusion of this study was that careful preparation of a mummy was not enough to guarantee it would endure: satisfactory environmental conditions were also necessary.

From 1994 to 1997, and then again in 2003, the same team studied the human remains from the necropolis of Ain Labakha, located (like Dush) in el-Kharga Oasis, but around nineteen miles north of the town of el-Kharga. The site of Ain Labakha includes a Roman Period fort, two temples, one of unbaked brick and the other a semi-speos (a little cave that was used as a shrine), and the remains of a town near the fort.[19] The necropolis lies to the west, in a cliff consisting of alternating strata of sandstone and marl. The tombs were excavated into the rock at a level much higher than that of the cultivated fields, creating excellent conditions for the preservation of mummified bodies. The remains suffered only from pillaging, which was itself much less serious than at Dush. For this reason, of the sixty-four complete mummies X-rayed, and the six isolated heads, a large number were in a good state of preservation. More than 20 percent were practically intact, with nearly all their bandaging preserved (figures 224 and 225), and even, in certain rarer cases, their cartonnages.

Since 1998, the team has been working at the site of el-Deir, located nearly nineteen miles northeast of the town of el-Kharga. This vast site, which had never been investigated, had fallen victim to many acts of pillaging. It included a large, square (246 feet per side) Roman fortress, some of whose towers were preserved to a height of 39 to 42 feet. Other buildings, almost entirely in ruins, are still visible at the site, including a small brick temple situated about 875 yards north of the fort.

The cemeteries are distributed in an arc around the fortress. Much older than the fortress, these cemeteries were related to a village that must have been large, but whose location is now marked only by numerous mounds of shards. Three groups of burials were identified and investigated. One-fourth of these were discovered in the course of the most recent campaign (2004); this was a Christian cemetery. Near this cemetery was a small building of unbaked brick, in large part collapsed, that we identified as an embalmer's workshop. Thirty-seven complete mummies and forty heads were X-rayed and studied.

Two hundred ninety-eight skulls, along with post-cranial bone remains, were measured and studied. Taking into account all categories of remains, the entire population of the cemetery can be estimated at about 750 individuals.

Methodological Approach

The first step, that of cleaning the mummies, was a tricky one that in certain cases took half a day for a single subject, for the bodies were often encrusted with a coating of caked-up, and sometimes moist, sand.[20] After that, pictures were taken from a distance of thirteen feet, using a 105mm telephoto lens (24mm x 36mm body), to assure minimal distortion.

The next step was X-ray examination (figures 226 and 227). Setting up a complete radiological facility in a desert environment, without running water, is not without problems. The X-ray equipment used was portable, in every way analogous to the equipment used by an army on campaign or by a radiologist who must go to the home of a patient who cannot be moved. This type of equipment, which is capable of providing 20mA and 90kV, is entirely sufficient for the type of radiology that was performed.[21] Its low power is compatible with the limited power provided by the electrical wiring at dig sites in Egypt, even those with generators.

In fact, our main problem was that of a laboratory for developing the X-rays, which required near total darkness. The developer bath had to be kept at a temperature of 68°F, which often meant warming the bath in the morning and sometimes postponing work when its temperature exceeded 71.6°F. Moreover, the baths were kept going as long as there were films to be processed, so as to maintain their chemical consistency as long as possible. In such field conditions, it is exceptional to have running water, which would make it convenient to wash the film on the spot. The solution is thus to concentrate effort on the quality of the developing and fixing of the negatives, which can later be reprocessed by machine (fix and water baths) after returning home to assure their permanence. This protocol has proved to be entirely reliable: negatives

Fig. 224. Three mummies waiting to be X-rayed at the Inspectorate of Kharga. Necropolis of Ain Labakha (el-Kharga Oasis).

Fig. 225. Completely bandaged mummy. Robbers in search of jewels tore off the bandaging at the neck. Necropolis of Ain Labakha, T6 (el-Kharga Oasis).

processed this way more than twenty years ago display no deterioration, and in particular, no trace of yellowing.

We chose to apply systematically the principle of teleradiography: as a general rule, the negatives are shot from a distance of at least ten feet, which makes it possible to take several shots of a mummy at one time without moving it, and later, as needed, to join the negatives together with absolute precision. The result is the same as if the mummy were X-rayed all at once using a single huge film holder. Moreover, care is taken to place a small (16 cm long) metric ruler made of lead in the shot of the mummy, making it possible later to take measurements directly on the negatives.

As a rule, the head and the entirety of the mummy were X-rayed from the front. Additionally, the head was always X-rayed in pro-file, and the trunk less systematically so, because the superposition of the arms sometimes rendered the interpretation quite difficult. On average, according to the case, four to eight X-rays were taken per mummy.

Most often, we chose to X-ray mummies that were rigid enough to be hung by two straps. This procedure made it possible to take multiple X-rays in rapid succession. In particular, if a negative does not come out, it is possible to try again under practically identical conditions.

In certain cases, when a mummy was "broken" at the base of the neck, we needed to X-ray an isolated head, always at a distance of ten feet. This procedure usually makes it possible to use what is called the Hirtz position to X-ray the base of the skull (basilaris), which is not ordinarily possible.[22]

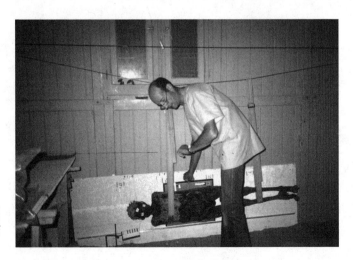

Fig. 226. Radiologist at work in his "laboratory" at the excavation site of Dush (el-Kharga Oasis).

Fig. 227. Equipment in place to X-ray mummies in a facility of the Inspectorate of Egyptian Antiquities at Kharga.

The study of mummies in the field has proven to be a rich source of information. While certain state-of-the-art techniques cannot be used under these conditions, the immense advantage of working on homogeneous groups consisting of numerous individuals largely compensates for these limitations. We are thus able to pass from the study of the individual, though such study remains necessary and fruitful, to that of an entire population, enabling more solid historical, anthropological, and medical conclusions.

The Results

X-ray study of human remains from el-Kharga Oasis was conducted on a group of 155 complete mummies, along with 60 isolated mummified heads. Additionally, about 700 skeletons were studied (figure 228).[23]

This large number enabled us to make dependable demographic and paleopathological assessments.

Age at death was on the order of thirty-five to thirty-eight, not taking into account the extremely high neonatal mortality rate. We found a relatively large number of newborns and fetuses; at Dush, they were buried in separate graves, while at el-Deir, they were placed with their parents in family tombs. Many remains of very young children have surely disappeared because of their fragility. From the ages of one year to eighteen months, however, they were often properly mummified and thus preserved.[24] As in most cemeteries, female mortality occurred in the majority of cases between twelve and forty years of age, a reflection of death during or just after labor.

The study of growth arrest lines, made pos-

Fig. 228. Anthropologist at work at the Inspectorate of Kharga.

sible by radiology, revealed that they were present in a large proportion (55–60 percent), a little lower at Ain Labakha and el-Deir than at Dush; it is probable that the nutritional level at Dush was slightly higher. At Dush, moreover, we noted a higher incidence of growth arrest lines among women (68 percent) than men (46 percent). Early pregnancies, lengthy periods of nursing, and malnutrition were probably the causes of this difference between the genders.

Cases of scoliosis were very much present, often complicated by osteoarthritis among adults. Osteoarthritis also was found in the major joints, mostly those of the legs. This type of condition was far more frequent at Dush than in the other two cemeteries. At el-Deir, one case of advanced ankylosing spondylarthritis was observed. Fractures were rather often noted in the skull, the forearms, and the neck of the femurs. Some wounds from a sharp weapon were noted at el-Deir, perhaps war injuries or simply the result of a brawl.

The study of mummies, which were often not eviscerated, enabled us to diagnose a large number of cases of schistosomiasis, which were detectable by densification in the area of the liver and spleen or by calcification of the vesical wall. Other parasitic conditions were noted, such as filariasis, which was observed twice. At the site of Ain Labakha, we discovered a spine with Pott's disease (tuberculosis vertebralis), unfortunately on the surface. Seven subjects with pulmonary tuberculosis were observed. In one and the same tomb (no. 20), there were three cases of this condition, and four cases of schistosomiasis; two individuals suffered from both conditions. Some tumors of the hypophyseal region were detected in children, including what was quite likely a glioma of the optic chiasma. One case of hydrocephalus was also identified.

Study of the human material at these three sites enabled us to determine that, contrary to widespread opinion, mummification technique had not become "degraded" in the Roman Period. In fact, our observations in the field included categories corresponding to the "classes" described by Herodotus, ranging from top-quality mummification, with abdominal evisceration and excerebration, to highly perfunctory procedures, by way of treatments that, although simplified, nonetheless yielded rather suitable results. Gilding of the body was found at all three sites in connection with high-quality mummification. Moreover, the "fine" mummies were often those in which less pathology was detected.

WORK AT SAQQARA

In 1992, R. Lichtenberg did on-site radiography of the remains of the vizier Aper-El, his wife, Taweret, and their son Huy, which had been discovered in their tomb in the cliff of the Bubasteion of Saqqara.[25] Though these remains were in skeletal condition, it could be seen that the subjects had been mummified, and that excerebration had been performed on the two males. The salient fact was the osteoporosis, including compression of the vertebrae, from which Aper-El had suffered. Aper-El also presented growth arrest lines, which are rather rare on high-ranking personages.[26]

In 2005, in the framework of the Louvre mission directed by C. Ziegler, M. and R. Lichtenberg X-rayed nine Dynasty 26 mummies that had been discovered in the vaults and galleries beneath some Old Kingdom mastabas located east of the pyramid of Wenis and a little to the north of its causeway.[27] With the exception of a single mummy that was X-rayed in a storeroom, through its sarcophagus, the others were X-rayed in situ in the subterranean galleries.

THE CEMETERIES OF ADAIMA

Since the beginning of the 1990s, a team directed by B. Midant-Reynes has been investigating the predynastic site of Adaima in the western desert between Esna and Hierakonpolis, across the river from the site of el-Kab.[28] Two cemeteries extending south-southwest of the settled area were in use from the end of Naqada I (c. 3800 B.C.E.) through the Naqada III era (c. 3200–3000 B.C.E.). The west cemetery, which is characterized by a large concentration of burials, is badly pillaged, though it is possible to study its organization and chronology. A more detailed study of funerary practices and tomb occupation has proved possible in the east cemetery, where the graves are relatively spread out and have only exceptionally been pillaged. The graves generally consist of individual pits, the latest of which in some cases have walls made of unbaked brick. There are also some double or even multiple burials: one grave contained six subjects who might have been buried at the same time, which poses a problem. The occupants, mostly in contracted, fetal position, were all in skeletal state, and there was apparently no spontaneous mummy. Yet, the remains included a foot wrapped in bandages, prefiguring the practice in use at a later date. The grave goods consisted basically of ceramics, with apparently some remains of leather and mats. In the east cemetery, the investigators noted an underrepresentation of adults. As for newborns, some were buried within the settlement area. Individuals were found with at least their arms severed. In two other cases, postmortem removal of the skull was noted. In two cases, traces of cut throats could be observed, possibly indicating, according to the investigators, a sacrificial practice.

Anthropological study revealed a marked sexual dimorphism, the men being distinctly taller than the women. With regard to paleopathology, the investigators noted that the teeth were affected by parodontosis and presented marked wear and apical cysts, while caries was rare. Scoliosis was observed, along with ankylosing spondylarthritis and degenerative osteoarthritis. Hyperostotic syndrome was also detected, as well as some cases of spinal articular tuberculosis. Fractures, especially of the arms, were rather frequent. Altogether, study of the population of Adaima revealed more similarities to African than to European reference groups.

THE ALEXANDRIAN CEMETERIES

The Italian missions investigating the vast cemeteries of Alexandria since the beginning of the twentieth century have discovered one funerary practice differing markedly from what was traditional in Egypt: cremation. Yet the earlier excavations of A. Adriani had brought to light mummified bodies in the latest cemeteries (first century B.C.E.), in particular, that of Ras el-Tin. Recent investigation of the necropolis of Gabbari by J. Y. Empereur and his team has yielded much new information.[29] Study of remains preserved in funerary urns (the hydras of Hadra) has revealed that the bones were often relatively well preserved and that it was possible to reconstruct skeletons, at least partially, and even to diagnose pathological conditions.[30] Moreover, the presence of unmummified bodies, along with bodies presenting traces of mummification, is well attested at Gabbari, as in other Alexandrian cemeteries.[31]

MUMMIES AT DEIR EL-MEDINA

In 2005, in the framework of a mission conducted by the Institut Français d'Archéologie Orientale, R. Lichtenberg X-rayed twenty mummies in the tomb of Pashed (DEM 323) at Deir el-Medina. These Ptolemaic Period mummies, some of them identified by their names, which were written on their bandages, proved to be well made, many of them with abdominal evisceration, though few had been cranially eviscerated. Many cases of vertebral scoliosis were observed.

Research continues on human remains exhumed in Egyptian cemeteries. No longer is it conceivable for archaeologists not to call on anthropologists and physicians to study the human material in tombs. Thus, E. Strouhal, a pioneer in this field, has recently worked on three mummies found in the royal necropolis of Abusir.[32] For some years now, cemeteries in the eastern delta have been under investigation, among them Minshat Abu Omar.[33] Recent investigations in this region continue to unearth human remains that are the object of studies conducted in coordination with the archaeological work.[34]

14 What We Learn from Mummies

The scientific study of human mummies affords insight into four areas of study: anthropology, paleodemography, paleopathology, and mummification.

The Study of Anthropology

Anthropology enables the determination of the ethnic characteristics of the population in question, its homogeneity, and the presence or absence of exogenous elements. To be sure, anthropology has long been done in the field, and in museum laboratories, based on remains preserved in skeletal state. But with regard to mummies, it goes without saying that the study of "populations" of known provenance (figure 229), as enabled by fieldwork, is much more fruitful than the study of mummies in museums. In fact, since the latter are most often of unknown provenance and in any case heterogeneous, we cannot call them, in the strictest sense, a "population." An anthropological study of an isolated individual can be done, of course, but only the study of a homogeneous group makes it possible to get beyond discrete anthropological characteristics, that is to say, anatomical variants that have no pathological value and that might have a certain genetic character without being part of the particular characteristics of an ethnic group.

Studies of groups of known origin permit a subtle approach to their composition. In fact, if exogenous subjects exist in a given population, they are in principle sufficiently different from the rest to be immediately recognized. At Dush, it has been possible to identify individuals of northern European origin in a population of Mediterranean type. It could be shown, however, that there were few African characteristics in this population, though a certain influx of such elements might have been expected, due to the geographical proximity of Nubia.[1]

The Study of Paleodemography

Paleodemography is a "spin-off" from the anthropological study of human remains. Since the latter makes it possible to determine gender and to know the average age at death, it is thus possible to prepare mortality charts for each sex. At Dush, the average age at death was thirty-five years for men and thirty-eight years for women. The rarity of remains of newborns is undoubtedly linked to their fragility, which led to their rapid destruction (it does not seem they were mummified); if we were able to take them into account, it would probably lead to a major lowering of this statistic. Nonetheless, it remains true that the paleodemographic study done by R. S. Bagnall on the Roman Period declarations that served as the basis for the head tax (*kat'oikian apographai*) led to similar figures.[2]

The table of ages at death of the population of Dush (figure 230) shows a slightly higher death rate for little boys than for little girls. After puberty and up to the age of forty, we note a higher female death rate, no doubt related to "difficult" births (this observation is repeated nearly everywhere in studies of ancient populations, including A. Macke's study of the population of the Valley of the

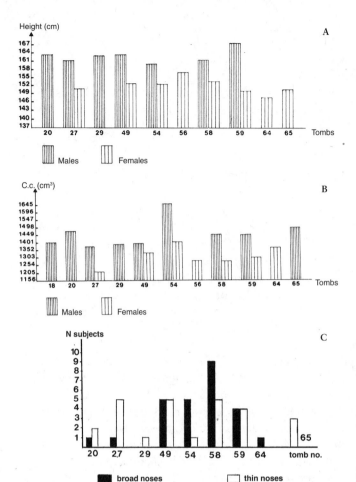

Height (cm)

A

Males | Females

C.c. (cm³)

B

Males | Females

N subjects

C

broad noses   thin noses

Fig. 229. Tables showing distribution: of average height according to sex and by tomb (A); of cranial capacity according to sex and by tomb (B); of nasal index according to tombs. Necropolis of Dush (el-Kharga Oasis).

Queens). After the age of fifty, there were no more men. Some women, however, seem to have reached a relatively advanced age. This pattern is similar to what we observe in Europe in the nineteenth century, prior to progress in hygiene and medicine. At the site of Ain Labakha, however, the division of the sexes by age is somewhat different, with a noticeable proportion of older men. This observation, added to that of a clearly higher standard of living, could indicate that the labors of the inhabitants were less hard than at Dush, with, perhaps, fewer peasants among the subjects comprising the sample that was studied. We can make a comparable remark regarding the population studied at el-Deir, where living conditions also seem to have been less harsh than at Dush. The existence of

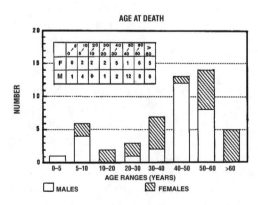

Fig. 230. Table of age at death. Necropolis of Dush (el-Kharga Oasis).

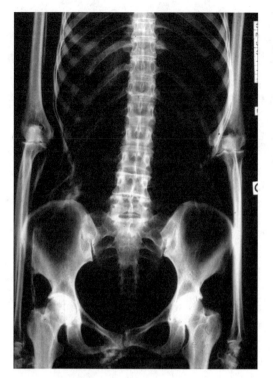

Fig. 231. X-ray of the thorax and abdomen of the mummy of a woman thirty-five to forty years of age, displaying a dense appearance of the liver: schistosomiasis. Necropolis of Dush, T58 (el-Kharga Oasis).

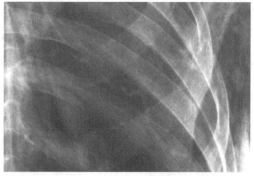

Fig. 232. X-ray of the thorax of the mummy of an elderly woman at least fifty years of age, displaying a calcified filaria (male) in an intercostal area. Necropolis of Dush, T58 (el-Kharga Oasis).

The Study of Paleopathology

Paleopathology, or the study of the illnesses from which ancient populations suffered, is far more easily done, in its diversity, by the study of mummies than of skeletons. We have sufficient remains of mummified tissues to be in a position to diagnose certain maladies that leave no traces on skeletons. In this way, investigators have been able to recognize conditions as diverse as schistosomiasis (figure 231), filariasis (figure 232),[3] and in certain cases, typhoid fever or appendicitis. At Dush, the mummy of a little girl of seven wore a wig: her hair had fallen out and grown back in a disordered manner, a characteristic result of the prolonged form of typhoid fever (figure 233). Also at Dush, a boy of five was still in a posture sug-

garrisons at Ain Labakha and el-Deir makes it likely that there were supplementary revenues (in-kind rations), though this hypothesis is perhaps valid only for a relatively late period in time (fourth century C.E.).

Fig. 233. Head of the mummy of a girl seven years of age. Her wig hides hair in the process of growing back, a symptom of the prolonged form of typhoid fever, the certain cause of her death. Necropolis of Dush, T20 (el-Kharga Oasis).

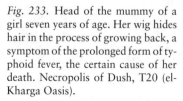

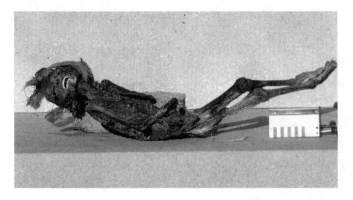

Fig. 234. Mummy of a boy five years of age, fixed in agony: probably appendicitis complicated by peritonitis. Necropolis of Dush, T92 (el-Kharga Oasis).

gesting agony, with his right hand clenched over the region of his appendix (figure 234). X-rays revealed a dense image in the abdomen, probably indicating an abscess of the appendix. We also found a fracture of the neck of the thighbone (figure 235) and a rectal prolapsus (figure 236), in both cases on old women. P. H. K. Gray detected kidney stones and gallstones, as well as arterial atheroma lesions; the same observations were made by E. Strouhal.[4] By the same token, tuberculosis can be demonstrated by means other than its classic traces on the skeleton. At the site of Ain Labakha, it was possible to detect signs of pulmonary tuberculosis in the form of thoracic calcifications (in mummies that were not eviscerated, of course).[5]

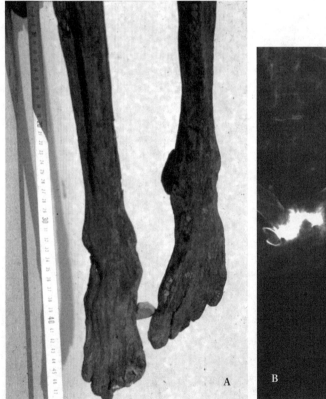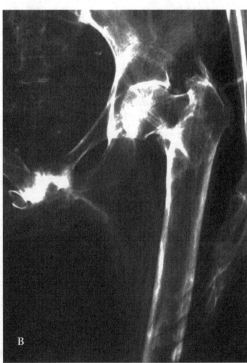

A   B

Fig. 235. Feet of the mummy of an elderly woman around sixty years of age displaying significant shortening of the left leg (A). The X-ray of the left hip reveals a fracture of the hip bone and considerable decalcification (B). Necropolis of Dush, T54 (el-Kharga Oasis).

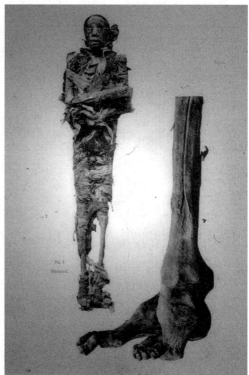

Fig. 237. Mummy of King Siptah displaying a significant shortening of the left leg: probably poliomyelitis. Cairo Museum.

Fig. 236. Close-up of the perineal region of a woman forty years of age, displaying rectal prolapse. Necropolis of Dush, T49 (el-Kharga Oasis).

Many years ago, clinical observation made it possible to identify poliomyelitis on King Siptah (figure 237), originally thought to have had a clubfoot, and smallpox on King Ramesses V (figure 238). More recently, an anomaly was observed on the skeleton of a general named Huy: a transitional vertebra L5 (figure 239). This anomaly is frequently noted on mummies or skeletons.

By making it possible to detect growth arrest lines (it is the only means of doing so), radiology supplies an approach to the health and dietary condition of an entire population. Thus, at the small town of Dush, where everything contributes to the impression that this was a place where life was hard, where pack animals were rare, and where the majority of the inhabitants were probably malnourished, growth arrest lines (figure 240) were present in 60 percent of the cases studied. At other sites in el-Kharga Oasis, Ain Labakha and el-Deir,

which seem to have been inhabited by more "comfortable" populations, growth arrest lines were present in 56 percent and 50 percent of the cases, respectively. In the large group of mummies in museums studied by Gray, who were probably individuals belonging to the upper classes of society, growth arrest lines were present in only 30 percent of the cases. Finally, in the royal mummies studied by J. E. Harris and E. F. Wente, these lines were identified in only about 5 percent of the total. The investigation of growth arrest lines is thus a good means of determining the living standards and the average health condition of a population.

As for dental health (figures 241 and 242), we know that throughout the pharaonic period, Egyptians suffered from severe and premature abrasion of their teeth. In the past, the cause cited has been the consumption of wheat containing particles of silica from the millstones used to grind it. Moreover, living in a

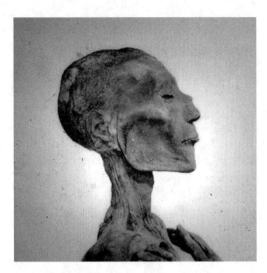

Fig. 238. Head of the mummy of King Ramesses V, displaying smallpox pustules.

Fig. 239. Lumbo-sacral segment of the spinal column of General Huy, son of Vizier Aper-El, displaying a left hemisacralization of L5. The intervertebral disks have been restored. Tomb of Aper-El (Dynasty 18), Saqqara.

semi-desert land, with frequent gusts of sand-bearing wind, persons often take in sand, not in the form of grains, as we might imagine, but in the form of a fine but nevertheless abrasive powder.

The Roman Period saw the appearance of caries, which was caused by a more regular consumption of sugar (honey). At Ain Labakha, out of sixty-four complete mummies and four isolated heads, 30 percent of the subjects presented caries, while those at Dush were free of it.

The Study of Ritual: Mummification

The study of mummies enables the study of mummification by tracing the process back through its most obvious effects. What is entailed is a sort of "reverse engineering."

For the most part, it was the royal mummies that benefited from the most elaborate treatment, which did not automatically lead to the best results. To successes like the mummy of Sethos I (figure 243), we must contrast the wretched mummy of Tutankhamun, which was literally scorched by the embalming products and, in modern times, damaged by the handling that occurred when it was separated from its gold coffin and mask.[6] The royal mummies of Tanis suffered heavily from bad conditions, principally humidity (figure 244). Throughout the New Kingdom, the external appearance of mummies displayed little variation. From Dynasty 20 on, and especially from Dynasty 21 on, embalmers had the habit of inserting various materials (sawdust, cloth) under the skin in order to simulate a more lifelike appearance;[7] the mummy of Queen Henuttawy, wife of Pinudjem I, is a good example.

The group of mummies studied by P. H. K. Gray displayed a certain variety in the appearance of their bodies and in the quality of their mummification. Gray attempted to draw information regarding their chronological order, but he prudently signaled the impossibility of dating mummies precisely on the basis of such characteristics. Like most investigators, though, he felt he could conclude that in the Roman Period, the quality of the treat-

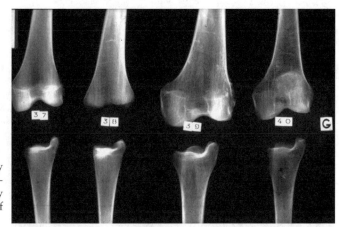

Fig. 240. X-ray of the lower extremity of the left femurs and tibias of four subjects. Nos. 38, 39, and 40 display growth arrest lines. Necropolis of Dush (el-Kharga Oasis).

ment declined severely, even when the external appearance of the mummies was especially meticulous.

Our own experience studying mummies in the field runs counter to this opinion. The mummies from Dush, Ain Labakha, and el-Deir, all undoubtedly somewhat small, outlying towns, have enabled us to determine that at this late date, far from being bad, the quality of mummification remained good, at least for part of the population: the know-how had not been lost. It is the spread of mummification that alone accounts for a lowering of the average level of quality. Thus, in the cemeteries of el-Kharga Oasis, we have been able to determine the rarity of abdominal evisceration (figure

245), which we can easily understand, for it was a long and tricky process. Removal of the brain was much more frequent. In the mummies of the Valley of the Queens, however, which were contemporary with those of el-Kharga, A. Macke noted an inverse proportion, with many cases of abdominal evisceration. R. Lichtenberg made the same observation regarding the twenty Ptolemaic Period mummies he investigated at Deir el-Medina.[8]

Observation and radiology of mummies have made it possible to discern the three classes of mummification described by Herodotus, which must have existed everywhere during the period when mummification became widespread. At Ain Labakha, where the

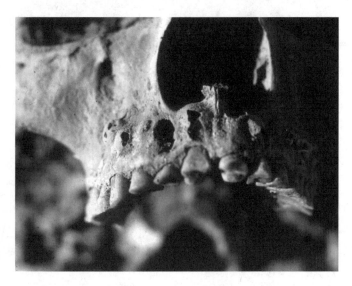

Fig. 241. Apical abscesses of the upper incisors and the upper right canine tooth of a mummy. Necropolis of Dush (el-Kharga Oasis).

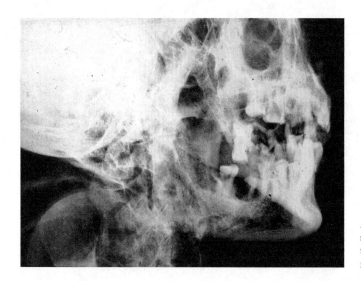

Fig. 242. X-ray of the jaw of Ramesses II in a position showing separately
the two horizontal branches of the
maxilla, displaying apical lesions.

Fig. 243. An example of an extremely well-made mummy: Sethos I. Cairo Museum.

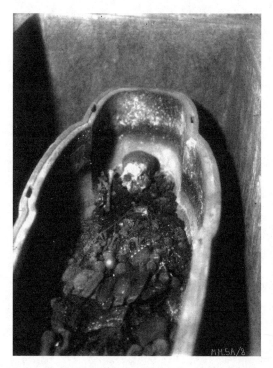

Fig. 244. An example of a poorly preserved mummy: Psusennes I in his coffin at Tanis. Now in the collection of Qasr el-Aini Hospital, Cairo.

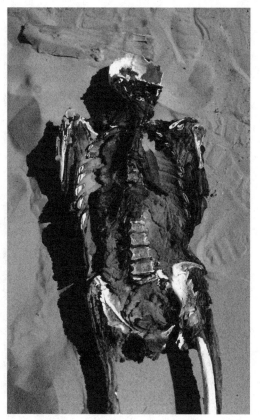

Fig. 245. Mummy removed from its tomb by pillagers and exposed to windblown sand, which stripped it, resulting in a veritable "autopsy." The lungs and the liver are still visible. Cemetery (uninvestigated) of Ain Ziyada (el-Kharga Oasis).

population seems to have had more means, the average quality of mummification seems to have been higher than at Dush, and abdominal and cranial evisceration more frequent, while often enough, we find high-quality mummies wrapped in an abundance of bandaging that was done "by the book" (figure 246).

Thus, the mummies with cranial and abdominal evisceration, some of them with gold leaf applied in greater or lesser quantity to the face (figure 247) and sometimes to other parts of the body, fall into the "first class" described by Herodotus. These first-class mummies are

Fig. 246. Evisceration orifice of a mummy. Left open, it enables the linen cloth used in packing the abdomen to be seen. Necropolis of Ain Labakha, T51 (el-Kharga Oasis).

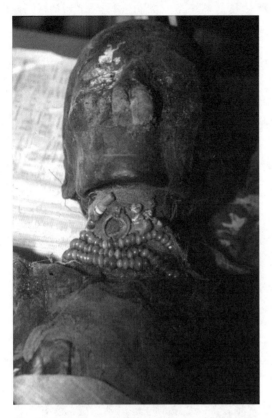

Fig. 247. Radiography detected the presence of two large collars on the mummy of a little girl twelve years of age, which had been entirely bandaged (no. 38.1.02). Traces of gold on the forehead area. Linen plugs in the nostrils. Necropolis of Ain Labakha, T38 (el-Kharga Oasis).

quite often adorned with jewels (figures 247, 248, 249, and 250). The "second class" could be represented by the mummies with cranial, but not abdominal, evisceration. The "third class" would consist of those mummies that were dehydrated but not eviscerated. All the mummies, whatever their class, are often covered by a black coating with a vitreous appearance. It goes without saying that these distinctions are somewhat schematic, and that we can observe variations in each of these categories. We should undoubtedly take into account not only the cost of the various aspects of the mummification process but also the customs peculiar to each "school of embalming," which could have varied from one region to another.

Another cause of variation in the final appearance of mummies seems to be the delay, which could have differed in duration, separating the death of the individual from the beginning of the mummification process. In some cases, treatment began rather late on bodies in a more or less advanced state of decomposition, as evidenced by the presence of stalks of *gerid* stuffed into the spinal column or used, with indifferent success, to assure an apparent connection of the bones. Not rarely, the head was held in place by a *gerid* (figure 251), a reflection of the importance the Egyptians attached to the preservation of the head.[9] In extreme cases, what we have are veritable bags of bones containing pieces of skeletons (the

Fig. 248. One of the collars from mummy no. 38.1.02, with carnelian beads and a silver *halal* (jewel in the shape of a crescent moon) pendant. Necropolis of Ain Labakha, T38 (el-Kharga Oasis).

Fig. 249. Right hand and wrist of mummy no. 38.1.02, wearing a bracelet and two adult rings too large for her fingers. Necropolis of Ain Labakha, T38 (el-Kharga Oasis).

bones sometimes coming from several individuals), with the "bag" consisting of pieces of cloth summarily held in place by large bandages, thus simulating the appearance of a mummy (figures 252 and 253).

The position of the arms of mummies can supply information of a ritual sort: as we know, arms crossed over the chest symbolically identified the deceased with Osiris. Such Christian mummies as have been studied to date never have their arms in this position. Let us also note the left arm bent at a right angle, the hand under the right breast, and the right arm alongside the body; this position is displayed by one female mummy (no. 49.1.1.2) from the necropolis of Dush. This position, which was already in use in the New Kingdom, has yet to be explained.[10] Crossed legs have been observed seven times at Ain Labakha and six times at Dush (figure 254), another position that has no explanation.

ANIMAL MUMMIES

The study of animal mummies can also contribute precious information. As in the case of human mummies, the noninvasive character of radiography makes it possible to study mummified animal remains without damaging them.[11]

Since they include most known species, these remains are a good reflection of the fauna of ancient Egypt. Of the many burial sites, Saqqara is one of the richest in the variety of its animal cemeteries, which include ibises, falcons, cats, dogs, baboons, bulls, and cows. Many other sites in Egypt also have cemeteries of animals that vary according to the local deity and the animal associated with him or her.[12]

The study of these mummies, along with that of the vegetal materials found in tombs, gives us a rather accurate idea of the ancient Egyptian environment. We thus note that a number

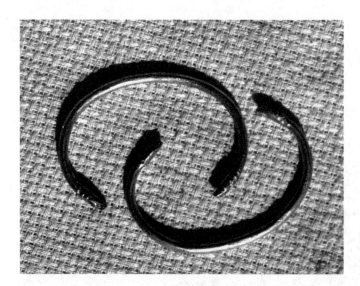

Fig. 250. Silver bracelets with serpents' heads found on the wrists of mummy no. 38.1.02. Necropolis of Ain Labakha, T38 (el-Kharga Oasis).

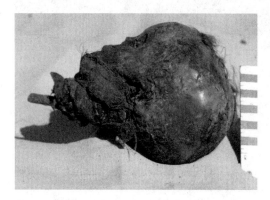

Fig. 251. Isolated head of the mummy of a child. Prior to pillaging, a stalk of *gerid* stuffed into the spinal canal had served to connect the head to the trunk. Necropolis of Ain Labakha, T6 (el-Kharga Oasis).

of species have disappeared, including the ibis; in this particular case, scholars have thought that its intensive use for cultic ends might have led to its extinction. In fact, though, this development occurred only in the nineteenth century of our own era, when artificial drainage of the delta occurred: the resulting deterioration of the biotope was the basic cause of the disappearance of these birds. Mummification cannot be the explanation, for most of the ibises that were mummified came from breeding facilities. Crocodiles, to judge from the cemeteries in the Faiyum and at Kom Ombo, were also numerous in the Roman Period. The disappearance of the crocodile (like that of the hippopotamus) resulted from excessive hunting to eliminate dangerous "neighbors," and also from climate change. After the construction of the High Dam, crocodiles became numerous in Lake Nasser, a situation that was not without prob-

Fig. 252. Mummy no. 88.1.1.1, whose superficial appearance is of high quality. Necropolis of Dush, T88 (el-Kharga Oasis).

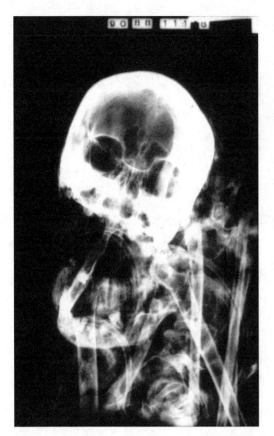

Fig. 253. X-ray of mummy no. 88.1.1.1, revealing that the skeleton is in utter disorder. Necropolis of Dush, T88 (el-Kharga Oasis).

lems, if only in that they had the habit of "sampling" the fish in the lake.

Radiography of animal mummies can aid in the identification of different species within a given family. This is the case with the falcons found in large numbers in the galleries of north Saqqara, which are being studied by a team directed by P. Nicholson. Several species have been identified.[13]

In the same way, the radiological study of more than three hundred cats from the Bubasteion carried out by R. and M. Lichtenberg under the direction of A. Zivie (French Archaeological Mission, Bubasteion), has enabled the identification of two species of cat, the large wild cat (*Felis chaus,* figure 255), little represented at Saqqara, and especially the much smaller cat (*Felis sylvestris libyca*), domesticated from the Middle Kingdom on, which is generally considered to be the ancestor of our modern domestic cat. Since they were raised to furnish mummies for ex-voto offerings, these were young animals, and almost no pathology was detected on them.

From 2001 to 2004, a rather large quantity of canine mummies was discovered at the site of el-Deir. Fifty-four mummies were X-rayed, and it proved possible to make the same observations as in the case of the cats at Saqqara: the canines were most often put to death, generally by strangulation, and then mummified to be offered for sale to pilgrims. This hypothesis is supported by the asymmetrical appearance of the mummies, which have a "good side" finely decorated with colored bandages arranged in meticulous geometric motifs, while the other side is often of much more mediocre quality. This observation leads us to suppose that the mummies were simply shown

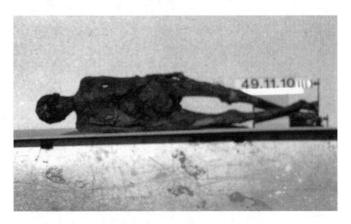

Fig. 254. Mummy of a woman, displaying the crossed position of the legs. Necropolis of Dush T49 (el-Kharga Oasis).

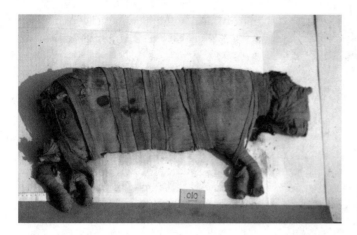

Fig. 255. Mummy of a large cat, probably *Felis chaus*. Saqqara, Bubasteion. Roman Period.

to the pilgrims, set aside, and then buried by the priests.[14]

At Elephantine, where ram (*Ovis platyura*) mummies have been found, L. Lortet and C. Gaillard noted traces of rheumatism on the skeletons, indicating to them that the animals must have lived in a confined space: these sacred animals probably spent their entire existence in a place located within the enclosure of the temple of Khnum. To us, it seems more likely that these were aged individuals, for these rams, incarnation of the god Khnum, were not put to death, quite unlike the animals intended to serve as ex-votos.

The tableau of mummified fauna does not, however, completely reflect the totality of the animals that inhabited ancient Egypt. Animals present in large number and indispensable to daily life and activities, such as the donkey and to a lesser degree the pig, have never been found mummified, undoubtedly because they were linked to the god Seth. Dangerous, feared animals, such as the hippopotamus and the scorpion, though associated with the beneficent goddesses Taweret and Selkis, also seem never to have been mummified.[15]

Conclusion

Here, at the end of this survey of more than three thousand years of a technique that developed slowly and laboriously, one at first reserved for an elite and then extended progressively down through all the strata of society, we may inquire as to the reasons for such an "investment" in the industry of death. For kings and important personages, considerable resources were dedicated to the construction of tombs and to the preservation and appearance of the deceased. Even the less wealthy did not hesitate, as their means allowed, to prepare a "beautiful burial." We must in fact put aside our twenty-first-century Western mentality, with its concern for profitability and its incomprehension of expenditures considered unproductive. It has not always been so: medieval European societies devoted considerable sums, for instance, to the construction of cathedrals. Mummification, too, cannot be separated from its religious context. By meeting a condition necessary for survival—the preservation of the body—it expressed one of the fundamental beliefs of Egyptian religion. In the eyes of the Egyptians, death was merely the temporary separation of the physical and spiritual elements that constituted a person. It was not an end, it was but a brief passage to the second life that could be attained, provided the funerary ritual assured that the invisible elements of the personality were reunited with the preserved body. This second life was not viewed as a compensation for human misery, but as an even happier continuation of the present life. No other civilization has approached this overwhelming attempt to negate death. We can understand how it was that the Greeks, upon conquering Egypt, rapidly adopted the Egyptian vision of the afterlife, which was far more reassuring and optimistic than their own.

For some of our contemporaries, who are fascinated by Egyptian mummies, this practice might seem an answer to their questions regarding death and the afterlife. It is no such thing: mummification will always remain a pseudoresponse to a genuine question.

Appendix

Royal (and Other) Mummies

ABBREVIATIONS

CGC   Catalogue générale Cairo (General
       Catalogue of the Cairo Museum)
KV   Kings' Valley (Valley of the Kings)
QA   Qasr el-Aini

THE ROYAL AND NONROYAL MUMMIES OF THE CACHES AT THEBES

Dynasty 17

TETISHERI (found at Deir el-Bahari, CGC 61056). Wife of King Senahktenre Tao I, found in a coffin bearing the name of Ramesses I. Mummy of an elder woman, her head mostly bald and separated from her body. Radiography revealed anthropological characteristics of the skull that occur over four generations, especially in regard to the teeth. The inscriptions on the coffin seem to show that the priests who carried out the reburial were persuaded this was the body of Ramesses I (whose mummy has yet to be found, or perhaps is the mummy now resting in the Luxor Museum). The identification of the queen's mummy rests essentially on its anthropological characteristics and on the mummification technique employed.

SEQENENRE TAO II (found at Deir el-Bahari, CGC 61051). Son of Queen Tetisheri and King Senakhtenre Tao I. Examination of the mummy showed that the king died a violent death, for there were severe wounds to the face and head, suggesting blows from several attackers using lances (or arrows) and battle axes. It could not be definitely determined whether he died in battle (in the course of a conflict with the Hyksos), or whether he had been surprised in his sleep. The quality of the mummification was indifferent, which argues in favor of a hasty embalming, perhaps in the vicinity of the battlefield, as suggested by G. Maspero. His age has been estimated at about thirty. His lips had been cut away, revealing teeth that were in good condition. The *rishi* coffin seems to be the one in which he was originally buried, but all the gilding, which had been removed by plunderers, was replaced by yellow paint, no doubt at the time of the reburial of the royal mummies.

AHMOSE-INHAPI (found at Deir el-Bahari, CGC 61053). Daughter of Senahktenre Tao I and wife of Seqenenre Tao II. The mummy is that of a robust, tall (about 5′6″) woman with a somewhat dark complexion. Her abundant hair is arranged in numerous small braids. Prior to unwrapping, the mummy still had its bandages, which were covered by garlands of flowers. The mummy was in a somewhat mediocre state of preservation. It was found in a coffin belonging to the lady Rai, who was also found in the cache at Deir el-Bahari but in another coffin.

AHMOSE-HENUTEMPET (found at Deir el-Bahari, CGC 61062). Daughter of Seqenenre Tao II and Queen Ahhotep. The unwrapping revealed a somewhat tall (about 5′3″) mummy, in bad condition, with both forearms broken. The head was covered with thick black hair. An enormous wig lay on the chest, beneath the bandages. The mummy had been placed in a "recycled" coffin of Dynasty 18 date, on which her name replaced that of the original owner.

189

AHMOSE-HENUTTAMEHU (found at Deir el-Bahari, CGC 61061). Daughter of Seqenenre Tao II and Queen Ahmose-Inhapi. The mummy, which had been damaged by plunderers, was rebandaged by the priests charged with transferring it to the cache. Height about five feet. Her coffin was found in bad condition, with the gilding and the inlaid eyes stolen by the plunderers.

From Dynasty 17, we lack the mummy of Kamose, who was its last ruler.

Dynasty 18

AHMOSE (found at Deir el-Bahari, CGC 61057). Son of Seqenenre Tao II and Queen Ahhotep; founder of Dynasty 18, he reunified Egypt after having expelled the Hyksos. The name of the king was found inscribed on the coffin and on the bandages in which the mummy was wrapped. This coffin, of cedar wood, dates to Dynasty 18 but was not originally his. The names of Amenhotep I, his successor, and of Pinudjem II, the high priest of Thebes who ordered the reburials, were also inscribed on the bandages. Around forty years of age at death, he was somewhat short (about 5'4") and of a frail constitution. Unlike many of the kings, he was not circumcised. Radiography revealed major similarities to Seqenenre, confirming their family ties. The mummy bore advanced osteoarthritis lesions.

SIAMUN (found at Deir el-Bahari, CGC 61059). His mummy was found in extremely bad condition, literally broken apart by plunderers. When it was reburied, the bones were placed pell-mell to form an oblong "packet" nearly 3'3" in length. The *rishi* coffin bears the name of this prince (which is unknown from elsewhere).

SITKAMOSE (found at Deir el-Bahari, CGC 61063). Probably a daughter of Kamose. A woman tall for the period (about 5'4"), poorly mummified. The body, which was covered with a thick coating, was damaged by plunderers. Absence of excerebration. The feet bore the mark of the thin cords used to hold the toenails in place. The abdominal cavity was filled with textile packing material. The position of the arms, which are extended, with the hands in front of the pubic area, is unusual for an adult female (age of death around thirty to thirty-five years): this is the position used for young boys. She was placed in a coffin bearing the name of a certain Pediamun.

AHMOSE-SIPAIR (found at Deir el-Bahari, CGC 61064). Son of Ahmose; young boy of indeterminate age. The body, which had been damaged by plunderers, was reinforced at the time of reburial with the help of a stick that was placed inside the bandaging. The coffin, which was not originally his, dates to the end of Dynasty 18.

AHMOSE-NOFRETARI (found at Deir el-Bahari, CGC 61055). Sister and wife of Ahmose. The mummy of this queen was unwrapped by E. Brugsch in 1885. The body had been damaged by plunderers; the left hand was missing, as were the right hand and forearm. Mummy of an older woman wearing a wig made of real hair. Her skeleton noticeably resembles that of her grandmother, Tetisheri. She displays an upper dental prognathism even more marked than Tetisheri's. She was lying in an enormous wooden coffin (nearly twelve feet long), which was beautifully made, with traces of inlays of stone or glass paste (stolen). The mummy of Ramesses III was also found in this coffin.

SITAMUN (found at Deir el-Bahari, CGC 61090). Daughter of Ahmose and Queen Ahmose-Nofretari. The mummy seemed to be in good condition, but after it was unwrapped, nothing was found but bones mixed with reed stalks. The body must have been torn apart by plunderers. What remained of it had been placed in a small anthropoid coffin that bore no decoration or inscription.

AMENHOTEP I (found at Deir el-Bahari, CGC 61058). Son of Ahmose and Queen Ahmose-Nofretari. A tomb discovered by Carter at Dra Abu el-Naga might have been his. A tall mummy (5'8"), left intact by the scholars because of the fine quality of the rebandaging carried out by the priests at the time of its reburial. The mummy was entirely covered with garlands of flowers, and a cartonnage mask was placed on the face. Radiography revealed that like his predecessors, the king had a rather marked prognathism. The arms were in the Osirian position. He was in a coffin of cedar wood inscribed with the name of a certain Djehutinefer, but an inscription containing the names and titles of the king had been added on the lid.

AHMOSE-MERITAMUN (found at Deir el-Bahari, CGC 61052). Daughter of Ahmose. Mummy in extremely bad condition, with some remnants of bandaging preserved on the legs. Cloth packing visible through holes in the abdominal cavity. The mummy, which is short of stature (about 4′10″), was found in a coffin that had belonged to the intendant Seniu (Dynasty 18).

TUTHMOSIS I (?) (found at Deir el-Bahari, CGC 61065). Born of an unknown father and a lady named Seseneb. His mummy, which is short (barely more than five feet), is of good quality and very well preserved. The arms are drawn together just above the genitals (the hands are missing). Radiography revealed a healed fracture of the pelvis. The identification of this mummy is subject to caution, because radiography enabled the age of the skeleton to be established as eighteen to twenty years, which does not square with the length of the reign of Tuthmosis I (eleven years and nine months), who would have died around the age of fifty. Based on mummification technique, G. Elliot Smith dated this mummy earlier than that of Tuthmosis II. J. E. Harris and E. F. Wente suggested that this is the mummy of an unidentified ancestor of the Tuthmosids. Two cedar coffins were used for his reburial, one dating to Dynasty 18, the other to Dynasty 21.

TUTHMOSIS II (?) (found at Deir el-Bahari, CGC 61066). Son of Tuthmosis I and Mutnofret, one of his wives. Unwrapped by G. Maspero in 1886. The body, which had been badly damaged by thieves (traces of ax blows, arms broken and right leg separated from the body), was restored by G. Elliot Smith. The head is well preserved. Medium height (about 5′6″). The arms are in the Osirian position. The skin of the thorax, the shoulders, and the arms is covered with rough pustules that are also on the bodies of Tuthmosis III and Amenhotep II. The age of death was around thirty years. The morphology is similar to that of the preceding mummy. In fact, it is probably necessary to identify this mummy no. 61066 as that of Tuthmosis I. The cedar coffin dates to Dynasty 18, but it was not originally intended for the use of a king.

TUTHMOSIS III (found at Deir el-Bahari, CGC 61068). Son of Tuthmosis II and one of his concubines, Isis. He assumed power only after the reign of his aunt and mother-in-law, Hatshepsut. His was the first of the royal mummies to be unwrapped. The mummy was in bad condition, which led the priests to use oars by way of "supports" to keep the body firm when they reburied it. These oars were probably part of the funerary equipment (they were also found in the tomb of Tutankhamun). The arms and legs were detached from the body; the arms were in the Osirian position. Radiography revealed that his morphology was similar to those of Tuthmosis I and Tuthmosis II. Documents from his reign indicate that he would have been about sixty-five years old at the time of his death (theoretically, he reigned fifty-five years), but the radiography does not seem to be in accord with such an age. His height was estimated at about 5′3″ by G. Elliot Smith, but the measurements made by G. Robins and C. C. D. Shute, who took into account the absence of the feet, indicated a height of about 5′7″. The coffin, which was badly damaged, was probably originally his. The interior was gilded, and the names and titles of the king are still identifiable on the inside of the lid.

AMENHOTEP II (found in his tomb in 1898 by V. Loret, CGC 61069). Son of Tuthmosis III and Queen Meritre-Hatshepsut. His tomb had been pillaged by thieves, but despite all, he was reburied in his own coffin, and other members of the royal family, including several kings, were placed in a side chapel of the burial chamber. After his discovery, he was left in his tomb, but he was soon "disturbed" by modern thieves, which led to his transfer to the Cairo Museum. His body, which is extremely damaged, bears a strong resemblance to those of his father, Tuthmosis III, and his son, Tuthmosis IV. Radiography permitted his age to be estimated at about forty-five, and it revealed that he suffered from osteoarthritis.

UNIDENTIFIED PRINCE (found in the tomb of Amenhotep II, CGC 61071). Found with two female mummies, one of whom was Teye, which enabled his possible identification with Prince Tuthmosis, the oldest son of Amenhotep III and Teye. He was a young boy around nine years of age (height about 4′1″). Except for the "sidelock of youth," the head of the mummy is shaved. The mummy, which was without a coffin, had been badly damaged by plunderers.

MERITAMUN (found in Deir el-Bahari tomb no. 358, CGC 55150). Daughter of Tuthmosis III and wife of Amenhotep II. Until her discovery in 1929, she remained in place in her own tomb, which was restored during Dynasty 21, after it had been plundered, and then also reused for a daughter of Pinudjem I. Her tomb, which is somewhat complex, was dug immediately under the northern portico of the first terrace of the temple of Hatshepsut. The body, which is well preserved, is that of a woman fifty years of age and short of stature (about 5′1″). The skin bears traces of jewels that were removed by thieves. The body had been covered with a liquid resinous product that formed a thick coating. Her features resembled those of her father, Tuthmosis III. She was preserved in her two original coffins, though their present-day appearance owes much to the restoration carried out during Dynasty 21. All their original inlays have disappeared, now evoked only by touches of paint. Fragments of the third coffin, which was quite large, have been found.

TUTHMOSIS IV (found in the tomb of Amenhotep II, CGC 61073). Son of Amenhotep II and Queen Tia. Died at age thirty or even earlier. Arms in the Osirian position. Strong resemblance to his father. Height about 5′5″. The team from Michigan who studied the mummy was struck by its particularly emaciated appearance, which could not have been caused by the mummification process alone; it might rather have been caused by the illness from which he died, though this cannot be identified. The work of the embalmers seems to have been done somewhat crudely and hastily. He was reburied in a sycamore coffin from Dynasty 20.

AMENHOTEP III (found in the tomb of Amenhotep II, CGC 61074). Son of Tuthmosis IV and Queen Mutemwia; short of stature (about 5′1″). Mummy in extremely bad condition (perhaps the worst of all the royal mummies). The head was separated from the body. The mummy is practically reduced to a skeletal state. The king was probably obese, as bas-reliefs and statues tend to indicate. He must have died around the age of fifty, according to the X-rays. The embalmers had placed resin and cloth underneath the skin to give the body a lifelike appearance, anticipating the technique of Dynasty 21. The coffin, which dates to Dynasty 20, is crudely made; it bears the names of Amenhotep III, but also those of Sethos II and Ramesses III.

TEYE (found in the tomb of Amenhotep II, CGC 61070). Principal wife of Amenhotep III, Queen Teye was of nonroyal parents. This mummy had neither a coffin nor any mark enabling its identification. It was long designated the "elder woman." In 1976, X-rays made by the team from Michigan showed that its morphology was quite similar to that of Yuya and Tuya, the parents of Teye. Moreover, a comparative study of the hair of this mummy and that found in the tomb of Tutankhamun, in a little coffer inscribed with the name of Teye, revealed that the hair was identical. Nevertheless, this identification has recently been placed in doubt. Some scholars think the mummy could be Ankhesenamun, the wife of Tutankhamun. The body is that of a middle-aged woman, short (around 4′9″), with her long, wavy hair preserved. The body suffered considerably from plunderers. The right arm is placed alongside the body, while the left arm is bent in front of the thorax.

SMENKHKARE (found in tomb KV 55, CGC 61075). Probably a son of Amenhotep III, he has posed major problems of identification. Tomb 55 contained many objects bearing the name of Teye, and scholars think that it was reused for royal burials at the time of the abandonment of Amarna and the return to Thebes. The body was at first thought to be that of Teye, but G. Elliot Smith demonstrated that it was a man aged twenty-five to twenty-six. The arms were, however, positioned like those of a woman, with the right arm alongside the body and the left bent over the thorax. Then, some began to identify it as Akhenaten. Today most scholars think it is Smenkhkare, though a recent study has attributed an age of thirty to thirty-five to it, again leading to thoughts of Akhenaten. The skeleton, which is incomplete, is quite similar to that of Tutankhamun and his immediate forebears. The coffin, which is well made, has preserved its inlays of gold and glass paste. The form of the wig is feminine, but the lid was modified for the use of a king, as shown by the addition of a uraeus and a wig. The presence of a cartouche is visible on the lid.

TUTANKHAMUN (found in his tomb, KV 62). Probably son of Amenhotep III and brother of Akhenaten. His tomb was discovered in 1922 by H. Carter and Lord Carnarvon. Despite some initial tomb robbery, his mummy was found completely intact in its three coffins, themselves placed in a quartzite sarcophagus, which in its turn was surrounded by four chapels of gilded wood. But the abundance of unguents smeared on the body had literally carbonized the flesh, to the extent that the condition of the mummy is quite mediocre. In the same way, the bandages were rendered quite friable. The mummy was examined in detail by D. Derry and Salah Bey Hamdin. In 1968, it was X-rayed, revealing an age at death of about twenty years. Several ribs and the sternum were lacking, which permitted the formulation of a hypothesis of accidental death—for example, a fall from a chariot; but we must remember that the body was broken in numerous places when it was removed from its coffin, a procedure that was rendered quite difficult by the abundance of hardened resin. The head and the extremities were better preserved than the rest of the body, probably because of the protection afforded by the gold mask and finger sheaths. The king was rather short (around 5′6″), and the anthropological measurements of his skull were quite similar to those of the skull from tomb KV 55 (Smenkhkare or Akhenaten), confirming that they were closely related. The position and appearance of the evisceration incision differ slightly from the usual: it is more median, beginning at the navel and continuing obliquely toward the left hip. The internal organs of the king, bathed in unguents and resin, were contained in small mummiform coffins of solid gold that were placed in an alabaster chest with four compartments closed by lids in the image of the king, the whole surmounted by a large lid. Let us recall the fine quality of the king's coffins, in particular the last one, of solid gold, which was extremely heavy, as well as that of the mask, also of gold, which is a veritable masterpiece of the goldsmith's art.

TWO FETUSES (found in the tomb of Tutankhamun). These were probably premature, stillborn children of the royal couple Tutankhamun and Ankhesenamun. The first (Catalog of the tomb 317a2) is probably a female fetus, whose estimated age is about four months (height about 9.8″); the arms were placed alongside the body. Absence of abdominal evisceration. The second child (Catalog of the tomb 317b2) is also a female fetus, whose estimated age is seven or eight months (height about 15.4″). The body had been eviscerated and packing material placed in the abdomen and the cranial cavity. X-ray examination in 1979 revealed skeletal anomalies: scoliosis, spina bifida, and Sprengel's deformity of the scapula. Each of these fetuses was placed in a double coffin, which were deposited in a wooden chest found in the room known as the "treasury."

Dynasty 19

SETHOS I (found at Deir el-Bahari, CGC 61077). Son of Ramesses I, the founder of Dynasty 19. The body was unwrapped by G. Maspero in 1886. The identification was made possible by hieratic inscriptions on the lid of the coffin, which also describe the work of the priests at the time of the reburial. Although the base of the neck was fractured, the mummy as a whole was in a remarkable state of preservation, in particular the head. The arms were in the Osirian position. The entire body was covered with bandages impregnated by blackened "resin." The embalmers had put the heart back in the thorax, on the right side. His age at death could not be precisely determined. His height was about 5′4″. The cedar coffin seems to have been part of the king's funerary equipment; its mask was restored at the time of reburial.

RAMESSES II (found at Deir el-Bahari, CGC 61078). Son of Sethos I. His is one of the most studied royal mummies. In fact, when it went to Paris in 1976 for purposes of restoration work, scientists took advantage of the opportunity to carry out studies that included X-ray examination; bacteriological, mycological, and parasitic examinations; and analyses of the packing material and the vegetal remains. The identification of the mummy was furnished by an inscription indicating that, in year 10 of Pinudjem (c. 1060 B.C.E.), the body was placed in the tomb of Amenophis I. Later, the mummy was deposited in the cache at Deir el-Bahari. When it was discovered, it was still perfectly bandaged and covered with garlands of flowers. The king bore a close resemblance to his father, Sethos I. The body was in a good state of preservation. The king was tall (about 5′8″). His yellowish hair was partially preserved; analysis showed that it had originally been red. The arms, which had originally been in the Osirian position, moved slightly away from the thorax after the unwrapping. The neck displayed an accentuated curve along the sagittal plane; radiography showed (A. C. Thuilliez and R. Lichtenberg, 1977) that this curve was due to a postmortem fracture of the cervical spine caused by the embalmers when they introduced the intracranial resin. The volume of the nose was preserved, thanks to the introduction of grains of pepper, while the nostrils were filled with resin. Radiological study of the mummy revealed ankylosing spondylitis scars, an ailment that must have caused the king a great deal of pain in his old age. Arteriosclerosis lesions were also visible. The teeth were in rather bad condition. The well-made cedar coffin dated to Dynasty 18. Its original gold decoration had disappeared and was replaced by yellow paint. The style of the coffin is comparable to that of Tutankhamun.

MERNEPTAH (found in the tomb of Amenhotep II, CGC no. 61079). The thirteenth son of Ramesses II and Queen Isetnofret, he became king as a middle-aged man. The mummy, unwrapped by G. Elliot Smith in 1907, was identified thanks to an inscription. It was damaged by plunderers, who had broken the right forearm and pierced a hole in the abdomen. The king was a bald man, probably corpulent, apparently aged, and somewhat tall (about 5′7″). The arms were in the Osirian position, and the hands seemed still to be holding the insignia of royalty. The body was covered with a crust of salt (sodium chloride). In the abdomen was a substance reminiscent of butter mixed with soda. Like his father, the king was emasculated (a custom going back to the myth of Osiris). Radiography revealed that, also like his father, he suffered from osteoarthritis and arteriosclerosis. There were also a hole on the right side of his skull and fractures of the heads of the femurs, all probably postmortem accidents. His teeth were in bad condition, and some of them were missing. The king was found lying at the bottom of a cartonnage coffin, probably originally made for Sethnakhte, while the mummy of an unidentified woman was found under the lid. The king's granite sarcophagus is still in his tomb.

SETHOS II (found in the tomb of Amenhotep II, CGC 61081). Son of Merneptah. His mummy was unwrapped by G. Elliot Smith in 1905. The mummification was particularly well done, the bandages were of high quality, and resin was spread over the body and the bandaging. The head and arms had been broken by plunderers. The arms were originally in the Osirian position. He was about thirty years of age at the time of his death. His height was about 5'5". Beads and scarabs, as well as two perfectly preserved shirts, were found in the thickness of the bandaging. The mummy was in the lower half of a wooden coffin; it was reused but inscribed with the name of Sethos II. The exact identity of the mummy has, however, been the object of discussion. G. Elliot Smith had already noted his resemblance to the kings of Dynasty 18. More recently, J. E. Harris and E. F. Wente, thinking it was unlikely that this mummy was that of a son of Merneptah, proposed that it was Tuthmosis II. In that case, the mummy identified as that of Tuthmosis II would be that of Tuthmosis I. The mummy officially identified as Tuthmosis I would then be an ancestor of the dynasty.

SIPTAH (found in the tomb of Amenhotep II, CGC 61080). Son of Sethos II. The body is that of a man of about twenty. The unwrapping done by G. Elliot Smith took three days, for the bandages had been entirely hardened by resinous products. Similarly, the face was entirely covered with a black product. The abdominal cavity contained lichens. The right forearm had been broken by thieves, and the priests of Dynasty 21 restored it with the help of wooden sticks. The left foot presented a major deformity at first thought to be a clubfoot, but the team from Michigan attributed it to a neuromuscular disorder, probably poliomyelitis. Height about 5'4". He was found in a coffin dating to Dynasty 19, reused and inscribed with the names and titles of the king.

Dynasty 20

RAMESSES III (found at Deir el-Bahari, CGC 61083). The mummy is that of a man about sixty-five years of age. The arms are in the Osirian position. The bandaging, which is well preserved, was carefully restored by the priests who reburied the royal mummies during Dynasty 21. The mummy is generally well preserved. Height about 5'6". Artificial eyes were inserted in the orbits. His dentition closely resembled that of the kings of Dynasty 19. Radiography revealed the presence of statuettes of the Sons of Horus located on the left side of the trunk. The mummy, in a rather crude cartonnage with the names and titles of the king inscribed on it, was found in the enormous coffin of Queen Ahmose-Nofretari, along with the mummy of that queen.

RAMESSES IV (found in the tomb of Amenophis II, CGC 61084). Son of Ramesses III. Mummy in good condition, with its arms in the Osirian position. Bald head. Presence of onions in the orbits and resin in the nostrils and the mouth. Lichens in the abdominal cavity. Unlike what we can observe on other kings of the same period, the genitals are in place, and the king seems to have been circumcised. When he was reburied, the bandaging was not well done. A shroud, however, was inscribed with the name of the king. He was in a rather modest coffin, inscribed with the names of the king and dating to Dynasty 20.

RAMESSES V (found in the tomb of Amenhotep II, CGC 61085). Perhaps a brother of Ramesses IV. The mummy is well preserved, and the face is painted with red ocher. The cranial cavity and the orbits contain fine cloth, and the nostrils and the mouth are filled with wax. The ear lobes are pierced and distended (the king must have worn large earrings during life). The arms are in the Osirian position. The skin is covered with small nodules that G. Elliot Smith proposed to interpret as signs of smallpox, a diagnosis that remains the most probable. The abdomen is filled with sawdust. A part of the viscera remains in the abdominal cavity. Height about 5'8". The mummy was found in a rectangular wooden coffin dating to Dynasty 18.

RAMESSES VI (found in the tomb of Amenhotep II, CGC 61086). Another son of Ramesses III and Queen Isis, and brother of Ramesses IV and V (?), whose reigns were quite brief. Mummy of a middle-aged man, found in bad condition, the head and the trunk having literally been hacked to pieces by plunderers; there were traces of postmortem knife and ax blows. The reburial seems to have been conducted hastily, with a mixture of mummy fragments belonging to other individuals. The restorers had attached the remains to a plank to give them the substance of a mummy. The anthropoid coffin, of sycamore wood, had been made for a priest of the reign of Tuthmosis III.

RAMESSES IX (found at Deir el-Bahari, Cairo Museum). Mummy in bad condition, found in the coffin of Nesikhons. It seems not to have been examined since the time of its discovery.

NEDJMET (found at Deir el-Bahari, CGC 61087). Wife of the high priest and king Herihor. Mummy vandalized by thieves: broken wrists, legs damaged, traces of blows on the face and thorax. The mummification technique was a harbinger of what would follow in the ensuing periods. In the abdomen, the viscera were replaced by statuettes of the four Sons of Horus, and the evisceration incision was filled with wax. Particular care seems to have been shown to the appearance of the body: sawdust and resin packing in the oral cavity, giving the face a swollen appearance; human hair used as substitutes for the eyebrows, which had disappeared; and artificial eyes of black and white stone inserted into the orbits. The mummy had retained its own long hair, to which false hair had been added. The hands were arranged alongside the body, according to a custom that would become more widespread in the following period. Radiology revealed bad teeth. Height five feet. Age at death about thirty to thirty-five years. The corpse was in two coffins, both reused and originally made for a man. The first coffin was badly damaged, and the original decoration had disappeared. The second, though damaged, retained part of its decoration, mostly on the interior, and even part of its exterior gilding and inlays.

Dynasty 21

PINUDJEM I (found at Deir el-Bahari, not inventoried in the CGC). High priest of Amun and founder of Dynasty 21. When papyri and funerary objects belonging to him and his family appeared on the antiquities black market, archaeologists were put on the trail of the modern thieves. The mummy was found well bandaged (arms and legs bandaged separately). It seems to have disappeared since its discovery.

HENUTTAWY (found at Deir el-Bahari, CGC 61090). Daughter of Ramesses XI and wife of Pinudjem I. The mummy was damaged by thieves, but it was in good condition. It had benefited from an elaborate treatment whose goal was to restore a lifelike appearance. The volume of the hair had been augmented by false hairs. The skin of the face was painted yellow, with the cheeks and lips painted red. The eyebrows were outlined in black. Each part of the body had been filled with various substances intended to give it a normal volume. Thus, in the neck, there was a greasy substance comparable to butter mixed with soda. The abdomen was filled with sawdust. The chest was remodeled with cloth. The treatment was not entirely successful, in particular the face, which literally exploded. Dr. N. Iskander recently restored this mummy. The internal organs, which were separately embalmed, had been put back in the abdominal cavity. A gold plate was still in place. Radiology indicated an age at death of about thirty to forty years. The height is about 4'11". The mummy was placed in two reused coffins, of the same type as those of Queen Nedjmet. They were both damaged, and the first one was also missing its lid.

MAATKARE (found at Deir el-Bahari, CGC 61088). Daughter of Henuttawy and Pinudjem I. Though more damaged by thieves than that of her mother, her mummy clearly received the same type of treatment. The breasts were ample. G. Elliot Smith, who examined the mummy in June 1909, stated that she might have died during or just after childbirth. The presence of a small, carefully wrapped mummy beside the princess led scholars to think that this was a baby. In fact, radiology revealed that it was the mummy of a female hamadryas baboon! The latter was thus probably a pet animal. The body of the princess was painted in yellow ocher. The ear lobes were pierced and distended. The hair, which was brown, showed traces of gray. Height about 4′11″. Three rings of gold and silver were found on her fingers. The mummy was placed in two coffins that belonged to her. Moreover, inside the second coffin, a mummy-board was placed directly on the mummy. The coffins were made of cedar and acacia. The first is in perfect condition, gilded and covered with funerary texts and scenes, while the second is damaged in the area of the mask and the hands, which have disappeared. The mask and hands of the mummy-board have also disappeared.

MASAHARTA (found at Deir el-Bahari, CGC 61092). Son of Pinudjem I and probably of Henuttawy. General and high priest of Amun. The treatment of the mummy is entirely comparable to that of his mother: the face also appears swollen, and along with the body, it is painted in red ocher. The body, which is intact, retains the imprint of jewels and bandages. It is that of a corpulent man. The arms are arranged alongside the body, and the hands are placed together above the pubic area. Height 5′6″. The mummy was found in two coffins, with a mummy-board on the body. The first coffin is almost intact, while the second, along with the covering plank, have lost their masks and their hands. The mummy is now kept on display at the Museum of Mummification in Luxor.

TAIUHERET (found at Deir el-Bahari, CGC 6104 1). Probably the wife of Masaharta, and God's Wife of Amun, i.e., in charge of the "harem" of Amun, according to an inscription on the bandages. The bandaging of the mummy was badly damaged by thieves, who took all the jewels. The body is practically intact, and it looks like those just described, with its face swollen by packing material. Pieces of cloth modeled in the form of breasts are still in place. Height about 5′3″. The two sycamore coffins and the mummy-board were originally made for a songstress of Amun. They were seriously damaged by thieves, who removed the gilded masks and the hands.

PINUDJEM II (found at Deir el-Bahari, CGC 61094). High priest of Amun and king. It was he who had the cache at Deir el-Bahari prepared for himself and his family, and who also had royal mummies of the preceding dynasties placed there. The mummy is intact, and radiography revealed amulets still in place. The embalming technique is characteristic of the period, with packing intended to restore a lifelike appearance to the body. Height about 5′7″. The arms were placed alongside the body. The mummy was found in two coffins, along with a mummy-board, all intact and made for it. The entire surface of the coffins is covered with funerary texts and scenes, and the masks are gilded.

ISETEMKHEB (found at Deir el-Bahari, CGC 61093). Wife of Pinudjem II. The excellent condition of the mummy and its funerary equipment leads us to think that she was originally buried in the cache. The extremely good quality of the bandaging saved the mummy from being examined by earlier scholars. Radiography revealed the presence of some rare amulets. It was also possible to detect the effects of osteoarthritis on the knees, abrasion of the teeth, and the presence of caries. Height about 5′2″. The mummy was found in two coffins, and it was provided with a mummy-board. The first coffin was intact, but the second coffin and the mummy-board had lost their gilded mask and hands (ancient or modern theft?).

NESIKHONS (found at Deir el-Bahari, CGC 61095). Another wife of Pinudjem II. An extremely good example of mummification in this period, with packing of the body, but without swelling. Long, wavy hair. Arms alongside the body. Height about 5′3″. The mummy was found inside two reused coffins that had belonged to a woman named Isiemkheb, and it was provided with a mummy-board. Again, the masks of the second coffin and the board had disappeared.

NESTANEBETISHERU (found at Deir el-Bahari, CGC 61096). Daughter of Pinudjem II and wife of Djedptahiufankh. God's Wife of Amun, in charge of his "harem." Good example of the advanced mummification technique of Dynasty 21. The packing was done carefully and without excess. Artificial eyes of white and black stone had been placed in the orbits. The arms were placed alongside the body. Height about 5'4". The mummy was found in two coffins probably made for her, along with a mummy-board, all in a rather bad state of preservation. The coffins were covered with a layer of "bitumen."

DJEDPTAHIUFANKH (found at Deir el-Bahari, CGC no. 61097). Husband of Nestanebetisheru. Mummy well made, like those listed above. Presence of packing in particular under the face. Artificial eyes inserted in the orbits. Presence of amulets and jewels still in place, in particular, bracelets. On its flank, a plate of copper alloy. Height about 5'6". The mummy was found in two coffins of cedar and a mummy-board, which had belonged to a certain Nesshuenopet. They were intact, except for one hand that was missing from the first coffin.

THE ROYAL NECROPOLIS OF TANIS

In the royal necropolis located in the enclosure of the temple of Amun at Tanis, P. Montet discovered three additional royal bodies. Unfortunately, these remains were reduced to a skeletal state because of the moisture in the tombs.

PSUSENNES I (Qasr el-Aini, QA 2). Found in his intact tomb. The king was resting in a coffin of solid silver, itself in a black granite anthropoid coffin, which in its turn was placed in a massive sarcophagus of red granite. The tomb contained a large quantity of funerary furnishings (canopic vases, *ushabtis*, etc.) The mummy had a splendid mask of solid gold and numerous gold jewels, as well as finger sheaths and a flank plate. Study of the remains revealed that the king was an old man who had suffered from advanced vertebral osteoarthritis. The teeth were in extremely bad condition, with a number of abscesses.

AMENEMOPE (Qasr el-Aini QA 40). Successor of Psusennes I. His tomb was also found intact. The mummy, which was in extremely bad condition, also had a gold mask and a complete assortment of jewels.

Dynasty 22

SHOSHENQ II (Qasr el-Aini, QA 3). Found in the tomb of Psusennes I in a coffin of solid silver whose "head" depicted that of a falcon. Inside it, the mummy was provided with a gold mask and with jewels inscribed with the name of the king. Four small silver coffins contained the viscera. The mummy was badly damaged by water, which must have penetrated into the coffin. Examination of the skull revealed that the brain had been removed and that the bridge of the nose had been broken. The skeleton was that of a man of more than fifty years of age. The probable cause of death was septicemia caused by an infected cranial wound.

OTHER MUMMIES FOUND WITH THE ROYAL MUMMIES OF THE THEBAN TOMBS

Mummies Contemporary with Dynasty 18

RAI (found at Deir el-Bahari, CGC 61054). Nurse of Ahmose-Nofretari and perhaps also of Ahmose, her brother and husband. Mummy of a short (about five feet), slender woman. Abundant hair, with many small tresses arranged on either side of the face. The abdominal cavity had been filled with pieces of cloth and the body sprinkled with a mixture of sand and a resinous product reduced to powder. The mummy was found in a coffin inscribed with the name of a certain Paheripedjet. Her own coffin had been used for the reburial of Queen Ahmose-Inhapi.

BAKT (found at Deir el-Bahari, CGC. 61076). Theoretically the mummy of a man named Bakt, according to the inscriptions on the coffin, but the skeletal characteristics favor the female sex. There thus remains the problem of identification. Few human tissues remain on the skeleton. Garlands of flowers had been arranged on the bandaging of the mummy. The cedar coffin dates to Dynasty 18 and must have been used once before for an unidentified royal mummy before being used for the reburial of Bakt.

UNIDENTIFIED WOMAN (found in the tomb of Amenhotep II, CGC 61072). Mummy without a coffin, in bad condition: it lacks nearly all the right arm, and it has a hole in the left cheek, as well as a large hole in the thorax. There are no formal means of identification. Its association with the mummy of Teye has led some to consider the possibility that this is Sitamun, daughter of Amenhotep III and Teye. Height about 5'2".

UNIDENTIFIED WOMAN (found in the Valley of the Kings, tomb KV 60). Partially unwrapped mummy, found lying without a coffin on the floor of the burial chamber. The left arm was bent above the thorax, while the right was alongside the body. The woman seemed to have been fat, if not obese, to judge by the large folds of skin. The teeth were quite worn, suggesting an advanced age. The evisceration seems to have been done via the perineum, perhaps because of the obesity of the subject. Certain scholars think this is the mummy of Hatshepsut. No identification has been possible to this day, for lack of a complete scientific examination. Height about 5'1".

MAHERPRA (found in the Valley of the Kings, tomb KV 36). Found in a tomb that had been disturbed by thieves, but had preserved a part of its equipment, in particular a beautiful Book of the Dead papyrus and some jars of oil. Weapons were also found, evidence that the occupant of the tomb had been a military man (his name means "lion on the battlefield"). The unwrapping in 1901 revealed small jewels. Age at death around twenty years. The cause of death has not been established. Height about 5'5". The appearance of the mummy, along with the representation of the deceased in the vignettes of his Book of the Dead, suggests a Nubian origin. The mummy was found in three coffins, the first of which was rectangular and entirely covered with black "bitumen"; it was decorated with deities and funerary inscriptions. The other two coffins were anthropoid and gilded. Another coffin, which was to have contained the body itself, was placed beside the others, empty; it was probably not used because it was too large. All these were cedar coffins of high quality. A gilded cartonnage mask was placed on the face of the mummy.

YUYA (found in the Valley of the Kings, tomb KV 46, CGC 51190). Priest of the god Min at Akhmim and father of Queen Teye. Appointed commandant of the cavalry after the marriage of his daughter to Amenhotep III. The fact of being buried in the Valley of the Kings constituted a rare privilege. Although it had been "visited," the tomb still contained a large quantity of funerary furnishings, in particular chairs and chests of extremely high quality, though the small precious objects had disappeared. Like that of his wife Tuya, his mummy is one of the best preserved from the New Kingdom. The body is that of an old man in the Osirian position. He had wavy white hair. There was beard and mustache stubble, probably because he was not shaved during his final illness. Linen plugs in the orbits and nostrils. Abdominal evisceration; canopic chest containing the viscera. Brain removed; intracranial resin. The mummy had gold finger sheaths on its hands. Height about 5'5". The body lay in three nested anthropoid coffins, all contained in a sort of bottomless box with runners that had been built in the tomb itself because of its large dimensions, which would have prevented its being brought in. The coffins, which were of extremely high quality, were intact and richly decorated: the third, which was closest to the body, was entirely covered with gold leaf on the outside and silver leaf on the inside. The face of the mummy was covered by a gilded stucco mask that had been badly damaged by plunderers in search of jewels. The masks of the three coffins still had their inlaid eyes. On the first and second coffins, the hands, represented in relief and crossed over the chest, held the Isis knot and the *djed*-pillar.

TUYA (found in the Valley of the Kings, tomb KV 46, CGC 51191). Wife of Yuya. She was "mistress of the robes" of the temple of Min at Akhmim. The mummy was remarkably well preserved despite having been disturbed by robbers. The abdominal evisceration incision had been sewn shut, but the stitches had broken, making it possible to see the cloths used as packing in the abdomen. The mummy still had resin plugs in the nostrils and the orbits, the latter with traces of paint imitating the pupils. The organs removed from the body were still in their canopic jars, which were found in the tomb. The arms of the mummy were arranged alongside the trunk and thighs. The age at death was fifty or more. X-rays revealed osteoarthritis lesions. The skull had not received the traditional evisceration. Height about 4′11″. The mummy had been placed in two anthropoid coffins that were in a rectangular boxlike sledge similar to that of Yuya, but smaller and with a bottom. To reach the mummy, thieves had removed one side of this sledge. The two coffins were well preserved and entirely covered with gold, except for the eyes and the collar, which were inlaid. The head was covered with a gilded stucco mask made of cloth.

NEBSENI (found at Deir el-Bahari, CGC 61067). A person of whom we know nothing besides his offices of priest and scribe, which are stated in the inscriptions on his coffin. The mummy was in good condition, despite having been "visited" by thieves and reburied by the priests in Dynasty 21. The face and hair were

in a perfect state of preservation. The arms were arranged alongside the body. Height about 5′9″. The anthropoid cedar coffin was painted in white, with inscribed bands painted in yellow.

UNIDENTIFIED MAN (found at Deir el-Bahari, CGC 61098). Mummy found in a white, uninscribed coffin. The body, which was wrapped in a sheepskin sewn shut, was that of a young man, his arms stretched out and the hands over the pubic area, though his genitals were gone. Height about 5′7″. The hands and feet were tied together at the wrists and ankles. There was no trace of evisceration. The head was in an extended position, its mouth wide open, and as a whole, the mummy gave the impression of deep suffering. The mummy otherwise gave out a bad odor, which was unusual. All these circumstances suggested that the individual had not died a natural death, and some have proposed that he had been buried alive. G. Elliot Smith noted that there was no real support for this hypothesis, and that death from illness could easily explain these facts. Still, there is no explanation for the burial in a sheepskin: we know that contact with wool was considered impure and that it was prohibited in religious and funerary contexts. The coffin, which is uninscribed, seems to have been reused.

UNIDENTIFIED WOMAN (found in the tomb of Amenophis II, CGC 61082). Woman found in the lid of the coffin of Sethnakhte. Small cloth packets were attached to the feet of the mummy; one contained bits of skin mixed with natron, and the other fragments of viscera, also mixed with natron. The arms were arranged alongside the trunk and the thighs. Presence of an epigastric orifice due to plunderers. The face had received a packing that gave it a slightly swollen appearance. The curly hair was extremely well preserved. The embalming technique was characteristic of the end of Dynasty 21. Height about 5′3″. The coffin was made of cartonnage. The trough contained the mummy of Merneptah.

Notes

1. From Prehistory to the First Two Dynasties

1. B. Midant-Reynes, *Préhistoire de l'Égypte, Des premiers hommes aux premiers pharaons* (Paris: Armand Colin, 1992), p. 33.

2. Ibid., pp. 60–62 and 85.

3. Ibid., pp. 147–160.

4. B. Midant-Reynes, *Aux Origines de l'Égypte: Du Néolithique à l'émergence de l'État* (Paris: Fayard, 2003), pp. 158–162.

5. A. J. Spencer, *Early Egypt: The Rise of Civilisation in the Nile Valley* (London: British Museum Press, 1993), pp. 22–33.

6. Midant-Reynes, *Aux Origines de l'Égypte,* pp. 158–162.

7. Now in the Turin Museum; E. D'Amicone, "Le Site archéologique de Gebeleyn," in *Civilisation des Égyptiens: Les Croyances religieuses,* ed. A. M. Donadoni-Roveri (Milan: Electra, 1988), pp. 41–42.

8. B. Midant-Reynes and N. Buches, *Adaïma,* vol. 1, *Économie et habitat,* Fouilles de l'Institute Français d'Archéologie Orientale 45 (Cairo: Institut Français d'Archéologie Orientale, 2002); E. Crubézy, T. Janin, and B. Midant-Reynes, *Adaïma,* vol. 2, *La Nécropole prédynastique,* Fouilles de l'Institute Français d'Archéologie Orientale 47 (Cairo: Institut Français d'Archéologie Orientale, 2002).

9. I. H. Takamiya, "Prestige Goods and Status Symbols in the Naqada Period Cemeteries of Predynastic Egypt," in *Egyptology at the Dawn of the Twenty-first Century: Proceedings of the Eighth International Congress of Egyptologists, Cairo, 2000,* ed. Z. Hawass (Cairo: American University in Cairo Press, 2003), vol. 1, pp. 486–492. On the question of social differentiation, see also the remarks of G. J. Tassie and J. van Wetering, "Early Cemeteries of East Delta: Kafr Hassan Dawood, Minshat Abu Omar and Tell Ibrahim Awaad, in Hawass, *Egyptology at the Dawn of the Twenty-first Century,* vol. 1, pp. 499–507.

10. Spencer, *Early Egypt,* figs. 25–26.

11. E. Delange, "Le Couteau dit 'du Djebel el-Arak,'" *Images et rites d'éternité en Égypte, Dossiers d'Archéologie,* no. 257 (October 2000): 52–59.

12. Spencer, *Early Egypt,* pp. 38–39 and figs. 20 and 23; E. Delange, "Le Couteau dit 'du Djebel el-Arak,'" pp. 58–59; Midant-Reynes, *Origines de l'Égypte,* pp. 331–336.

13. Crubézy, Janin, and Midant-Reynes, *Adaïma,* vol. 2, pp. 178–182, with mention (p. 194) of the presence of jars filled with ashes in tomb T5 at Naqada.

14. C. Andrews, *Egyptian Mummies* (London: British Museum Publications, 1984), p. 4, fig. 1.

15. The idea of survival seems all the more probable in that objects of daily life were deposited along with the body.

16. W. M. F. Petrie and J. Quibell, *Nagada and Ballas,* repr. ed. (Warminster, U.K.: Aris & Phillips, 1974), pp. 31–32.

17. See Pyramid Texts §§ 447 and 828 a–c, R. O. Faulkner, *The Ancient Egyptian Pyramid Texts* (Oxford: Clarendon Press, 1969).

18. W. B. Emery, *Archaic Egypt,* repr. ed. (Harmondsworth, U.K.: Penguin, 1984), pp. 71–73.

19. Ibid., plates 28–29.

20. Ibid., p. 135 and fig. 80.

21. Midant-Reynes, *Origines de l'Égypte,* pp. 230–236, raises the question of the interpretation of these annex burials and of their discontinuation in Dynasty 2.

22. Emery, *Archaic Egypt,* pp. 66–68.

23. R. Macramallah, *Fouilles à Saqqara: Un Cimetière archaïque de la classe moyenne du peuple à Saqqarah* (Cairo: Imprimerie Nationale, 1940).

24. J. Quibell, *Excavations at Saqqara (1911–1912)* (Cairo: Institut Français d'Archéologie Orientale, 1913).

25. Petrie, *Seventy Years in Archaeology* (London: S. Low, Marston & Co., 1931), p. 175, cited by A. J. Spencer, *Death in Ancient Egypt* (Harmondsworth, U.K.: Penguin, 1982), pp. 34–35 and fig. 4.

26. See T. O. Tucker, "Bioarchaeology of Kafr Hassan Dawood: Preliminary Investigations," in Hawass, *Egyptology at the Dawn of the Twenty-first Century,* vol. 1, pp. 530–535.

27. Evisceration was an entirely different process from that of dismemberment of the body for the purpose of reinhumation.

28. Diodorus Siculus, *Library of History,* book 1, chap. 91, sec. 4. See *Diodorus on Egypt,* trans. E. Murphy (Jefferson, N.C.: McFarland & Company, 1985), p. 118.

2. The Old Kingdom

1. A. Dodson and S. Ikram, *The Mummy in Ancient Egypt: Equipping the Dead for Eternity* (London: Thames and Hudson, 1998), p. 110 and fig. 110.

2. G. A. Reisner and W. S. Smith, *History of the Giza Necropolis,* vol. 2 (Cambridge, Mass.: Harvard University Press, 1955), pp. 21–22 and pl. 44. Cf. A. Dodson, "Visceral History," *KMT* 3, no. 4 (1992–93): 53–54.

3. "The Oldest Royal Mummy in Cairo," *KMT* 8, no. 4 (1997–98): 83–85.

4. W. M. F. Petrie, *Medum* (London: D. Nutt, 1892), pp. 17–18; Dodson and Ikram, *The Mummy,* p. 110 and fig. 111.

5. A. J. Spencer, *Death in Ancient Egypt* (Harmondsworth, U.K.: Penguin, 1982) pp. 36–37.

6. Mummy discovered by Reisner; see B. Adams, *Egyptian Mummies* (Aylesbury, U.K.: Shire Egyptology, 1988), pp. 14–16.

7. Adams, *Egyptian Mummies,* pp. 13–14.

8. Dodson and Ikram, *The Mummy,* pp. 110–111 and fig. 112. This mummy was left in its tomb, and for this reason, it was neither X-rayed nor studied with any great care.

9. S. D'Auria, P. Lacovara, and C. H. Roehrig, eds., *Mummies and Magic: The Funerary Arts of Ancient Egypt* (Boston: Northeastern University Press, 1988), pp. 91–92.

10. E. D'Amicone, "Les Édifices religieux et la nécropole de Gébeleyn dans le IIIe millénaire avant notre ère," in *Civilisation des Égyptiens: Les Croyances religieuses,* ed. A. M. Donadoni-Roveri (Milan: Electra, 1988), fig. 70 and pp. 73–77.

11. An example is the black basalt sarcophagus of King Mycerinus; as a result of the shipwreck of the vessel transporting it to Europe, this sarcophagus is now at the bottom of the Mediterranean.

12. The complex of Sekhemkhet was barely begun, probably because of the premature death of the king; see Z. Goneim, *The Lost Pyramid* (New York: Rinehart & Company, 1956).

13. One of Cheops's boats, discovered in a pit near the south face of the pyramid, has been restored and is now on display at Giza in a little museum constructed especially for it.

14. These boats are now in the Cairo Museum.

15. On, inter alia, funerary architecture, see J. L. de Cenival. *Architecture universelle: Égypte* (Fribourg, Switz.: Office du Livre, 1964).

16. See Z. Hawass, "The Pyramids' Builders," in *Guide to the Pyramids of Egypt,* ed. A. Siliotti (Cairo: American University in Cairo Press, 1997), pp. 86–89.

17. For translations of these texts, see S. A. B. Mercer, *The Pyramid Texts in Translation and Commentary* (New York: Longmans, Green, 1952), and R. O. Faulkner, *The Ancient Egyptian Pyramid Texts* (Oxford: Clarendon Press, 1969). The passages cited in the text are from Faulkner's translation.

18. See C. Berger-El Naggar, "Des Textes des Pyramides dans des tombes de reines à Saqqara," *Images et rites d'éternité en Égypte, Dossiers d'Archéologie,* no. 257 (October 2000): 26–29.

19. See C. Barocas, "La Décoration des chapelles funéraires égyptiennes," in *La mort, les morts dans les sociétés anciennes,* ed. G. Gnoli and J. P. Vernant, pp. 429–440 (Cambridge: Cambridge University Press, 1982).

3. The Middle Kingdom

1. The text is published by A. H. Gardiner, *The Admonitions of an Egyptian Sage, from a Hieratic Papyrus in Leiden (Pap. Leiden 344 recto),* repr. ed. (Hildesheim, Ger.: Georg Olms Verlag, 1969). The passages cited here are from Gardiner's translation.

2. *Mummies and Magic: The Funerary Arts of Ancient Egypt* (Boston: Northeastern University Press, 1988), no. 38, pp. 105–106.

3. For an example from the Museum of Fine Arts in Boston, see *Mummies and Magic,* no. 34, p. 101.

4. The tombs of these princesses were discovered by H. Winlock and published by him in *Excavations at Deir el-Bahri 1911–31* (New York: Macmillan, 1942). See also A. Dodson and S. Ikram, *The Mummy in Ancient Egypt: Equipping the Dead for Eternity* (London: Thames and Hudson, 1998), pp. 114–115.

5. *Mummies and Magic,* no. 43, pp. 109–117.

6. See H. E. Winlock, "The Mummy of Wah Unwrapped," *Bulletin of the Metropolitan Museum of Art* 35 (1940): 253–259; Dodson and Ikram, *The Mummy,* p. 156, fig. 176–181.

7. A. J. Spencer, *Death in Ancient Egypt* (Harmondsworth, U.K.: Penguin, 1982), pp. 115–116.

8. See C. Desroches-Noblecourt, *Life and Death of a Pharaoh: Tutankhamen* (New York: New York Graphic Society, 1963), p. 59; S. J. Allen, "Tutankhamun's Embalming Cache Reconsidered," in *Egyptology at the Dawn of the Twenty-first Century: Proceedings of the Eighth International Congress of Egyptologists, Cairo, 2000,* ed. Z. Hawass (Cairo: American University in Cairo Press, 2003), vol. 1, pp. 23–29.

9. H. Winlock, *The Slain Soldiers of Neb-hepet-re Mentuhetep* (New York: Metropolitan Museum of Art, 1945).

10. H. Hartleben, *Champollion, sa vie et son oeuvre (1790–1832)* (Paris: Pygmalion, 1983), pp. 121–124.

11. M. A. Murray, *The Tomb of Two Brothers* (Manchester, U.K.: Sherratt & Hughes, 1910).

12. The mummy of a certain Ipi from Beni Hasan, which dates to Dynasty 12, has such a beard; see Dodson and Ikram, *The Mummy,* p. 115, fig. 115.

13. This coffin dates from Dynasty 11 and is now in the Cairo Museum. Its decoration includes a representation of the milking of a cow.

14. I. E. S. Edwards, *The Pyramids of Egypt,* rev. ed. (Baltimore: Penguin, 1961), pp. 225–226.

15. See A. Bongioanni and M. S. Croce, eds., *The Illustrated Guide to the Egyptian Museum in Cairo* (Cairo: American University in Cairo Press, 2001), pp. 446–452.

16. G. Pinch, *Magic in Ancient Egypt* (London: British Museum Press, 1994), pp. 64–65 and 131, and p. 57, fig. 27.

17. C. Carrier and B. Mathieu, *Les Textes des Sarcophages* (Paris: Rocher, 2004).

18. Here we follow the translation of P. Barguet, *Les Textes des sarcophages égyptiens du Moyen Empire* (Paris: Le Cerf, 1986).

4. The New Kingdom

1. M. Bietak, "La Ville de Pi-Ramsès," *L'Égypte, IIIe–IIe millénaires et la Bible, Le Monde de la Bible* 41 (November–December 1985): 39–44 and figs. 38–39.

2. Cairo Catalogue général no. 61051; see G. E. Smith, *The Royal Mummies* (Cairo: Institut Français d'Archéologie Orientale, 1912), pl. 2.

3. A. J. Spencer, *Death in Ancient Egypt* (Harmondsworth, U.K.: Penguin, 1982), p. 117.

4. Z. Hawass, "Luxor Museum Addition," *KMT* 15, no. 3 (2004): 20–32.

5. G. Maspero, *La Trouvaille de Deir el-Bahari* (Cairo: Imprimerie Française, 1881).

6. D. C. Forbes, "Cache KV 35," *KMT* 3, no. 4 (1992–93): 30–33 and 86–87.

7. See C. Aldred, *Akhenaten, King of Egypt* (London: Thames and Hudson, 1988), pp. 195–218.

8. Ibid., pp. 201–202.

9. H. Carter, *The Tomb of Tut-ankh-Amen, Discovered by the Late Earl of Carnarvon and Howard Carter,* repr. ed. (New York: Cooper Square Publishers, 1965), vol. 1, pp. 182–183.

10. Ibid., vol. 2, p. 45.

11. S. Curto, "Espace réel et symbolique: L'Architecture rituelle," in *Civilisation des Égyptiens: Les Arts de la célébration,* ed. A. M. Donadoni-Roveri (Milan: Electra, 1989), p. 89 and figs. 134–135.

12. Z. Hawass, "King Tut Returns," *KMT* 16, no. 2 (2005): 20–37.

13. Smith, *Royal Mummies,* pl. 2.

14. J. E. Harris and K. R. Weeks, *X-Raying the Pharaohs* (New York: Scribner's, 1973); J. E. Harris and E. F. Wente, *An X-Ray Atlas of the Royal Mummies* (Chicago: University of Chicago Press, 1980).

15. See L. Balout et al., eds., *La Momie de Ramsès II* (Paris: Recherches sur les Civilisations, 1985).

16. R. Lichtenbnerg and A. C. Thuilliez, "Étude Radio-chromo-densitographique," in *La Momie de Ramsès II,* ed. Balout et al., pp. 84–95.

17. R. H. Partridge, *Faces of Pharaohs: Royal Mummies and Coffins from Ancient Thebes* (London: The Rubicon Press, 1994). pp. 102–117.

18. According to some scholars, the so-called Osirian position of the arms was the prerogative of pharaohs. This, however, was not the case. In our personal experience with Graeco-Roman mummies in el-Kharga Oasis, we discovered a rather large number that displayed this characteristic.

19. The two sarcophagi are now in the Cairo Museum; see A. Bongioanni and M. S. Croce, eds., *The Illustrated Guide to the Egyptian Museum* (Cairo: American University in Cairo Press, 2001), pp. 438–439.

20. A. Dodson and S. Ikram, *The Mummy in Ancient Egypt: Equipping the Dead for Eternity* (London: Thames and Hudson, 1998), pp. 254–265.

21. These were not boomerangs but throw sticks, which we see rather often in the hands of notables fowling in the marshes. The tomb of Nebamun furnishes an especially beautiful example of such a scene; see G. Robins, *The Art of Ancient Egypt* (Cambridge, Mass.: Harvard University Press, 2000), p. 22, fig. 11.

22. E. Schiaparelli, *Relazioni sui lavori della missione archeologica italiana in Egitto (anni 1903–1920),* vol. 2, *La Tomba intatta dell'architetto Cha nella necropoli di Tebe* (Turin: R. Museo di Antichità, 1927).

23. J. L. de Cenival, in *Tanis, l'or des pharaons* (Paris: Grand Palais, 1987), pp. 273–280.

24. J. H. Breasted, trans., *Records of Ancient Egypt,* repr. ed. (New York: Russell & Russell, Inc.), vol. 2, p. 43; see also Spencer, *Death in Ancient Egypt,* p. 99.

25. P. Vernus, *Affairs and Scandals in Ancient Egypt* (Ithaca: Cornell University Press, 2003), p. 40.

26. Translation based on that of F. Daumas, *La Civilisation de l'Égypte Pharaonique* (Paris: Arthaud, 1982), p. 30.

27. E. Hornung and E. Staehelin, *Sethos—ein Pharaonengrab* (Basel: Antikenmuseum, 1991).

28. A long, straight descending corridor extending more than 145 feet from the sarcophagus chamber: it led to a stretch of subterranean water, a materialization of the primordial ocean from which it was believed that the king, like the sun, emerged every day. See ibid., pp. 81–82; A. Dodson, *Egyptian Rock-Cut Tombs* (Aylesbury, U.K.: Shire Egyptology, 1991), p. 43.

29. K. R. Weeks, *The Lost Tomb* (New York: William Morrow, 1998), Weeks, *KV 5: A Preliminary Report on the Excavation of the Tomb of the Sons of Ramesses II in the Valley of the Kings,* Publications of the Theban Mapping Project 2 (Cairo: American University in Cairo Press, 2000).

30. This is the case with tombs 290 and 359.

31. A. Zivie, *Les Tombeaux retrouvés de Saqqara* (Paris: Rocher, 2003).

32. One mummy found in the necropolis of Dush had its arms in the Osirian position, and it had been emasculated. Between its thighs was a little mummy that was thought to be the separately mummified phallus. In fact, it turned out to be the mummy of a frog, which points directly to the myth of Osiris and the notion of the rebirth of the deceased.

33. Diodorus Siculus, *Library of History* book 1, chap. 14. See *Diodorus on Egypt*, trans. E. Murphy (Jefferson, N.C.: McFarland & Company, 1985), p. 18.

34. The passages cited here are from Book of the Dead chapter 125, translated by R. O. Faulkner in *The Egyptian Book of the Dead: The Book of Going Forth by Day*, ed. E. von Dassow, p. 115 and pl. 31 (San Francisco: Chronicle Books, 1994).

35. This scene is regularly represented in the vignettes to the Book of the Dead—for example, the papyrus of Ani now in the British Museum; see von Dassow, *The Egyptian Book of the Dead*, pl. 31, and E. Dondelinger, *Das Totenbuch des Schreibers Ani* (Graz, Austria: Akademische Druck-Verlagsanstalt, 1987), pp. 56–57.

36. See the papyri of Hunefer and Neferwebenef; J. L. de Cevival, *Le Livre pour sortir le jour* (Paris: Réunion des Musées Nationaux, 1992), p. 82.

5. The Later Stages of Pharaonic History

1. R. Partridge, *Faces of Pharaohs: Royal Mummies and Coffins from Ancient Thebes* (London: Rubicon Press, 1994), pp. 190–194; Partridge, "Cache DB 320," *KMT* 3, no. 4 (1992–93): 26–27.

2. Partridge, *Faces of Pharaohs*, pp. 183–187.

3. Ibid., pp. 200–203.

4. Ibid., pp. 221–224.

5. Mummification is essentially a process of dehydration, which stabilizes the condition of the body. If the ambient moisture increases, the corpse rehydrates, enabling putrefaction to resume.

6. See *Tanis: L'Or des pharaons* (Paris: Grand Palais, 1987), p. 40, fig. On the discovery of the royal tombs, see P. Montet, *Tanis: Douze années de fouilles dans une capitale oubliée du Delta égyptien* (Paris: Payot, 1942). The excavation of Tanis was resumed and pursued by P. Brissaud.

7. J. Lipinska, "Bab el-Gusus: Cache-tomb of the Priests and Priestesses of Amen," *KMT* 4, no. 4 (1993–94): 48–59; A. Niwinski, *21st Dynasty Coffins from Thebes: Chronological and Typological Studies*, Theben 5 (Mainz, Ger.: Philipp von Zabern, 1988).

8. These sarcophagi are now dispersed among about thirty museums, in particular, the Cairo Museum, the British Museum, the Louvre, and the Leiden Museum.

9. Notable examples are the goddess Nut on the sarcophagus of Takhateru in the Leiden Museum (Dynasty 22), the Osiris-Djed on that of Pamiu in the Hildesheim Museum (Dynasty 22 or 23), and the Goddess of the West on that of Tabaketkhons in the Vienna Museum (Dynasty 21).

10. C. V. A. Adams, "The Manufacture of Ancient Egyptian Cartonnage Cases," *Smithsonian Journal of History* 1, no. 3 (1966): 55–66.

11. A. J. Spencer, *Death in Ancient Egypt* (Harmondsworth, U.K.: Penguin, 1982), pp. 240–241.

12. See n. 7 above.

13. Histories book 2, chap. 89; *Herodotus: The Histories*, trans. A. de Sélincourt, 2d ed. (Harmondsworth, U.K.: Penguin, 1972), p. 161.

14. W. M. F. Petrie, *Amulets* (London: Constable, 1914), plates 51, nos. 11–12 and 52, nos. 13–14.

15. Spencer, *Death in Ancient Egypt*, pp. 132–133.

16. J. H. Taylor, *Egyptian Coffins* (Aylesbury, U.K.: Shire Egyptology, 1989), pp. 53–54 and fig. 42.

17. H. D. Schneider and M. J. Raven, *De egyptische oudheid* (Leiden, Netherlands: Rijksmuseum van Oudheden, 1981), p. 127.

18. J. P. Lauer, *Les Pyramides de Sakkara* (Cairo: Institut Français d'Archéologie Orientale, 1991), pp. 33–35 and fig. 50.

19. See A. Dodson and S. Ikram, *The Mummy in Ancient Egypt: Equipping the Dead for Eternity* (London: 1998), p. 269, fig. 386.

20. A. Fakhry, *The Oases of Egypt*, vol. 2, *Bahriyah and Farafra Oases* (Cairo: American University in Cairo Press, 1974), pp. 137–153. Z. Hawass has rediscovered several tombs from the same period that were noted by Fakhry; see Z. Hawass, *Valley of the Golden Mummies* (New York : Harry N. Abrams, 2000), pp. 183–192.

21. Spencer, *Death in Ancient Egypt*, pp. 106–108.

22. Published by G. Lefebvre, *Le Tombeau de Pétosiris*, 2 vols. (Cairo: Institut Français d'Archéologie Orientale, 1923–1924). See also the articles by B. Menu under the title "Le Tombeau de Pétosiris" in *Bulletin de l'Institut Français d'Archéologie Orientale* 94–98 (1994–98).

23. Lefebvre, *Le Tombeau de Pétosiris*, vol. 2, p. 136.

6. The Graeco-Roman Period

1. F. Dunand, with the collaboration of R. Lichtenberg, "Pratiques et croyances funéraires en Égypte romaine," in *Aufstieg und Niedergang der römischen Welt*, vol. 2/18/5 (Berlin and New York: W. de Gruyter, 1995), pp. 3216–3315.

2. A. K. Bowman, *Egypt after the Pharaohs* (London: British Museum Publications, 1986), pp. 17–20.

3. W. R. Dawson and P. H. K. Gray, *Mummies and Human Remains*, Catalogue of Egyptian Antiquities in the British Museum 1 (London: British Museum Press, 1968), and A. R. David et al., *The Manchester Museum Mummy Project: Multidisciplinary Research on Ancient Egyptian Mummified Remains* (Manchester, U.K.: Manchester University Press, 1979), are precursors of the many other studies published in the meanwhile, such as the recent work of M. J. Raven and W. K. Taconis, *Egyptian Mummies: Radiological Atlas of the Collections in the National Museum of Antiquities in Leiden* (Turnhout: Brepols, 2005).

4. For more than twenty years, there has been an ongoing study of mummies in the cemeteries of Dush, Ain Labakha, and el-Deir in el-Kharga Oasis. See F.

Dunand, J. L. Heim, N. Henein, and R. Lichtenberg, "La Nécropole d'Ayn el-Labakha (oasis de Kharga): Recherches archéologiques et anthropologiques," in *Egyptology at the Dawn of the Twenty-first Century: Proceedings of the Eighth International Congress of Egyptologists, Cairo, 2000,* ed. Z. Hawass (Cairo: American University in Cairo Press, 2003), vol. 1, pp. 154–161. The study of mummies in the field has also been pursued in the Valley of the Queens by A. Macke and C. Macke-Ribet; see A. Macke, C. Macke-Ribet, and J. Connan, *Ta Set Neferou: Une Nécropole de Thèbes Ouest et son histoire,* vol. 5 (Cairo: Dar Namatallah Press, 2002).

5. This representation of the deceased colored entirely black has, however, generally been interpreted as the "shadow" of the deceased.

6. See J. Connan, "Le Bitume des momies égyptiennes, un passeport pour l'éternité," *La Recherche* 22, no. 238 (December 1991): 1503–1504. See also Macke, Macke-Ribet, and Connan, *Ta Set Neferou,* vol. 5.

7. R. Lichtenberg, "Plusieurs cas de tuberculose diagnostiqués par la radiographie des momies de la nécropole d'Aïn-Labakha, Oasis de Kharga (Égypte)," *Anthropologie* 39, no. 1 (2001): 75–77.

8. This puffy appearance is most often observed in mummies of young children.

9. J. C. Goyon and P. Josset, *Un Corps pour l'éternité: Autopsie d'une momie* (Paris: Le Léopard d'Or, 1988).

10. A. Bongioanni and M. S. Croce, eds., *The Illustrated Guide to the Egyptian Museum in Cairo* (Cairo: American University in Cairo Press, 2001), p. 438.

11. G. E. Smith and F. W. Jones, *Archaeological Survey of Nubia,* vol. 2, *Report on the Human Remains* (Cairo: National Printing Department, 1910), pp. 195 and 201.

12. F. Dunand, J. L. Heim, N. Henein, and R. Lichtenberg, *La Nécropole de Douch,* vol. 1 (Cairo: Institut Français d'Archéologie Orientale, 1992), pp. 235–236 and 249.

13. Dunand, Heim, Henein, and Lichtenberg, "La Nécropole d'Ayn el-Labakha," p. 156.

14. British Museum inventory nos. 30362 and 30363; Dush, mummy 58.2.2.7; Aïn el-Labakha, mummies 06.1.06, 38.1.02, and 51.1.15.

15. Translation based on that of J. C. Goyon, "Le Rituel de l'embaumement," in *Rituels funéraires de l'ancienne Égypte* (Paris: Cerf, 1972), p. 71.

16. See L. H. Corcoran, *Portrait Mummies from Roman Egypt (I–IV Centuries* A.D.), Studies in Ancient Oriental Civilization 56 (Chicago: University of Chicago Press, 1995), plates 1–11.

17. British Museum inventory no. 6704.

18. Mummy 20.2.1.4; see F. Dunand and R. Lichtenberg, "Une Tunique brodée de la nécropole de Douch," *Bulletin de l'Institut Français d'Archéologie Orientale* 85 (1985): 133–148; *La Nécropole de Douch,* vol. 1, pp. 51–52.

19. Goyon and Josset, *Un Corps pour l'éternité.*

20. Tomb LXVI; see W. Hauser, "The Christian Necropolis in Khargeh Oasis," *Bulletin of the Metropolitan Museum of Art* 2 (March 1932): 42–50. One of the coffins is now in the Cairo Museum, the other in the Metropolitan Museum of Art, New York.

21. See F. R. Herbin, *Padiimenipet, fils de Soter* (Paris: Réunion des Musées Nationaux, 2002), p. 12, fig. 9. The same motif appears on other coffins of the same family, such as that of Cleopatra, the daughter of Soter.

22. Coffin in the Cairo Museum, Catalogue générale 33123; see G. Grimm, *Die Römischen Mumienmasken aus Ägypten* (Wiesbaden, Ger.: F. Steiner, 1974), plate 123, nos. 1–3.

23. J. Y. Empereur, *A Short Guide to the Graeco-Roman Museum Alexandria* (Alexandria: Sarapis, 1995), p. 18, fig. 23.

24. Berlin, Äg. inventory nos. 17039/40 and 17126/7; see K. Parlasca, *Mumienporträts und verwandte Denkmäler* (Wiesbaden, Ger.: F. Steiner, 1966), plate 1, nos. 1–2.

25. A torso lacking its head and limbs, found in tomb 62; see Dunand et al., *La Nécropole de Douch,* vol. 1, pp. 160 and 245.

26. Now in the Cairo Museum, Journal d'entrée no. 41097; see Grimm, *Die römischen Mumienmasken aus Ägypten,* plate 114, no. 2.

27. See A. Schweitzer, "L'Évolution stylistique et iconographique des parures de cartonnage d'Akhmîm du début de l'époque ptolémaïque à l'époque romaine," *Bulletin de l'Institut Français d'Archéologie Orientale* 98 (1998): 325–352.

28. See Grimm, *Die römischen Mumienmasken aus Ägypten,* plate 60, nos. 1–3. There are others in the Berlin Museum; see D. Wildung, "Geheimnisvolle Gesichter," *Antike Welt,* no. 4 (1990): 206–221.

29. D. L. Thompson, *Mummy Portraits in the J. Paul Getty Museum* (Malibu, Calif.: J. Paul Getty Museum, 1982), no. 8, pp. 46–51.

30. See S. Walker and M. Bierbrier, *Ancient Faces: Mummy Portraits from Roman Egypt* (London: British Museum Press, 1997), no. 117, pp. 121–127. See also E. Doxiadis, *The Mysterious Fayum Portraits: Faces from Ancient Egypt* (New York: H. N. Abrams, 1995).

31. Walker and Bierbrier, *Ancient Faces,* nos. 180–181, pp. 160–161.

32. G. Grimm, *Die römischen Mumienmasken aus Ägypten,* plate 112, nos. 1–5.

33. In reality, the coffin was surely of extremely thin, translucent alabaster.

34. New studies on the practice of cremation are currently in progress; see G. Grévin and P. Bailet, "La Crémation en Égypte au temps des Ptolémées," in *La Mort n'est pas une fin,* ed. A. Charron, pp. 62–65 (Arles, Fr.: Musée de l'Arles Antique, 2002).

35. J. Y. Empereur and M. D. Nenna, *Nécropolis,* vol. 2, Études Alexandrines 7 (Cairo: L'Institut Français

d'Archéologie Orientale, 2003), parts 1–2; see also Charron, *La Mort n'est pas une fin.*

36. T. Schreiber, *Die Nekropole vom Kom esh Shugafa, Expedition Von Sieglin,* vol. 1, *Text* (Leipzig, Ger.: Giesecke & Devreint, 1908).

37. Among the many publications pertaining to this necropolis, see Abd el-Hafeez Abd el-Al, J. C. Grenier, and G. Wagner, *Stèles funéraires de Kom Abu Bellou* (Paris: Éditions Recherches sur les Civilisations, 1985).

38. S. Gabra, E. Drioton, P. Perdrizet, and W. G. Wadell, *Rapport sur les fouilles d'Hermoupolis Ouest (Touna el-Gebel)* (Cairo: Institut Français d'Archéologie Orientale, 1941).

39. C. Leblanc, *Ta Set Neferou: Une Nécropole de Thèbes Ouest et son histoire,* vol. 1 (Cairo: Dar el-Kutûb, 1989).

40. J. Osing et al., *Denkmäler der Oase Dachla aus dem Nachlass von Ahmed Fakhry,* Archäologische Veröffentlichungen 28 (Mainz, Ger.: Philipp von Zabern, 1982).

41. K. Lembke, "Aus der Oase des Sonnengottes—Das Grab des Siamun in Siwa," *Stadel—Jahrbuch* 19 (2004): 363–373.

42. E. Bernand, *Inscriptions métriques de l'Égypte Gréco-Romaine* (Paris: Belles-Lettres, 1969).

43. J. Yoyotte, "Bakhthis: Religion égyptienne et culture grecque à Edfou," in *Religions en Égypte hellénistique et romaine* (Paris: Presses Universitaires de France, 1969), pp. 127–141.

44. L. Coulon and F. Leclère, "À Karnak, les catacombes d'Osiris," *Le Monde de la Bible* 145 (September–October 2002): 46–49.

45. M. Lichtheim, *Ancient Egyptian Literature,* vol. 3, *The Late Period* (Berkeley: University of California Press, 1980), pp. 138–141.

7. The Passage from This Life to the Next

1. Herodotus, *Histories,* book 2, chaps. 85–90. See the commentary by A. B. Lloyd, *Herodotus, Book II* (Leiden, Netherlands: E. J. Brill, 1976).

2. In the case of pharaohs, these procedures took place in the proximity of the valley temple.

3. Such a structure has been discovered at the site of el-Deir in el-Kharga Oasis. In it was found, in particular, a bag of natron, along with a large number of ceramic vessels of various sizes and types, undoubtedly intended as containers for the products used in the mummification process.

4. See H. C. Youtie, *Scriptiunculae,* vol. 1 (Amsterdam: A. M. Hakkert, 1973), pp. 90–97.

5. See A. Macke, *Ta Set Neferou: Une Nécropole de Thèbes Ouest et son histoire,* vol. 5 (Cairo: Dar Namatallah Press, 2002), p. 85. We have made the same observation in the case of mummies at el-Deir.

6. A good example is that of the mummy of Ramesses II; see R. Lichtenberg and A. C. Thuilliez, "Étude Radio-chromo-densitographique," in *La Momie de Ramsès II,* ed. L. Balout et al. (Paris: Recherches sur les Civilisations, 1985), pp. 84–95.

7. Translation based on that of J. L. de Cenival, *Le Livre pour sortir le jour* (Paris: Réunion des Musées Nationaux, 1992), p. 58.

8. See chapter 2 above, p. 13.

9. A. Lucas, "The Use of Natron in Mummification," *Journal of Egyptian Archaeology* 18 (1932): 125–140; R. Garner, "Experimental Mummification," in *Manchester Museum Mummy Project: Multidisciplinary Research on Ancient Egyptian Mummified Remains,* ed. A. R. David (Manchester, U.K.: Manchester University Press, 1979), pp. 19–24.

10. Genesis 50:2–3 (New Revised Standard Version).

11. M. Lichtheim, *Ancient Egyptian Literature,* vol. 3, *The Late Period* (Berkeley: University of California Press, 1980), p. 132.

12. J. C. Goyon, *Rituels funéraires de l'ancienne Égypte* (Paris: Cerf, 1972) pp. 17–84.

13. Embalming Ritual, chapter 7, words spoken during the wrapping of the head; translation based on that of Goyon, *Rituels funéraires,* p. 57.

14. See A. J. Spencer, *Death in Ancient Egypt* (Harmondsworth, U.K.: Penguin, 1982), p. 134 and fig. 46.

15. These two coffins are reproduced in *La Mort n'est pas une fin,* ed. A. Charron (Arles, Fr.: Musée de l'Arles Antique, 2002), p. 95, fig. 70 and p. 97, fig. 73.

16. See chapter 3 above, p. 28.

17. See *Ägypten: Geheimnis der Grabkammern* (Mainz, Ger.: Philipp von Zabern, 1993), no. 3, pp. 34–35.

18. On the funeral ritual and the texts recited on this occasion, see J. Assmann, *Death and Salvation in Ancient Egypt* (Ithaca: Cornell University Press, 2005), pp. 299–329. Assmann stresses the importance of the word in the funerary rites.

19. We may view the *ba,* one of the immaterial components of the individual, as the equivalent of the "conscience," while the *ka* is the "life force."

20. W. B. Emery, *Archaic Egypt* (Harmondsworth, U.K.: Penguin, 1984), p. 145 and figs. 28–29.

21. C. Desroches-Noblecourt, *Life and Death of a Pharaoh: Tutankhamen* (New York: New York Graphic Society, 1963), p. 59.

22. See F. Dunand, J. L. Heim, N. Henein, and R. Lichtenberg, *La Nécropole de Douch,* vol. 1 (Cairo: Institut Français d'Archéologie Orientale, 1992), pp. 252–254.

23. de Cenival, *Le Livre pour sortir le jour,* p. 47.

24. In the specific case of Tutankhamun, certain ushabtis, of large size and remarkable quality, are of cedar wood inlaid with gold and bronze. See A. Bongioanni and M. S. Croce, eds., *The Illustrated Guide to the Egyptian Museum in Cairo* (Cairo: American University in Cairo Press, 2001), pp. 272–277.

25. See chapter 4 above, n. 23. J. L. de Cenival, *Tanis, l'or des pharaons* (Paris: Grand Palais, 1987), pp. 273–280.

8. Animal Mummies

1. Translation based on that of J. Yoyotte, in G. Posener, ed., *Dictionnaire de la civilisation égyptienne* (Paris: F. Hazan, 1970), p. 15c.

2. F. Dunand and R. Lichtenberg, with the collaboration of A. Charron, *Des Animaux et des hommes: Une Symbiose égyptienne* (Paris: Rocher, 2005).

3. The spread of the mummification of animals, especially in the Roman Period, could be at least partly connected with confiscation of temple goods and an increased need for the temples to procure subsidies.

4. See P. T. Nicholson, "The Sacred Animal Necropolis at North Saqqara," in *Divine Creatures: Animal Mummies in Ancient Egypt*, ed. S. Ikram (Cairo: American University in Cairo Press, 2005), pp. 44–71.

5. D. Kessler and Abd el Haim Nur el-Din, "Tuna al-Gebel: Millions of Ibises and Other Animals," in Ikram, *Divine Creatures*, pp. 120–163.

6. See A. Zivie and R. Lichtenberg, "Les Chats du Bubasteion de Saqqâra, état de la question et perspectives," in *Egyptology at the Dawn of the Twenty-first Century: Proceedings of the Eighth International Congress of Egyptologists, Cairo, 2000*, ed. Z. Hawass (Cairo: American University in Cairo Press, 2003), vol. 2, pp. 587–593; Zivie and Lichtenberg, "The Cats of the Goddess Bastet," in Ikram, *Divine Creatures*, pp. 106–119.

7. *Library of History* book 1, chap. 83. See *Diodorus on Egypt*, trans. E. Murphy (Jefferson, N.C.: McFarland & Company, 1985), pp. 107–108.

8. It is unlikely that it was a wolf, for this animal does not seem to have existed in Egypt.

9. See F. Dunand and R. Lichtenberg, "Des Chiens momifiés à El Deir (oasis de Kharga)," to appear in *Bulletin de l'Institut Français d'Archéologie Orientale* 105 (2005): 75–87.

10. Frog of the species *Rana mascareniensis;* see F. Dunand, J. L. Heim, N. Henein, and R. Lichtenberg, *La Nécropole de Douch*, vol. 1 (Cairo: Institut Français d'Archéologie Orientale, 1992), p. 120.

11. R. B. Partridge, *Faces of Pharaohs: Royal Mummies and Coffins from Ancient Thebes* (London: The Rubicon Press, 1994), pp. 195–197.

12. In the case of the hippopotamus, the size of the adult animal rendered mummification impossible. Still, archaeologists have found skeletal remains of this animal still wrapped in cloth; see Dunand and Lichtenberg, *Des Animaux et des hommes*, pp. 208–209.

13. An exhaustive list of animal cemeteries is given by D. Kessler, "Tierkult," in *Lexikon der Ägyptologie*, ed. W. Helck and E. Otto, vol. 6 (Wiesbaden, Ger.: Otto Harrassowitz, 1992), cols. 579–580.

14. Aelian, *The Personality of Animals* book 11, chap. 10; this text is not available in an English translation.

15. Diodorus Siculus, *Library of History* book 1, chap. 85, sec. 2. See *Diodorus on Egypt*, trans. E. Mur-

phy (Jefferson, N.C.: McFarland & Company, 1985), p. 110.

16. R. L. Voss, *The Apis Embalming Ritual: P. Vindob. 3873* (Louvain, Belgium: Peeters, 1993).

17. A. Mariette, *Le Sérapéum de Memphis*, vol. 1 (Paris: F. Vieweg, 1882).

18. See J. Vercoutter, *Textes biographiques du Sérapéum de Memphis* (Paris: Librairie Ancienne H. Champion, 1962), pp. 37–43.

19. See the decrees of Canopus (237 B.C.E.), W. Dittenberger, *Orientis Graeci Inscriptiones Selectae*, repr. ed. (Hildesheim, Ger.: G. Olms, 1960), no. 56, and Memphis (186 B.C.E.), ibid., no. 90.

20. R. Mond and O. H. Myers, *The Bucheum*, vol. 1, *The History and Archaeology of the Site;* vol. 2, *The Inscriptions;* vol. 3, *The Plates*, Memoirs of the Egypt Exploration Society 41 (London: Egypt Exploration Society, 1934).

21. P. Derchain, "Portraits d'un divin crocodile," in *Religions méditerranéennes et orientales de l'Antiquité*, ed. F. Labrique, pp. 79–99 (Cairo: Institut Français d'Archéologie Orientale, 2002).

22. C. Dolzani, *Il Dio Sobk* (Rome: Accademia Nazionale dei Lincei, 1961), p. 196.

23. E. Breccia, *Teadelfia e il tempio di Pneferôs* (Bergamo, 1926), pl. 64.1.

24. Ibid., pl. 64.4.

25. See Dunand and Lichtenberg, *Des Animaux et des hommes*, p. 160 and fig. 86.

26. E. Bresciani and A. Giammarusti, "Le Temple de Sobek sur la colline de Medinet Madi," *Comment construisaient les égyptiens, Dossiers d'Archéologie*, no. 265 (July–August 2001): 139–140.

27. Strabo, *Geography* book 17, part 1, chap. 38. See the *Geography of Strabo*, trans. H. L. Jones, vol. 8 (New York: G. P. Putnam's Sons, 1932), p. 107.

28. Herodotus, *Histories* book 2, chap. 69. See *Herodotus: The Histories*, trans. A. de Sélincourt, 2d ed. (Harmondsworth, U.K.: Penguin, 1972), p. 156.

29. V. Rondot, *Tebtynis*, vol. 2, *Le Temple de Soknebtynis et son dromos* (Cairo: Institut Français d'Archéologie Orientale, 2004).

30. The recent discovery of cat remains in a neolithic tomb on Cyprus would seem to demonstrate that the cat was domesticated earlier there than in Egypt.

31. See J. Malek, *The Cat in Ancient Egypt* (London: British Museum Press, 1993).

32. Ibid., pp. 66–67, figs. 42–43.

33. Ibid., pp. 84–85, figs. 51 and 55.

34. E. Naville, *Bubastis (1887–1889)*, Memoirs of the Egypt Exploration Fund 8 (London: Trübner, 1891).

35. Malek, *The Cat in Ancient Egypt*, 126–128.

36. J. Clutton-Brock, *Domesticated Animals from Early Times* (London: British Museum, 1981).

37. See note 6 above.

38. See E. Valtz, "Religion et coutumes funéraires à l'époque des Ptolémées et à l'époque romaine," in *La*

Civilisation des Égyptiens: Les Croyances religieuses, ed. A. M. Donadoni-Roveri, pp. 228–229, fig. 315 (Milan: Electra, 1988).

39. See D. Kessler, J. Boessneck, and A. von den Driesch, *Tuna el-Gebel,* vol. 1, *Die Tiergalerien,* Hildesheimer ägyptologische Beiträge 24 (Hildesheim, Ger.: Gerstenberg, 1987).

40. See note 4 above.

41. Mendes stela; H. de Meulenaere, *Mendes,* vol. 2 (Warminster, U.K.: Aris & Phillips, 1976), pp. 176–177.

42. See L. Lortet and C. Gaillard, *La Faune momifiée de l'ancienne Égypte,* 3d ser. (Lyon: Museum d'Histoire Naturelle, 1907–1909), pp. 89 ff.

9. The Last Mummies

1. See E. H. Pagels, *The Gnostic Gospels* (New York: Vintage Books, 1979).

2. See W. Hauser, "The Christian Necropolis in Khargeh Oasis," *Bulletin of the Metropolitan Museum of Art* 27 (1932): 38–50.

3. G. Castel, "Étude d'une momie copte," in *Hommages à la mémoire de Serge Sauneron,* vol. 2, Bibliothèque d'Étude 82 (Cairo: Institut Français d'Archéologie Orientale, 1979), pp. 121–143.

4. E. Prominska, "Ancient Egyptian Traditions of Artificial Mummification in the Christian Period in Egypt," in *Science in Egyptology,* ed. R. A. David (Manchester, U.K.: Manchester University Press, 1986), pp. 113–121.

5. H. E. Winlock and W. E. Crum, *The Monastery of Epiphanius at Thebes,* vol. 1, Publications of the Metropolitan Museum of Art Egyptian Expedition 3 (New York: Metropolitan Museum of Art, 1926).

6. H. Ranke, *Koptische Friedhöfe bei Karara* (Berlin-Leipzig: W. de Gruyter & Co., 1926).

7. See F. Dunand et al., *La Nécropole de Douch,* vol. 2 (Cairo: Institut Français d'Archéologie Orientale, 2005).

8. H. Buschhausen, "Das Mönschwesen in Abu Fano," in *Ägypten, Schatze aus dem Wüstensand* (Wiesbaden, Ger.: L. Reichert, 1996).

9. See F. Dunand, F. Letellier-Willemin, and M. Coudert, "Découverte d'une nécropole chrétienne à El Deir (oasis de Kharga)" (Journées d'études coptes, Lyon, May 19–21, 2005; conference volume in preparation).

10. C. Francot et al., *Les Momies égyptiennes des Musées Royaux d'Art et d'Histoire à Bruxelles et leur étude radiographique* (Turnhout: Brepols, 1999).

11. S. Walker and M. Bierbrier, *Ancient Faces: Mummy Portraits from Roman Egypt* (London: British Museum Press, 1997), pp. 160–161.

12. The translation follows that of. L. T. Lefort, *Vies coptes de saint Pachome,* Spiritualité Orientale 38 (Bellefontaine: Abbaye de Bellefontaine, 1984), pp. 144–145.

13. H. C. Puech, *En quête de la Gnose,* vol. 2 (Paris: Gallimard, 1978), pp. 59–62.

14. A. N. Athanassakis, *The Life of Pachomius (Vita Prima Graeca),* Society of Biblical Literature, Texts and Translations 7 (Missoula, Mont.: Society of Biblical Literature, 1975), p. 47.

15. Athanasius, *Life of Saint Anthony,* § 90; E. A. W. Budge, *Stories of the Holy Fathers* (London, 1934), p. 97.

16. See F. Dunand, "Between Tradition and Innovation: Egyptian Funerary Practices in Late Antiquity," in *Egypt in the Byzantine World, 450–700,* ed. R. Bagnall (in press).

17. A. Fakhry, *The Necropolis of El Bagawât in Kharga Oasis* (Cairo: Government Press, 1951).

18. "Macarius the Egyptian," § 38; B. Ward, *The Sayings of the Desert Fathers: The Alphabetical Collection,* Cistercian Studies 59 (Kalamazoo, Mich.: Cistercian Publications, 1975), p. 115.

10. Historical Background

1. S. H. Aufrère, *La Momie et la tempête: Nicolas-Claude Fabri de Peiresc et la curiosité égyptienne en Provence au début du XVIIe siècle* (Avignon: A. Barthélemy, 1990).

2. This was apparently the case with the tomb of the vizier Kar (Dynasty 6), located between Saqqara and Abusir.

3. P. Vernus, *Affairs and Scandals in Ancient Egypt* (Ithaca: Cornell University Press, 2003), pp. 1–49.

4. F. Dunand, J. L. Heim, N. Henein, and R. Lichtenberg, *La Nécropole de Douch,* vol. 1 (Cairo: Institut Français d'Archéologie Orientale, 1992), pp. 174–177.

5. Ahmed bey Kamal, *Le Livre des perles enfouies et du mystère précieux,* 2 vols. (Cairo: Institut Français d'Archéologie Orientale, 1907).

6. See B. Brier, *Egyptian Mummies: Unraveling the Secrets of an Ancient Art* (New York: William Morrow, 1994), pp. 148–149.

7. A. Paré, *Discours de la Mumie, des venins, de la licorne et de la peste* (Paris: Gabriel Buon, 1582), chap. 8.

8. Ibid., chap. 7.

9. An American industrialist, Augustus Stanwood, supposedly made a deal to turn tons of linens into paper, according to C. El Mahdy, *Mummies, Myth and Magic* (London: Thames and Hudson, 1989), p. 33.

10. *Description de l'Égypte,* repr. ed., vol. 2 (Cologne: Taschen, 1994), pls. 49–50 (mummies from the rock-cut tombs at Thebes) and pls. 52 and 55 (animal mummies).

11. T. Pettigrew, *History of Egyptian Mummies, and an account of the Worship and Embalming of the Sacred Animals by Egyptians, with remarks on the funeral ceremonies of different nations and observations on the mummies of the Canary Islands, of the ancient Peruvians, Burman priests, etc.* (London: Longman, Rees, Orme, Brown, Green and Longman, 1834; Los Angeles: North American Archives, 1985).

12. See S. H. Aufrère, *Collections égyptiennes* (Rouen: Musées départementaux de Seine Maritime, 1987), pp. 14–15.

13. G. Maspero and E. Brugsch, *La Trouvaille de Deir el-Bahari* (Cairo: F. Mourès, 1881).

14. See El Mahdy, *Mummies, Myth and Magic,* p. 75.

15. G. E. Smith, "The Physical Characters of the Mummy of Thoutmôsis IV," in T. M. Davis, *The Tomb of Thoutmôsis* (London: A. Constable, 1904; London: G. Duckworth, 2002), pls. 41–45.

16. It must be noted that the identification of the royal mummies is not absolutely certain, particularly as concerns some of the kings of Dynasty 18. At the time they were transferred to the tomb of Amenhotep II and the cachette at Deir el-Bahari, some of these mummies were rebandaged and placed in coffins that were not in fact theirs.

17. L. Lortet and C. Gaillard, "La Faune momifiée de l'ancienne Égypte," *Archives du Muséum d'Histoire naturelle de Lyon* 8 (1903): 1–205; 9 (1905): 1–130; and 10 (1907–1908): 1–336. See F. Dunand and R. Lichtenberg, with the collaboration of A. Charron, *Des Animaux et des hommes: Une Symbiose égyptienne* (Paris: Rocher, 2005), pp. 178–189.

18. M. A. Murray, *The Tomb of the Two Brothers* (Manchester: Manchester University Press, 1910).

19. A. R. David, ed., *The Manchester Museum Mummy Project* (Manchester: Manchester University Press, 1979), pp. 1 and 160. See also G. Reeder, "The Eunuch and the Web Priest: Another Look at the Mysterious Manchester Museum Mummies," *KMT* 16, no. 1 (2005): 54–63.

20. M. A. Ruffer, "Note on the Presence of Bilharzia Haematobia in Egyptian Mummies of the Twentieth Dynasty (1250–1000 B.C.)," *British Medical Journal* (1910): 1–16. See also Ruffer, "Histological Studies on Egyptian Mummies," *Mémoires présentés à l'Institut d'Égypte* 6, no. 3 (1911): 1–39 and Ruffer, *Studies on the Palaeopathology of Egypt* (Chicago: University of Chicago Press, 1921).

21. Later studies confirmed the diagnosis of leprosy; see A. T. Sandison, "Diseases in Ancient Egypt," in *Mummies, Disease and Ancient Cultures,* ed. A. and E. Cockburn (Cambridge: Cambridge University Press, 1980), pp. 30–31.

22. Dr. M. Bertolotti, "Une vertèbre lombaire surnuméraire complète chez une momie égyptienne de la 11e dynastie," *Nouvelle Iconographique de la Salpêtrière,* no. 26 (1913): 63–65.

23. See C. Leleux and M. Gouineau, "Que révèle la radiographie d'une momie," *Je Sais Tout* 243–244 (March–April 1926): 33–36 and 93.

24. R. L. Moodie, *Roentgenologic Studies of Egyptian and Peruvian Mummies,* Memoirs of the Field Museum of Natural History and Anthropology 3 (Chicago: Field Museum of Natural History, 1931).

25. The X-rays made it possible for us to detect growth arrest lines on two children of the Roman Period, and also, on another mummy, calcifications of the liver and the bladder that were signaled without comment by the author, and which we were able to identify as signs of schistosomiasis.

26. Moodie, *Roentgenologic Studies,* pl. 14.

27. L. C. Wyman and W. C. Boyd, "Human Blood Groups and Anthropology," *American Anthropologist* 37, no. 2 (1935): 181–200.

28. P. B. Candela, "Blood-Group Tests on Stains, Mummified Tissues, and Cancellous Bone," *American Journal of Physical Anthropology* 25, no. 2 (1939): 187–214.

29. F. Jonckheere, *Autour de l'autopsie d'une momie: Le Scribe royal Boutehamon* (Brussels: Fondation Égyptologique Reine Elisabeth, 1942). It has since been noted that the mummy is from the Ptolemaic Period; see C. Francot et al., *Les Momies égyptiennes des Musées Royaux d'Art et d'Histoire à Bruxelles* (Turnhout: Brepols, 1999).

30. A. T. Sandison, "The Histological Examination of Mummified Material," *Stain Technology* 30 (1955): 277–283.

31. P. H. K. Gray, "Radiological Aspects of the Mummies of Ancient Egyptians in the Rijksmuseum van Oudheden," in *Oudheidkundige Mededelingen uit het Reijksmuseum van Oudheden te Leiden* 47 (Leiden: E. J. Brill, 1966), pp. 1–31.

32. W. R. Dawson and P. H. K. Gray, *Mummies and Human Remains,* Catalogue of Egyptian Antiquities in the British Museum 1 (London: British Museum Press, 1968); P. H. K. Gray and D. Slow, "Egyptian Mummies in the City of Liverpool Museum," *Liverpool Bulletin* 15 (1968): 28–32.

33. The work at Gebel Adda was published in J. E. Harris and K. R. Weeks, *X-Raying the Pharaohs* (New York: Scribner's, 1973), pp. 60–72. On the exhaustive study of the royal mummies, see J. E. Harris and E. F. Wente, *An X-Ray Atlas of the Royal Mummies* (Chicago: University of Chicago Press, 1980).

34. N. B. Millet et al., "ROM I: Mummification for the Common People," in A. and E. Cockburn, *Mummies, Disease and Ancient Cultures,* pp. 71–84.

35. L. Balout et al., eds., *La Momie de Ramsès II* (Paris: Recherches sur les Civilisations, 1985).

36. A. R. David et al., *The Manchester Museum Mummy Project* (Manchester: Manchester University Press, 1979).

37. E. Strouhal and L. Vyhnánek, *Egyptian Mummies in Czechoslovak Collections* (Prague: Národního Muzea, 1979).

38. A. Cockburn, R. A. Barraco, W. H. Peck, and T. A. Reyman, "A Classic Mummy: PUM II," in A. and E. Cockburn, *Mummies, Disease and Ancient Cultures,* pp. 52–70; on PUM III and IV: T. A. Reyman and W. H. Peck, "Egyptian Mummification with Evisceration per Ano," in Cockburn, *Mummies, Disease and Ancient Cultures,* pp. 85–100.

39. E. Delorenzi and R. Grilletto, *Le Mummie del*

Museo Egizio di Torino, N 13001–13026: Indagine antroporadiologia (Milan: La Goliardica, 1989).

40. R. Drenkhahn and R. Germer, eds., *Mumie und Computer: Ein multidisziplinäres Forschungsprojekt in Hannover* (Hannover: Kestner-Museum, 1991).

41. See n. 29 above.

42. *Mummy: Results of Interdisciplinary Examination of the Egyptian Mummy of Aseh-Iri-Khet-es from the Archaeological Museum in Cracow,* ed. H. Szymánska (Cracow, Polish Academy of Arts and Sciences, 2001).

43. J. H. Taylor, *Mummy: The Inside Story* (London: British Museum Press, 2004).

44. M. J. Raven and W. K. Taconis, *Egyptian Mummies: Radiological Atlas of the Collections in the National Museum of Antiquities in Leiden* (Turnhout: Brepols, 2005).

45. Siemens Scanner financed by the National Geographic Society.

46. Z. Hawass, "The EMP: Egyptian Mummy Project," *KMT* 15, no. 4 (2004–5): 29–38.

47. See C. Roubet and R. Lichtenberg, "Dush: Rapport préliminaire de la campagne de fouille 1982," *Annales du Service des Antiquités de l'Égypte* 70 (1984–85): 194–200.

48. I. Morimoto, Y. Naito, K. Hirata, and T. Wakebe, *Ancient Human Mummies from Qurna, Egypt,* 2 vols., Studies in Egyptian Culture 4–7 (Tokyo: Waseda University Press, 1986–88).

49. A. Macke, C. Macke-Ribet, and J. Connan, *Ta Set Neferou: Une Nécropole de Thèbes Ouest* (Cairo: Dar Namatallah Press, 2002); A. Macke, "Les Momies de la Vallée des Reines," in F. Dunand and R. Lichtenberg, with P. Soto-Heim, J.-L. Heim and A. Macke, *Momies d'Égypte et d'ailleurs: La mort refuse* (Monaco: Rocher, 2002), pp. 78–91.

50. F. Dunand, J. L. Heim, and R. Lichtenberg, "La Nécropole d'Ayn el-Labakha (Oasis de Kharga): Recherches archéologiques et anthropologiques," in *Egyptology at the Dawn of the Twenty-first Century: Proceedings of the Eighth International Congress of Egyptologists, Cairo, 2000,* ed. Z. Hawass (Cairo: American University in Cairo Press, 2003), vol. 1, pp. 154–161.

51. Excavation of Tebtunis directed by Professor C. Galazzi in collaboration with B. Mathieu (Institut Français d'Archéologie Orientale).

52. In the framework of a mission of the Institut Français d'Archéologie Orientale directed by N. Cherpion.

53. These were tombs containing mummies of Dynasties 25–26. Excavations of the team from the Louvre directed by Madame C. Ziegler.

54. E. Crubézy, T. Janin, and B. Midant-Reynes, *Adaïma,* vol. 2, *La Nécropole prédynastique,* Fouilles de l'Institut Français d'Archéologie Orientale 47 (Cairo: Institut Français d'Archéologie Orientale, 2002).

55. M. Birrell, "Excavations in the Cemeteries of el-Kharab," in *Preliminary Reports on the 1992–1993 and 1993–1994 Field Seasons,* ed. C. A. Hope and A. J. Mills (London: Oxbow Books, 1999), pp. 29–41.

56. The most recent publication is that of S. Ikram and N. Iskander, *Non Human Remains* (Cairo: The Supreme Council of Antiquities Press, 2002).

57. Excavation directed by A. Zivie. During the campaigns of 1994 and 1995, M. and R. Lichtenberg were able to X-ray 120 falcons, 1 vulture, and 25 shrews, all of them mummified, from the excavation of P. Nicholson in North Saqqara.

58. See F. Dunand and R. Lichtenberg, "Des chiens momifiés à El Deir," *Bulletin de l'Institut Français d'Archéologie Orientale* 105 (2005): 75–87.

59. S. Pääbo and A. Di Rienzo, "A Molecular Approach to the Study of Egyptian History," in *Biological Anthropology and the Study of Ancient Egypt,* ed. W. V. Davies and R. Walker (London: British Museum Press, 1993).

11. Methods of Studying Mummies

1. It was this method, along with photographs, that was used by G. E. Smith in making his general description of the royal mummies.

2. A well-known example is that of the supposed mummy of the "royal scribe Butehamun" in Brussels, which was studied by Dr. Jonckheere. It turned out to be that of an individual who lived a good seven centuries later (see page 138 above).

3. R. Lichtenberg and A. C. Thuilliez, "Étude radio-chromodensitographique," in *La Momie de Ramsès II,* ed. L. Balout et al. (Paris: Recherches sur les Civilisations, 1985), pp. 84–95.

4. P. F. Ceccaldi et al., "Les Cheveux de Ramsès II," in *La Momie de Ramsès II,* ed. L. Balout et al., pp. 212–255.

5. J. E. Harris and E. F. Wente, *An X-Ray Atlas of the Royal Mummies* (Chicago: University of Chicago Press, 1980), pp. 346 and 355.

6. See J. R. Pérez-Accino, "Where Is the Body of Akhenaten?" in *The Seventy Great Mysteries of Ancient Egypt,* ed. B. Manley, pp. 84–87 (London: Thames & Hudson, 2003).

7. See Z. Hawass, *Valley of the Golden Mummies* (New York: Harry N. Abrams, 2000), p. 89.

8. A small group of Roman Period mummies in the necropolis of el-Deir was the object of DNA analysis that bore essentially on cytoplasmic DNA. See A. S. Delmas, "Apports de l'ADN ancien à l'anthropologie: Étude d'une population de momies de l'Oasis de Kharga" (Mémoire de DEA, Muséum National d'Histoire Naturelle, Paris, October 2000).

12. Mummies in Museums

1. G. E. Smith and W. R. Dawson, *Egyptian Mummies* (London: Allen and Unwin, 1924; repr., New York: Kegan Paul International, 1991), p. 7.

2. See chapter 10, note 33.

3. J. E. Harris had identified ankylosing spondylarthritis on the mummy of Amenhotep II; see *An X-Ray Atlas of the Royal Mummies* (Chicago: University of Chicago Press, 1980), pp. 292–293. Later, study of the mummy of Ramesses II led to the same diagnosis.

4. The appearance of the left foot of King Siptah had originally been attributed to clubfoot.

5. E. Strouhal, "Traces of a Smallpox Epidemic in the Family of Ramesses V of the Egyptian 20th Dynasty," *Anthropologie* 34, no. 3 (1966): 315–319.

6. See chapter 10, notes 31 and 32.

7. P. Soto-Heim, P. Le Floch-Prigent, and M. Laval-Jeantet, "Scannographie d'une momie égyptienne antique de nourrisson et de deux fausses momies de nouveau-nés," *Bulletin et Mémoires de la Société d'Anthropologie de Paris* 14 (1985): 115–140.

8. This reuse of coffins has caused special problems with regard to determining the age and sex of the royal mummies.

9. Similar "prostheses" involving feet are described by A. Macke, "Les Momies de la Vallée des Reines," in F. Dunand and R. Lichtenberg, with P. Soto-Heim, J.-L. Heim and A. Macke, *Momies d'Égypte et d'ailleurs: La mort refuse* (Monaco: Rocher, 2002), pp. 88–89 and fig. 55.

10. The interpretation advanced by Gray is now favored by most researchers. See F. J. Rühli, R. K. Chhem, and T. Boni, "Diagnostic Paleoradiology of Mummified Tissue: Interpretation and Pitfalls," *Canadian Association of Radiologists Journal* 55, no. 4 (October 2004), p. 221.

11. The results of the team's work were published in *Mummies, Disease, and Ancient Cultures,* ed. A. and E. Cockburn (Cambridge: Cambridge University Press, 1980).

12. At the time of Cockburn's study, CAT scanners were already in existence. They were not yet widespread, however, and he did not make use of this technology.

13. This mummy, which belongs to the Philadelphia Art Museum, had been loaned to the Paleopathology Association. Later, it was loaned to the National Museum of Natural History in Washington, D.C.

14. Let us recall that the conus medullaris is located at the dorsal lumbar joint.

15. According to the authors, this was the date of the mummification. But because the inscribed pieces of cloth were reused, the mummification could have occurred at a slightly later date.

16. The exceptional nature of this mummy's clothing does not seem to have been noted. We must bear in mind that the practice of dressing mummies in everyday clothing, which became widespread in the Christian community, is almost never found prior to the fourth century C.E.

17. See N. B. Millet, G. D. Hart, T. A. Reyman, M. R. Zimmerman, and P. K. Lewin, "ROM 1: Mummi-

fication for the Common People," in Cockburn, *Mummies, Disease, and Ancient Cultures,* pp. 71–84.

18. The use of a CAT scanner for ROM 1 was the first time this technology was applied to the study of mummies.

19. F. Dunand and R. Lichtenberg, "Une Tunique brodée de la nécropole de Douch," *Bulletin de l'Institut Français d'Archéologie Orientale* 85 (1985): 133–148.

20. A. R. David, ed., *The Manchester Museum Mummy Project* (Manchester: Manchester University Press, 1979).

21. We note here that our own work on a "population" of more than 190 mummies from the Ptolemaic and Roman Period cemeteries of Dush, Ain Labakha, el-Deir, and Deir el-Medina has led us to an altogether different conclusion.

22. See David, *The Manchester Museum Mummy Project,* pp. 37–38 and nn. 31–32. In our own opinion, the slightly higher frequency of ochronosis in present-day populations proves nothing with regard to the ancient Egyptians.

23. This hypothesis does not hold: while the condition has been identified with certainty, its cause is unknown. See A. M. Fournier, P. Vague, and J. Lafon, "L'Auto-résorption en bande symétrique du diploé pariétal (*malum biparietale*)," *Journal de Radiologie et d'Électrologie* 49, no. 5 (1968): 347–356.

24. See E. Strouhal and L.Vyhnánek, *Egyptian Mummies in Czechoslovak Collections.* (Prague: Národní Muzeum, 1979).

25. J. C. Goyon and P. Josset, *Un Corps pour l'éternité: Autopsie d'une momie* (Paris: Le Léopard d'Or, 1988).

26. R. Drenkhahn and R. Germer, *Mumie und Computer: Ein multidisziplinäres Forschungsprojekt in Hannover* (Hannover, Ger.: Kestner-Museum, 1991).

27. We ourselves have rather often observed this practice at Dush, Ain Labakha, and el-Deir (el-Kharga Oasis).

28. A. R. David and Dr. E. Tapp, *The Mummy's Tale: The Scientific and Medical Investigation of Natsef-Amun, Priest in the Temple at Karnak* (London: M. O'Mara Books, 1992).

29. See J. H. Taylor, *Unwrapping a Mummy: The Life, Death and Embalming of Horemkenesi* (London: British Museum Press, 1995).

30. C. Francot, L. Limme, F. Van Elst, M. P. Vanlathem, and B. Van Rietveld, *Les Momies égyptiennes des Musées Royaux d'Art et d'Histoire à Bruxelles et leur étude radiographique* (Turnhout: Brepols, 1999).

31. In the catalog, nos. 10 and 11 are children dated to the Graeco-Roman Period. It seems to us that these two individuals can be more precisely dated to the Ptolemaic Period, given the position of their arms, which are crossed over the chest.

32. M. J. Raven and W. K. Taconis, *Egyptian Mummies: Radiological Atlas of the Collections in the Na-*

tional Museum of Antiquities at Leiden (Turnhout: Brepols, 2005).

33. The animal mummies were X-rayed in the classic manner.

34. We feel that the small number of subjects, spread out over a long period of time (more than a thousand years), stands in the way of any statistical approach, which the investigators, in any event, did not attempt to make.

35. This proportion seems relatively high, given that the mummies belonged to a higher class than the peasants, among whom proportions of 60 percent are not rare (cf. our studies of the populations of el-Kharga Oasis). We must also bear in mind that Gray found Harris lines in only 30 percent of the 133 mummies he studied, which included those in Leiden. This discrepancy could be attributed to different radiographic protocols.

36. G. J. R. Maat, "Dating and Rating of Harris's Lines," *American Journal of Physical Anthropology* 63 (1984): 291–299 (cited by Raven and Taconis).

37. See n. 23 above.

38. F. Parsche and G. Ziegelmayer, "Munich Mummy Project: A Preliminary Report," in *Science in Egyptology,* ed. A. R. David (Manchester, U.K.: Manchester University Press, 1986), pp. 81–89; G. Ziegelmayer, *Münchner Mumien,* Schriften aus der ägyptischen Sammlung 2 (Munich: Staatliche Sammlung Ägyptischer Kunst, 1985).

39. J. Bourriau and J. Bashford, "Radiological Examination of Two Mummies of the Roman Era," *Museum Applied Science Center for Archaeology* 1, no. 6 (1980): 161–171.

40. M. Marx and S. H. D'Auria, "CT Examination of Eleven Egyptian Mummies," *Radiographics* 6 (1986): 321–330.

41. A. Macke, "Les momies égyptiennes du Muséum d'Histoire Naturelle de Lille: Radiographie, scannographie et endoscopie," *Anthropologie et Préhistoire* 102 (1991): 97–110.

42. L. Lortet and C. Gaillard, "La Faune momifiée de l'ancienne Égypte," *Archives du Muséum d'Histoire Naturelle de Lyon* 8 (1903): 1–205; 9 (1905): 1–130; 10 (1907–1909): 1–336.

43. C. Gaillard and G. Daressy, *La Faune momifiée de l'antique Égypte* (Cairo: Institut Français d'Archéologie Orientale, 1905).

44. This observation accords with those we ourselves have made on the cat mummies at Saqqara and the dog mummies at el-Deir.

45. This association is less surprising than it seems: the shrew was connected with Horus Mekhenti-irti.

46. R. L. Moodie, *Roentgenologic Studies of Egyptian and Peruvian Mummies,* Field Museum of Natural History and Anthropology Memoirs 3 (Chicago: Field Museum of Natural History, 1931).

47. We have made the same observations on the cats of the Bubasteion at Saqqara and the canines in the necropolis at el-Deir.

13. Mummies at Excavation Sites

1. J. E. Harris and K. R. Weeks, *X-Raying the Pharaohs* (New York: Scribner's, 1973).

2. A. Macke, C. Macke-Ribet, and J. Connan, *Ta Set Neferou: Une nécropole de Thèbes Ouest et son histoire,* vol. 5 (Cairo: Dar el-Kutûb, 2002); see also A. Macke and C. Macke-Ribet, "Les Recherches anthropologiques," *Égypte: Vallée des Reines, Vallée des Rois, Vallée des Nobles, Dossiers d'Archéologie,* nos. 149–150 (May–June 1990): 34–39.

3. C. Leblanc, "L'Archéologie et l'histoire de la Vallée des Reines, *Égypte: Vallée des Reines, Vallée des Rois, Vallée des Nobles, Dossiers d'Archéologie,* nos. 149–150 (May–June 1990): 22–29. See especially C. Leblanc, *Ta Set Neferou: Une nécropole de Thèbes Ouest et son histoire,* vol. 1 (Cairo: Dar el-Kutûb, 1989).

4. These observations confirm the depopulation of certain villages as attested in tax documents, especially in the second century of our own era.

5. These observations concur entirely with those of R. Lichtenberg concerning a group of Ptolemaic mummies from tomb DEM 323 at Deir el-Medina. Nevertheless, the mummies of the cemeteries of el-Kharga Oasis, which date to the Ptolemaic and Roman Periods, furnished an opposite ratio.

6. The balms have been analyzed by J. Connan, *Ta Set Neferou,* vol. 5, pp. 129–187.

7. C. A. Hope and A. J. Mills, eds., *Dakhleh Oasis Project: Preliminary Reports on the 1992–1993 and 1993–1994 Field Seasons* (Oxford: Oxbow Books, 1999); C. A. Hope and G. E. Bowen, eds., *Dakhleh Oasis Project: Preliminary Reports on the 1994–1995 to 1998–1999 Field Seasons* (Oxford: Oxbow Books, 2002).

8. M. Birrell, "Excavations in the Cemeteries of Ismant el-Kharab," in Hope and Mills, *Dakhleh Oasis Project,* pp. 29–41.

9. C. A. Hope and J. McKenzie, "Interim Report on the West Tombs," in Hope and Mills, *Dakhleh Oasis Project,* pp. 53–68.

10. Birrell, "Excavations in the Cemetries of Ismant el-Kharab," pp. 38–41.

11. According to the investigators, this number would represent about 10 percent of the estimated total.

12. J. E. Molto, "Bio-archaeological Research of Kellis 2: An Overview," in Hope and Bowen, *Dakhleh Oasis Project,* pp. 239–255.

13. R. L. Parr, "Mitochondrial DNA Sequence Analysis of Skeletal Remains from the Kellis 2 Cemetery," in Hope and Bowen, *Dakhleh Oasis Project,* pp. 257–261.

14. F. Calament, *La Révélation d'Antinoé par Albert Gayet: Histoire, archéologie, muséographie,* 2 vols. (Cairo: Institut Français d'Archéologie Orientale, 2005).

15. Ibid., vol. 1, pp. 293 ff.

16. R. Grilletto, "Premiers résultats anthropologiques des fouilles de la nécropole d'Antinoé en Égypte," *Bulletin et Mémoires de la Société d'Anthropologie de Paris*, 13th ser., 8, no. 3 (1981): 281–287.

17. F. Dunand, J. L. Heim, N. Henein, and R. Lichtenberg, *La Nécropole de Douch*, vol. 1 (Cairo: Institut Français l'Archéologie Orientale, 1992), and vol. 2 (Cairo: Institut Français d'Archéologie Orientale, 2005); F. Dunand, J. L. Heim, and R. Lichtenberg, "La Vie dans l'extrême: Douch, Ier S. È. CHR.—IVe S. È. CHR.," in *Life on the Fringe: Living in the Southern Egyptian Deserts During the Roman and Early Byzantine Periods*, ed. O. E. Kaper (Leiden, Netherlands: Research School CNWS, 1998), pp. 95–138; F. Dunand, J. L. Heim, and R. Lichtenberg, "La Nécropole d'Ayn el-Labakha (oasis de Kharga): Recherches archéologiques et anthropologiques," in *Egyptology at the Dawn of the Twenty-first Century: Proceedings of the Eighth International Congress of Egyptologists, Cairo 2000*, ed. Z. Hawass (Cairo: American University in Cairo Press, 2002), vol. 1, pp. 154–161.

18. The current excavations by a team from the Institut Français d'Archéologie Orientale, under the direction of M. Wattmann, at the site, which is close to Manawir (and which fell under the administrative authority of Dush), has uncovered the remains of a brick temple dating to the Persian Period, as well as numerous ostraca from the same era. The occupation of Dush thus dates back earlier than had been thought.

19. On the semi-speos temple, see A. Hussein, *Le Sanctuaire rupestre de Piyris à Ayn al-Labakha* (Cairo: Institut Français d'Archéologie Orientale, 2000).

20. At Dush, in particular, mummies have been found in this condition.

21. This piece of equipment, a Massiot 90/20, is old, dating to 1956.

22. On the technical conditions of work in the field, see F. Dunand and R. Lichtenberg, with P. Soto-Heim, J.-L. Heim and A. Macke, *Momies d'Égypte et d'ailleurs: La mort refuse* (Monaco: Rocher, 2002), Annexe, pp. 207–220.

23. Part of the long bones (femurs and tibias) of the skeletons were X-rayed in search of Harris lines.

24. In the Christian cemetery currently under investigation at el-Deir, there are a very large number of newborns and fetuses, buried in small individual pits.

25. R. Lichtenberg, "La Radiographie des ossements retrouvés dans la chambre funéraire du vizir Aper-El," *Bulletin de la Société Française de l'Égypte* 126 (March 1993): 38–43. On this tomb, see A. Zivie, *Découverte à Saqqarah: Le Vizir oublié* (Paris: Seuil, 1990). Aper-El probably held office under Amenhotep III and Akhenaten.

26. M. and R. Lichtenberg X-rayed thirty cat mummies at the same site; see A. Zivie and R. Lichtenberg, "The Cats of the Goddess Bastet," in *Divine Creatures: Animal Mummies in Ancient Egypt*, ed. S. Ikram, pp. 106–119 (Cairo: American University in Cairo Press, 2005).

27. The mastaba of Akhethotep, whose offering chapel is in the Louvre, is part of this group.

28. B. Midant-Reynes and N. Buchez, *Adaïma*, vol. 1, *Économie et habitat*, and B. Midant-Reynes, E. Crubézy, and T. Janin, *Adaïma*, vol. 2, *La Nécropole prédynastique* (Cairo: Institut Français d'Archéologie Orientale, 2002).

29. J. Y. Empereur and M. D. Nenna, *Nécropolis*, vol. 1, Études Alexandrines 5 (Cairo: Institut Français d'Archéologie Orientale, 2001), and *Nécropolis*, vol. 2, Études Alexandrines 7 (Cairo: Institut Français d'Archéologie Orientale, 2003).

30. G. Grévin and P. Bailet, "La Crémation en Égypte au temps des Ptolémées," in *La Mort n'est pas une fin*, ed. A. Charron (Arles: Musée de l'Arles Antique, 2002), pp. 62–65.

31. E. Boës, P. Georges, and G. Alix, "Des Momies dans les ossuaires de la Nécropolis d'Alexandrie: Quand l'éternité a une fin . . . ," in Charron, *La Mort n'est pas une fin*, pp. 68–71.

32. E. Strouhal, "Three Mummies from the Royal Cemetery at Abusir," in Hawass, *Egyptology at the Dawn of the Twenty-first Century*, vol. 1, pp. 478–785.

33. K. Kroeper and D. Wildung, *Minshat Abu Omar: Ein vor- und frühgeschichtlicher Friedhof im Nildelta*, vol. 1, *Gräber 1–114* (Mainz: Philipp von Zabern, 1994).

34. T. L. Tucker, "Bioarchaeology of Kasr Hassan Dawood: Preliminary Investigations," in Hawass, *Egyptology at the Dawn of the Twenty-first Century*, vol. 1, pp. 530–535; W. M. Van Haarlem, "The Excavations at Tell Ibrahim Awad (Sharqiya Province) Seasons 1995–2000," in Hawass, *Egyptology at the Dawn of the Twenty-first Century*, vol. 1, pp. 536–540.

14. What We Learn from Mummies

1. The other sites we have investigated in el-Kharga Oasis display no sensible difference in the composition of their population.

2. See R. S. Bagnall and B. W. Frier, *The Demography of Roman Egypt* (Cambridge: Cambridge University Press, 1994), but in this case as well, infants who died shortly after death were not taken into account.

3. See the studies by A. R. David and A. Cockburn and their collaborators.

4. L. Vyhnánek and E. Strouhal, "Arteriosclerosis in Egyptian Mummies," *Anthropologie* 13, no. 3 (1975): 219–221.

5. See R. Lichtenberg, "Plusieurs cas de tuberculose diagnostiqués par la radiographie des momies de la nécropole d'Aîn-Labakha, oasis de Kharga (Égypte)," *Anthropologie* 39, no. 1 (2001): 75–77.

6. See H. Carter, *The Tomb of Tut-ankh-Amen*, vols. 2–3 (London: Cassell, 1927–33).

7. This fact should not surprise: mummies were

not made to be seen, but this lifelike appearance was yet another way of denying death.

8. These could be individuals of Greek origin, as shown by their unusual stature and the few names inscribed on their bandages.

9. Otherwise, as on a mummy at Dush that was practically reduced to skeletal state, one leg was held in place by a *gerid* passing through an obturating hole of the pelvis. See F. Dunand, J. L. Heim, N. Henein, and R. Lichtenberg, *La Nécropole de Douch,* vol. 1 (Cairo: Institut Français d'Archéologie Orientale, 1992), mummy no. 27.2.1.1, p. 64 and pl. 8.2–3.

10. We can see this position of the arms represented on the sarcophagus of the lady Isis, daughter-in-law of Sennedjem, in the Cairo Museum, and in particular, it is the position of the arms of the mummy of Teye (Cairo Catalogue générale 61070) and of the mummy of the "unknown woman" from tomb 60 of the Valley of the Kings.

11. F. Dunand and R. Lichtenberg, with the collaboration of A. Charron, *Des Animaux et des hommes: Une Symbiose égyptienne* (Paris: Le Rocher, 2005).

12. See D. Kessler, "Tierkult," in *Lexikon der Ägyptologie,* ed. W. Helck and E. Otto, vol. 6 (Wiesbaden: Harrassowitz, 1992), cols. 579–581, and Kessler, *Die heiligen Tiere und der König,* vol. 1 (Wiesbaden: Harrassowitz, 1989).

13. One hundred twenty of these birds were X-rayed by R. and M. Lichtenberg in 1994–95.

14. See F. Dunand and R. Lichtenberg, "Des Chiens momifiés è El Deir (Oasis de Kharga)," *Bulletin de L'Institut Français d'Archéologie Orientale* 105 (2005): 75–87.

15. Hippopotamus skeletons wrapped in cloths have been found at many sites, however.

Glossary

GENERAL

Amenti. The "West," a designation of the realm of the dead.

ansate cross. The Egyptian "sign of life," *ankh,* which was adopted by the Christians of Egypt as a form of the Christian cross.

ba. Invisible component of the personality of an individual, often translated imperfectly as "soul"; represented as a human-headed bird.

bitumen. Term generally used to designate a black product widely used in the mummification process, especially in the later stages of Egyptian history, but which is not necessarily to be identified as true bitumen.

canopic jars. Four jars intended to contain the mummified viscera; each jar was placed under the protection of one of the four genies known as the "Sons of Horus."

cartonnage. Mummy container made of compacted papyri or pieces of cloth covered with a thin layer of stucco.

Choiak. Fourth month of the "Inundation" season, during which the "passion" of Osiris was commemorated during the sowing season.

Chora. In the Greek texts of Egypt, the designation of the "flat land," the Nile delta and valley, as opposed to "the City," Alexandria.

concubines of the dead. Expression used, undoubtedly incorrectly, to designate statuettes of naked women found in tombs, including those of women, from the Middle Kingdom down to the Roman Period.

gerid. Ligneous stalk bearing the leaves of the date palm.

heb-sed. Jubilee festival theoretically commemorating the thirtieth year of the reign of a pharaoh.

heqa-scepter. A "crook" that along with the flabellum (fly-whisk) was a characteristic attribute of Osiris; these two objects became symbols of royal power.

ka. Life force, an invisible component of the personality of an individual, sometimes translated as "double"; represented by two upraised arms.

mammisi. Small temple in which the birth of a god was celebrated in the Ptolemaic and Roman temples.

mastaba. Arabic word meaning "bench"; designation of the benchlike superstructure of a type of tomb in use from the Archaic Period down to the first millennium B.C.E.

muna. Mixture of unfired clay and straw used as a filler.

mumia. Black product of variable chemical composition (resins, bitumen); the word is the origin of our word "mummy."

natron. Natural mixture of sodium salts containing carbonate, sulfate, and chloride in variable proportions; used by the ancient Egyptians to dry out dead bodies.

rishi. Type of coffin with a characteristic decoration made up of wings (the wings of Isis, or perhaps those of the *ba*), used at the end of the Second Intermediate Period.

sem-priest. Priest wearing a panther skin; he carried out the "Opening of the Mouth" ritual during a funeral.

senet. A popular game that was played with seven pieces used to move around a board with thirty squares; depictions of the deceased playing *senet* might have a symbolic meaning.

serdab. Walled-up room with a single small opening, serving to contain the statue of the deceased; the *serdab* was part of the funerary chapel of mastabas and of the funerary temples of Old Kingdom pyramids.

shawabti. Mummiform funerary figurine placed in tombs from the Middle Kingdom on; this term, of unknown etymology, was replaced in the later periods of Egyptian history by *ushabti,* which can be translated as "answerer" (the statuette was believed to take the place of the deceased and "answer" for his obligations).

Tomb. In the expression "the Tomb," the institution and organization of the community of artisans living in Deir el-Medina, who excavated and decorated the tombs of the Valley of the Kings in the New Kingdom.

udjat-eye. "Eye of Horus," symbol of bodily integrity and of protection, often represented on coffins and amulets.

ushabti. See *shawabti.*

MEDICAL

adenopathy. Inflammatory or tumoral condition of a gland, causing enlargement of the tissue.

ankylosing spondylitis. Rheumatic condition beginning in the young adult (most often male) and leading to fusing of the vertebrae to one another. More rarely, joints such as the hips are affected.

atheroma. Cholesterol and calcareous deposits on the walls of arteries, entailing a decrease in their diameter.

Filaria medinensis. Parasitic worm, endemic in Egypt, that infects the lymph nodes. Also called *Dracunculus medinensis,* or Guinea worm.

foramen magnum. Opening in the skull connecting the cranial cavity and the spinal column.

hemisacralization. Congenital deformity consisting of the fusion of a transverse process of the last lumbar vertebra with the corresponding ala sacralis. Frequent cause of lumbago and sciatica.

hyperostasis. Reaction of the bone to multiple agents, causing an increase in its volume and its density (on X-rays).

inguinal. Adjective designating the region of the groin. An inguinal hernia.

ochronosis. Genetic condition entailing metabolic difficulties, with depositing of homogentistic acid on the intervertebral disks.

osteogenesis imperfecta. Genetic condition entailing anomalies in the development and number of the bones.

Paget's disease. Osseous condition of middle age entailing major change in the bones. These increase in volume and become deformed, and X-rays reveal modification of the bone structure, which becomes coarse.

pneumoconiosis. Pulmonary fibrosis caused by regular inhalation of air filled with particles such as silica. Also called silicosis.

Pott's disease. Tuberculosis of the spine, caused by the Koch bacillus.

rheumatoid polyarthritis. Destructive joint condition that mostly affects females. Also called progressive chronic polyarthritis.

Schistosoma haematobium. Parasite responsible for schistosomiasis. The disease is contracted by walking barefoot in infested water. A freshwater snail is the intermediate host of the parasite.

schistosomiasis. Parasitic condition caused by the *Schistosoma haematobium* worm, endemic in Egypt. It most often affects the urinary system, kidneys, and bladder, resulting in the presence of blood in the urine. Not rarely, it affects the liver and the spleen. Also called bilharziasis.

Schmorl node. Concave defects of upper and lower vertebral endplates resulting from herniation of disk material.

spina bifida occulta. Somewhat common, benign spinal deformity in which the posterior arches of the vertebrae fail to fuse.

Sprengel's deformity of the scapula. Congenital deformity in which a scapula is underdeveloped and positioned horizontally.

Strongyloides. Parasitic worm.

tomodensitometry (CAT scanning). Method that, like tomography, enables the obtaining of cross-section X-ray images, but is much more effective.

tomography. Radiographic technique enabling the obtaining of cross-section X-ray images.

Bibliography

Abd el-Hafeez, Abd el-Al, J. C. Grenier, and G. Wagner. *Stèles funéraires de Kom Abu Bellou.* Paris: Recherche sur les Civilisations, 1985.

Adams, B. *Egyptian Mummies.* Aylesbury, U.K.: Shire Egyptology, 1984.

Adams, C. V. A. "The Manufacture of Ancient Egyptian Cartonnage Cases." *Smithsonian Journal of History* 1, no. 3 (1966): 55–66.

Aegyptica Animalia: Il Bestiario del Nilo. Turin: Museo delle Antichità Egizie di Torino, 2000.

Ägyptischer Mumiensarg: Analysen—Konservierung—Restaurierung. Fribourg: Museum für Völkerkunde, 1990.

Altenmüller, H. *Grab und Totenreich der alten Ägypter.* 2d ed. Hamburg: Hamburgisches Museum für Völkerkunde, 1982.

Andrews, C. *Egyptian Mummies.* London: British Museum Press, 1984.

Archéologie funéraire. Paris: Errance, 2000.

Assmann, J. *Death and the Afterlife in Ancient Egypt* Ithaca: Cornell University Press, 2005.

——.*Images et rites de la mort dans l'Égypte ancienne.* Paris: Cybèle, 2000.

Baines, J., and J. Malek. *Cultural Atlas of Ancient Egypt.* New York: Checkmark Books, 2000.

Balout, L., et al., eds. *La Momie de Ramsès II.* Paris: Recherche sur les Civilisations, 1985.

Barguet, P. *Le Livre des Morts des anciens Égyptiens.* Paris: Cerf, 1967.

——. *Textes des Sarcophages égyptiens du Moyen Empire.* Paris: Cerf, 1986.

Barta, W. *Die altägyptische Opferliste von der Frühzeit bis zur griechisch-römischer Epoche.* Müncher ägyptologische Studien 3. Berlin: Hessling, 1963.

Batrawi, A. "The Racial History of Egypt and Nubia." *Journal of the Royal Anthropological Institute* 75 (1945): 81–101 and 76 (1946): 131–155.

Berry, A. C., R. J. Berry, and P. J. Ucko. "Genetical Chance in Ancient Egypt." *Man* 2 (1967): 551–567.

Bierbrier, M. I., ed. *Portraits and Masks: Burial Customs in Roman Egypt.* London: British Museum Press, 1997.

Bissing, W. Fr. von. "Tombeaux d'époque romaine à Akhmim." *Annales du Service des Antiquités de l'Égypte* 50 (1950): 547–576.

Borg, B. *Mumienporträts: Chronologie und kultureller Kontext.* Mainz: Philipp von Zabern, 1996.

Botti, G. *Le Casse di mummie e i sarcofagi da el Hibeh nel Museo Egizio di Firenze.* Florence: Oleschki, 1958.

Brech-Neldner, R., and D. Budde. *Der Mumiensarkophag des Nes-pa-kai-schuti.* Detmold: Lippische Landesmuseum, 1992.

Bresciani, E. *Il Volto di Osiri: Tele funerarie dipinte nell'Egitto romano.* Lucca: M. Pacini Fazzi, 1996.

Brier, B. *Egyptian Mummies: Unraveling the Secrets of an Ancient Art.* New York: Morrow, 1994.

Budge, E. A. W. *The Mummy: A Handbook of Egyptian Funerary Archaeology.* 2d ed. Cambridge: Cambridge University Press, 1925. Repr., New York: Kegan Paul International, 1974.

Capart, J. "Le Cercueil et la momie de Boutehamon." *Bulletin des Musées Royaux d'Art et d'Histoire*, 3d ser., 7 (1935): 111–113.

Capasso, I., M. La Verghetta, and R. d'Anastasio. "L'Homme du Similaun: Une Synthèse anthropologique et paléo-ethnologique. *L'Anthropologie* 103, no. 3 (1999): 447–470.

Carter, H. *The Tomb of Tut-ankh-amen.* Vols. 2–3. London: Cassell, 1927–33.

Carter, H., and A. C. Mace. *The Tomb of Tut-ankh-amen.* Vol. 1. London: Cassell, 1923.

Cénival, de, J. L. *Le Livre pour sortir le jour.* Paris: Réunion des Musées Nationaux, 1992.

Charron, A., ed. *La Mort n'est pas une fin: Pratiques funéraires en Égypte d'Alexandre à Cléopâtre.* Arles: Musée de l'Arles Antique, 2002.

Cockburn, A., E. Cockburn et al. *Mummies, Disease and Ancient Cultures.* Cambridge: Cambridge University Press, 1980.

Corcoran, L. H. *Portrait Mummies from Roman Egypt (I–IV Centuries A.D.).* Chicago: University of Chicago Press, 1995.

Crubézy, E. *Archéologie funéraire.* Paris: Errance, 2000.

Daressy, G. *Cerceuils des cachettes royales.* Cairo: Institut Français d'Archéologie Orientale, 1909.

——. "Les Cercueils des prêtres d'Amon (deuxième trouvaille de Deir el-Bahari)." *Annales du Service des Antiquités de l'Égypte* 8 (1907): 3–38.

Daressy, G., and C. Gaillard. *La Faune momifiée de*

l'antique Égypte. Cairo: Institut Français d'Archéologie Orientale, 1905.

Daresssy, G., and G. E. Smith. "Ouverture des momies provenant de la seconde trouvaille de Deir el-Bahari." *Annales du Service des Antiquités de l'Égypte* 4 (1903): 150–160.

Dart, R. "Population Fluctuation over 7,000 Years in Egypt." *Transactions of the Royal Society of South Africa* 27 (1939): 95–145.

David, A. R. et al. *The Manchester Museum Mummy Project.* Manchester, U.K.: Manchester University Press, 1979.

——. *Science in Egyptology.* Manchester, U.K.: Manchester University Press, 1986.

Davies, V. W., and R. Walker. *Biological Anthropology and the Study of Ancient Egypt.* London: British Museum Press, 1993.

Dawson, W. R., "Making a Mummy." *Journal of Egyptian Archaeology* 13 (1927): 40–49.

——. "References to Mummification by Greek and Latin Authors." *Aegyptus* 9 (1928): 106–112.

Dawson, W. R., and P. H. K. Gray. *Mummies and Human Remains.* Catalogue of Egyptian Antiquities in the British Museum 1. London: British Museum Press, 1968.

Dilorenzi, E., and R. Grilletto. *Le Mummie del Museo Egizio di Torino, N. 13001–26: Indagine antropo-radiologica.* Milan: La Goliardica, 1989.

Derry, D. E. "An X-ray Examination of the Mummy of King Amenophis I." *Annales du Service des Antiquités de l'Égypte* 34 (1934): 47–48.

Dodson, A. *Egyptian Rock-Cut Tombs.* Princes Risborough, U.K.: Shire Egyptology, 1992.

Drenkhahn, R., and R. Germer. *Mumie und Computer* Hannover, Ger.: Kestner-Museum, 1991.

Dunand, F., J. L. Heim, N. Henein, and R. Lichtenberg. *La Nécropole de Douch (Oasis de Kharga, Égypte).* Vol. 1, *Tombes 1 à 72.* Cairo: Institut Français d'Archéologie Orientale, 1992.

——. *La Nécropole de Douch (Oasis de Kharga, Égypte).* Vol. 2, *Tombes 73 à 92.* Cairo: Institut Français d'Archéologie Orientale, 2005).

Dunand, F., J. L. Heim, and R. Lichtenberg. "La Nécropole d'Aïn Labakha: Recherches archéologiques et anthropologiques." In *Egyptology at the Dawn of the Twenty-first Century: Proceedings of the Eighth International Congress of Egyptologists,* edited by Z. Hawass, vol. 1, pp. 154–161. Cairo: American University in Cairo Press, 2003.

——. "La Vie dans l'extrême: Douch, Ier s. è. chr.—IVe s. è chr." In *Life on the Fringe: Living in the Southern Egyptian Deserts During the Roman and early-Byzantine Periods,* edited by O. Kaper, pp. 95–138. Leiden: Research School CNWS, 1998.

Dunand, F., and R. Lichtenberg. "Des Chiens momifiés à El Deir (Oasis de Kharga)." *Bulletin de l'Institut Français d'Archéologie Orientale* 105 (2005): 75–87.

——. *Les Égyptiens.* Paris: Chêne, 2004.

——. *Momies de l'Égypte et d'ailleurs.* Paris: Rocher, 2002.

——. *Mummies: A Voyage Through Eternity.* New York: Abrams, 1994.

——. "Pratiques et croyances funéraires en Égypte romaine." In *Aufstieg und Niedergang der römischen Welt* 2/18/5, pp. 3216–3315. Berlin: De Gruyter, 1995.

Dunand, F., R. Lichtenberg, and A. Charron. *Des Animaux et des Hommes: Une Symbiose égyptienne.* Paris: Rocher, 2005.

Dunand, F., G. Tallet, and F. Letellier-Willemin. "Un Linceul peint de la nécropole d'El Deir (Oasis de Kharga)." *Bulletin de l'Institut Français d'Archéologie Orientale* 105 (2005): 89–101.

Dunand, F., and C. Zivie-Coche. *Gods and Men in Egypt: 3000 B.C.E. to 395 C.E.* Ithaca: Cornell University Press, 2004.

Dzierzykray-Rogalski, T. "Contribution à la paléodémographie de l'oasis de Dakhleh (Égypte)." *Africana Bulletin* 27 (1979): 161–165.

——. "Poursuite des recherches archéologiques dans l'oasis de Dakhleh (Balat)." *Bulletin de l'Institut Français d'Archéologie Orientale* 81 (1981): 215–217.

——. "Sur la paléopathologie de l'oasis de Dakhleh à l'Ancien Empire." *Bulletin de l'Institut Français d'Archéologie Orientale* 81 (1981): 219–221.

Edgar, C. C. *Graeco-Egyptian Coffins, Masks and Portraits.* Cairo: Institut Français d'Archéologie Orientale, 1905.

El-Mahdy, C. *Mummies, Myth and Magic in Ancient Egypt.* London: Thames and Hudson, 1991.

Emery, W. B. *Archaic Egypt.* Harmondsworth, U.K.: Penguin, 1961.

Empereur, J. Y., and M. D. Nenna. *Nécropolis.* Vol. 1. Études Alexandrines 5. Cairo: Institut Français d'Archéologie Orientale, 2001.

——. *Nécropolis.* Vol. 2. Études Alexandrines 7. Cairo: Institut Français d'Archéologie Orientale, 2003.

Engelbach, R., and D. E. Derry. "Mummification." *Annales du Service des Antiquités de l'Égypte* 41 (1942): 233–265.

Fakhry, A. *The Necropolis of El Bagawât in Kharga Oasis.* Cairo: Government Press, 1951.

Fischaber, G. *Mumifizierung im koptischen Ägypten: Eine Untersuchung zur Körperlichkeit im 1. Jahrtausend n. Chr.* Ägypten und Altes Testament 39. Wiesbaden: Otto Harrassowitz, 1997.

Fleming, S. et al. *The Egyptian Mummy: Secrets and Science.* Philadelphia: University of Pennsylvania Press, 1980.

Francot, C., L. Limme, F. Van Elst, M. P. Vanlathem, and B. Van Rietveld. *Les Momies égyptiennes des Musées Royaux d'Art et d'Histoire à Bruxelles et leur étude radiographique.* Turnhout: Brepols, 1999.

Frankfurter, D. *Religion in Roman Egypt.* Princeton: Princeton University Press, 1998.

Froment, A. "Origines du peuplement de l'Égypte Ancienne: L'Apport de l'anthropolobiologie." *Archéonil* 2 (1992): 79–98.

Gaillard, C., and G. Daressy. *La Faune momifiée de l'antique Égypte*. Cairo: Institut Français d'Archéologie Orientale, 1905.

Gardiner, A. H. *The Attitude of the Ancient Egyptians to Death and the Dead*. Cambridge: Cambridge University Press, 1935.

Garstang, J. A. *The Burial Customs of the Ancient Egyptians*. London: A. Constable, 1907.

Germer, R. et al. *Mummies: Life after Death in Ancient Egypt*. Munich: Prestel, 1997.

———. "Untersuchungen der altägyptische Mumien des Ägyptischen Museums der Universität Leipzig und des Museums für Völkerkunde Leipzig." *Zeitschrift für ägyptische Sprache und Altertumskunde* 122 (1995): 137–154.

Glob, P. V. *The Bog People: Iron-Age Man Preserved*. London: Faber and Faber, 1998.

Goyon, J. C. *Rituels funéraires de l'ancienne Égypte*. Paris: Cerf, 1972.

Goyon, J. C., and P. Josset. *Un Corps pour l'éternité: Autopsie d'une momie*. Paris: Le Léopard d'Or, 1988.

Gray, P. H. K. *Radiological Aspects of the Mummies of Ancient Egyptians in the Rijksmuseum van Oudheden,* Oudheidkundige Mededelingen uit het Rijksmuseum van Oudheden te Leiden 47. Leiden, Netherlands: Brill, 1966.

Gray, P. H. K., and D. Slow, "Egyptian Mummies in the City of Liverpool Museum." *Liverpool Museum Bulletin* 15 (1968): 28–32.

Grimal, N. *History of Ancient Egypt*. Oxford: Blackwell, 1992.

Grimm, G. *Die römischen Mumienmasken aus Ägypten*. Wiesbaden: Steiner, 1974.

Hamilton-Peterson, J., and C. Andrews. *Mummies: Death and Life in Ancient Egypt*. London: Collins British Museum Publications, 1978.

Hansen, J. P. H. "Les Momies du Groenland." *La Recherche* 183 (December 1986): 1490–1498.

Harris, J. E., and K. R. Weeks. *X-Raying the Pharaohs*. New York: Scribner's, 1973.

Harris, J. E., and E. F. Wente. *An X-Ray Atlas of the Royal Mummies*. Chicago: University of Chicago Press, 1980.

Hawass, Z. *Valley of the Golden Mummies*. New York: Abrams, 2000.

Heim, J. L., and R. Lichtenberg, "Étude des stries d'arrêt de croissance des restes humains momifiés de l'oasis de Kharga (Égypte—époque romaine)." In *L'Identité humaine en question: Nouvelles problématiques et nouvelles technologies en Paléontologie humaine et en Paléoanthropologie biologique, Colloque 26–28 mai 1999*, pp. 258–264. Crétail: Artcom, 2000.

Herodotus. *Herodotus: The Histories*. Trans. A. de Sélincourt. 2d ed. Harmondsworth, U.K.: Penguin, 1972.

Hope, C. A., and G. E. Bowen, eds. *Dakhleh Oasis Project: Preliminary Reports on the 1994–1995 to 1998–1999 Field Seasons*. Oxford: Oxbow Books, 2002.

Hope, C. A., and A. J. Mills, eds. *Dakhleh Oasis Project: Preliminary Reports on the 1992–1993 and 1993–1994 Field Seasons*. Oxford: Oxbow Books, 1999.

Hornung, E. *Ägyptische Unterweltsbücher*. Zurich: Artemis, 1972.

———. *Conceptions of God in Ancient Egypt: The One and the Many*. Ithaca: Cornell University Press, 1982.

———. "Vom Sinn des Mumifizierung." *Die Welt des Orients* 14 (1983): 167–175.

Humphreys, S. C., and H. King, eds. *Mortality and Immortality: The Anthropology and Archeology of Death*. London: Academic Press, 1981.

Ikram, S., ed. *Divine Creatures: Animal Mummies in Ancient Egypt*. Cairo: American University in Cairo Press, 2005.

Ikram, S., and A. Dodson. *The Mummy in Ancient Egypt: Equipping the Dead for Eternity*. London: Thames and Hudson, 1998.

Ikram, S., and N. Iskander. *Non-Human Mummies*. Cairo: Supreme Council of Antiquities Press, 2002.

Jonckheere, F. *Autour de l'autopsie d'une momie*. Brussels: Fondation Égyptologique Reine Elisabeth, 1942.

Kessler, D. "Tierkult." In *Lexikon der Ägyptologie*, edited by W. Helck and E. Otto, vol. 6, cols. 571–587. Wiesbaden: Otto Harrassowitz, 1986.

Kurth, D. *Der Sarg des Teüris*. Mainz: Philipp von Zabern, 1990.

Lalouette, C. *Textes sacrés et textes profanes de l'ancienne Égypte*. 2 vols. Paris: Gallimard, 1984–87.

Lauer, J. P. *Les Pyramides de Saqqarah*. Cairo: Institut Français d'Archéologie Orientale, 1972.

Lauer, J. P., and Z. Iskander, "Données nouvelles sur la momification dans l'Égypte ancienne." *Annales du Service des Antiquités de l'Égypte* 53 (1955): 167–198.

Leca, A. P. *La Médecine égyptienne au temps des pharaons*. Paris: Dacosta, 1971.

———. *Les Momies*. Paris: Hachette, 1976.

Leek, F. "The Problem of Brain Removal During Embalming by the Ancient Egyptians." *Journal of Egyptian Archaeology* 55 (1969): 112–116.

Leospo, E. *Io vivrò per sempre: Storia di un sacerdote nell antico Egitto*. Genoa: Tormena, 1999.

Lichtenberg, R. "La momification en Égypte à l'époque tardive." In *Aufstieg und Niedergang der römischen Welt* 11/37/3, pp. 2741–2760. Berlin: De Gruyter, 1996.

Llagostera Cuenca, E. *Radiological Examination of the Egyptian Mummies of the Archaeological Museum of Madrid*. Madrid: Raycar, 1978.

Loret, V. "Le Tombeau d'Aménophis II et la cachette royale de Biban el Molouk." *Bulletin de l'Institut Égyptien*, 3d ser., 9 (1898): 98–112.

Lortet, C., and C. Gaillard. *La Faune momifiée de l'ancienne Égypte*. 5 vols. Lyon: Muséum d'Histoire Naturelle, 1903–1909.

Lucas, A., *Ancient Egyptian Materials and Industries.* 4th ed. Revised by J. R. Harris. London: E. Arnold, 1962.

———. "The Use of Natron in Mummification." *Journal of Egyptian Archaeology* 18 (1932): 125–140.

Lustig, J., ed. *Anthropology and Egyptology: A Developing Dialogue.* Monographs in Mediterranean Archaeology 8. Sheffield, U.K.: Sheffield Academic Press, 1997.

Macke, A., C. Macke-Ribet, and J. Connan. *Ta Set Neferou: Une Nécropole de Thèbes-Ouest et son histoire.* Vol. 5. Cairo: Dar El-Kutûb, 2002.

Mallory, J. P., and V. H. Mair. *The Tarim Mummies.* London: Thames and Hudson, 2000.

Marx, M., and S. d'Auria. "CT Examination of Eleven Egyptian Mummies." *Radiographics* 6 (1986): 321–330.

———."Three-Dimensional Reconstruction of an Ancient Human Egyptian Mummy." *American Journal of Roentgenology* 150 (January 1988): 147–149.

Masali, M. "Physical Anthropology of Early Egyptians." In *Physical Anthropology of European Populations,* edited by I. Schwidetzky, B. Chiarelli, and O. Necrasov, pp. 369–376. Lahaye, Belgium: Mouton, 1980.

Maspero, G. *Les Momies royales de Deir el-Bahari.* Mémoires Publiés par les Membres de la Mission Archéologique Française au Caire 1, fasc. 4. Cairo: Institut Français d'Archéologie Orientale, 1889.

Midant-Reynes, B. *Aux Origines de l'Égypte: Du Néolithique à l'émergence de l'État.* Paris: Fayard, 2003.

———. *Préhistoire de l'Égypte: Des premiers hommes aux premiers pharaons.* Paris: Armand Colin, 1992.

Midant-Reynes, B., and N. Buchez. *Adaïma.* Vol. 1, *Économie et habitat.* Cairo: Institut Français d'Archéologie Orientale, 2002.

Midant-Reynes, B., E. Crubézy, and T. Janin. *Adaïma.* Vol. 2, *La Nécropole prédynastique.* Cairo: Institut Français d'Archéologie Orientale, 2002.

Moodie, R. L. *Palaeopathology: An Introduction to the Study of Ancient Evidences of Disease.* Urbana: University of Illinois Press, 1923.

———. *Roentgenologic Studies of Egyptian and Peruvian Mummies.* Chicago: Field Museum Press, 1931.

Morimoto, I., Y. Naito et al. *Ancient Human Mummies from Qurna, Egypt.* 2 vols. Tokyo: Waseda University Press, 1986–88.

Mummies and Magic: The Funerary Arts of Ancient Egypt. Boston: Northeastern University Press, 1988.

Needler, W. *Egyptian Mummies.* Toronto: University of Toronto Press, 1950.

Osing, J. et al. *Denkmäler der Oase Dachla aus dem Nachlass von Ahmed Fakhry.* Archäologische Veröffentlichungen 28. Mainz: Philipp von Zabern, 1982.

Parlasca, K. *Mumienporträts und verwandte Denkmälker.* Wiesbaden: Steiner, 1966.

Parlasca, K., and H. Seeman, eds. *Augenblicke: Mumienporträts und ägyptische Grabkunst aus römischer Zeit.* Munich: Klinkhardt & Biermann, 1999.

Partridge, R. B. *Faces of Pharaohs: Royal Mummies and Coffins from Ancient Thebes.* London: Rubicon Press, 1994.

Petrie, W. M. F. *Hawara, Biahmu and Arsinoe.* London: Field & Tuer, 1889.

———. *The Hawara Portfolio: Paintings from the Roman Age.* London: Quaritch, 1913.

———. *Roman Portraits and Memphis.* London: School of Archaeology in Egypt, University College, 1911.

———. *The Royal Tombs of the Earliest Dynasties.* Vol. 2. London: Egypt Exploration Fund, 1901.

Raven, M. J. "Corn Mummies." In *Oudheidkundige Mededelingen uit het Rijksmuseum van Oudheden te Leiden* 63, pp. 7–34. Leiden, Netherlands: Brill, 1982.

Raven, M. J., and W. K. Taconis. *Egyptian Mummies: Radiological Atlas of the Collections in the National Museum of Antiquities in Leiden.* Turnhout: Brepols, 2005.

Reymann, T. A. "Les Momies égyptiennes." *La Recherche* 145 (June 1983): 792–799.

Reymond, E. A. E. *Embalmers' Archives from Hawara.* Catalogue of Demotic Papyri in the Ashmolean Museum 1. Oxford: Griffith Institute, 1973.

Romano, J. F. *Death, Burial and Afterlife in Ancient Egypt.* Pittsburgh: Carnegie Museum of Natural History, 1990.

Ruffer, M. A. "Histological Studies on Egyptian Mummies." In *Mémoires présentés à l'Institut d'Égypte,* vol. 6/3, pp. 1–39. Cairo: L'Institut d'Égypte, 1911.

———. *Studies on the Palaeopathology of Egypt.* Chicago: University of Chicago Press, 1921.

Sandison, A. T. "The Use of Natron in Mummification in Ancient Egypt." *Journal of Near Eastern Studies* 22 (1963): 259–267.

Schneider, H. D. *Shabtis: An Introduction to the History of Ancient Egyptian Funerary Statuettes with a Catalogue of the Collection of Shabtis in the National Museum of Antiquities at Leiden.* 3 vols. Leiden, Netherlands: Rijksmuseum van Oudheden, 1977.

Schreiber, T. *Die Nekropole von Kom esch Schugafa.* Expedition von Sieglin 1. Leipzig, Ger.: Giesecke & Devrient, 1908.

Seeber, C. *Untersuchungen zur Darstellung des Totengerichts im alten Ägypten.* Münchner ägyptologische Studien 35. Munich: Deutscher Kunstverlag, 1976.

Settgast, J. *Untersuchungen zu altägyptischen Bestattungsdarstellungen.* Abhandlungen des Deutschen Archäologischen Instituts Kairo 3. Glückstadt, Ger.: Augustin, 1963.

Smith, G. E. "Report on the Unrolling of the Mummies of the Kings Siptah, Seti II, Ramses IV, Ramses V and Ramses VI in the Cairo Museum." *Bulletin de l'Institut Égyptien,* 5th ser., 1 (1907): 45–67.

——. *The Royal Mummies.* Cairo: Institut Français d'Archéologie Orientale, 1912.

Smith, G. E., and W. R. Dawson. *Egyptian Mummies.* London: Allen & Unwin, 1924. Repr. New York: Kegan Paul International, 1991.

Smith, G. E., and F. Wood-Jones. *Report of the Human Remains: The Archeological Survey of Nubia.* Cairo: National Printing Department, 1910.

Spencer, A. J. *Death in Ancient Egypt.* Harmondsworth, U.K.: Penguin, 1982.

——. *Early Egypt: The Rise of the Ancient Egyptians.* London: British Museum Press, 1993.

Strouhal, E. "Rassengeshichte Ägyptens." In *Rassengeschichte der Menschheit,* edited by I. Schwidetzky, vol. 3, *Afrika,* Part 1, pp. 9–89. Munich: R. Oldenbourg, 1975.

——. "Temporal and Spatial Analysis of Some Craniometric Features in Ancient Egyptians and Nubians." In *Population Biology of the Ancient Egyptians,* edited by D. Brothwell and B. Chiarelli, pp. 121–142. London: Academic Press, 1973.

Strouhal, E., and J. Jungwirth. "Palaeopathology of the Late Roman—Early Byzantine Cemeteries at Sayala, Egyptian Nubia." *Journal of Human Evolution* 9 (1980): 61–70.

Strouhal, E., and L. Vyhnánek. *Egyptian Mummies in Czechoslovak Collections.* Prague: Národniko Muzea, 1979.

Taylor, J. H. *Egyptian Coffins.* Aylesbury, U.K.: Shire Egyptology, 1989.

——. *Mummy: The Inside Story.* London: British Museum Press, 2004.

——. *Unwrapping a Mummy: The Life, Death and Embalming of Horemkenesi.* London: British Museum Press, 1995.

Thomas, L. V. *Anthropologie de la mort.* Paris: Payot, 1980.

Vercoutter, J., J. Leclant, F. M. Snowden Jr., and J. Desanges. *The Image of Black in Western Art.* Vol. 1, *From the Pharaohs to the Fall of the Roman Empire.* New York: William Morrow, 1976.

Vermeersch, P. et al. "Le Paléolithique de la Vallée du Nil égyptien." *L'Anthropologie* 94 (1990): 77–102.

Vernus, P. *Affairs and Scandals in Ancient Egypt.* Ithaca: Cornell University Press, 2003.

Vila, A. "Les Masques funéraires." In *Mirgissa,* edited by J. Vercoutter, vol. 3, *Les Nécropoles,* pp. 151–263. Paris: P. Geuthner, 1976.

Vos, R. L. *The Apis Embalming Ritual: P. Vindob. 3873.* Louvain, Belgium: Peeters, 1993.

Walker, R. et al. "Tissue Identification and Histologic Study of Six Lung Specimens from Egyptian Mummies." *American Journal of Physical Anthropology* 72 (1987): 43–48.

Walker, S., and M. Bierbrier. *Ancient Faces: Mummy Portraits from Roman Egypt.* London: British Museum Press, 1997.

Wendorf, F. *Prehistory of Nubia.* Dallas: Fort Burgwin Research Center, 1968.

Winlock, H. E. "The Mummy of Wah Unwrapped." *Bulletin of the Metropolitan Museum of Art* 35 (1940): 253–259.

Zandee, J. *Death as an Enemy According to Ancient Egyptian Conceptions.* Studies in the History of Religions (Supplements to *Numen*) 5. Leiden, Netherlands: Brill, 1960.

Ziegelmayer, G. *Münchner Mumien.* Munich: Anthropologischen Staatssammlung München, 1985.

Zivie, A., and R. Lichtenberg. "The Cats of the Goddess Bastet." In *Divine Creatures: Animal Mummies in Ancient Egypt,* edited by S. Ikram, pp. 106–119. Cairo: American University in Cairo Press, 2005.

Illustration Sources

PHOTOGRAPHS

Archives, Metropolitan Museum of Art: *figs. 112, 113, 127, 203*
Archives, Mission Montet: *fig. 244*
British Museum: *figs. 2, 5, 22*
A. R. David, 1979: *figs. 217, 219, 220, 221*
W. R. Dawson and P. H. K. Gray, 1968: *figs. 86, 109*
F. Dunand: *figs. 99, 103, 132, 133, 138, 160, 174, 184, 226, 247, 248, 250*
M. Fayein-Lichtenberg: *fig. 114*
S. Fleming, 1980: *figs. 216, 223*
J. L. Heim: *fig. 241*
P. Josset: *fig. 222*
A. Lecler, Institut Français d'Archéologie Orientale: *figs. 115, 131, 153, 162*
R. Lichtenberg: *figs. 8, 9, 11, 12, 14, 15, 17, 19, 20 A and B, 21, 24, 25, 26, 27, 28, 31, 33, 34, 35, 36, 39, 40, 41, 42, 54, 57, 59, 60, 64, 65, 67 A and B, 68, 70, 71, 72, 73, 83, 84, 85, 89, 95, 97, 100, 101, 102, 104, 105, 106, 107, 108, 110, 111, 117, 118, 119, 120, 121, 122, 123, 126, 128, 129, 130, 134, 135, 136, 137, 139, 141, 143, 144, 145, 146, 147, 148, 152, 155, 156, 157, 164, 165, 167, 168, 169, 170, 171, 172, 173, 176, 177, 178, 179, 180, 182, 183, 185, 187, 188, 189, 190, 191, 192, 193, 194, 196, 197, 199, 200, 201, 210, 211, 212, 213, 218, 224, 225, 227, 228, 231, 232, 233, 234, 235 A and B, 236, 239, 240, 242, 245, 246, 249, 251, 252, 253, 254, 255*
G. E. Smith, 1912: *figs. 38, 43, 44, 45, 46, 47, 49, 49, 50, 51, 52, 55, 56 A and B, 76, 77, 78, 79, 80, 81, 87, 142, 237, 238, 243*
Terres cuites gréco-romaines d'Égypte, Musée du Louvre, 1990: *fig. 163*
G. Wagner: *fig. 125*

DRAWINGS

M. Bietak, *Mitteilungen des Deutschen Archäologischen Instituts Kairo*, 1968: *fig. 37*
B. Bruyère, *La tombe n° 1 de Sen-nedjem à Deir el-Medineh*, 1959: *fig. 66*
Description de l'Égypte: *fig. 203*
F. Dunand (sources of the author's drawings): *fig. 1* J. E. Quibell and F. W. Green, *Hierakonpolis*, vol. 2,

1902; *fig. 4* photo Petrie Museum, University College, London; *fig. 7* A. M. Donadoni-Roveri, *Civilisation des Égyptiens, les croyances religieuses*, 1988; *fig. 23* A. Dodson and S. Ikram, *The Mummy in Ancient Egypt*, 1998; *fig. 30* J. Garstang, *The Burial Customs of Ancient Egypt*, 1907; *fig. 32 The British Museum Book of Ancient Egypt*, 1992; *fig. 58* exhibit catalog *Götter Pharaonen*, 1978, *fig. 61 KMT*, 1994; *fig. 62* A. M. Donadoni-Roveri, *Civilisation des Égyptiens, La Vie quotidienne*, 1987; *fig. 53* M. Bierbrier, *The Tombbuilders of the Pharaohs*, 1982; *fig. 63 Univers des formes, l'Égypte des Conquérants*, 1979; *fig. 82 Tanis, l'or des pharaons*, 1987; *fig. 88* R. Czerner, *KMT*, 1993–94; *fig. 90* J. H. Taylor, *Egyptian Coffins*, 1989; *fig. 91* exhibit catalog *Ägypten, Gehemnis der Grabkammern*, 1993; *fig. 92* exhibit catalog *Osiris Kreuz Halbmond*, 1984; *fig. 93* G. Botti, *Le casse di mummie . . . di Firenze*, 1958; *fig. 98* G. Lefebvre, *Le tombeau de Pétosiris*, 1923–24; *fig. 116* C. Andrews, *Egyptian Mummies*, 1984; *figs. 150 and 151* exhibit catalog *Ägypten, Geheimnis der Grabkammern*, 1993; *fig. 154* exhibit catalog *Ägypten, Geheimnis der Grabkammern*, 1993; *fig. 158* papyrus of Nebqed, Louvre; *fig. 159 Univers des formes, l'Égypte des Conquérants*, 1979; *fig. 161 The British Museum Book of Ancient Egypt*, 1992; *fig. 166* J. D. Ray, *The Archive of Hor*, 1976; *fig. 181* R. Mond and O. H. Myers, *The Bucheum*, vol. 1, 1934; *fig. 186* J. Malek, *The Cat in Ancient Egypt*, 1993; *fig. 195* exhibit catalog *Osiris Kreuz Halbmond*, 1984; *fig. 202 A and B* E. Prominska, in R. A. David, ed., *Science in Egyptology*, 1986
G. Ebers, *Ägypten*, 1879: *figs. 18, 206*
W. B. Emery, 1961: *figs. 3 A and B, 6 A and B*
J. E. Harris and E. F. Wente, 1980: *fig. 215*
J. L. Heim: *fig. 229 A, B, C*
E. Hornung, *The Ancient Egyptian Books of the Afterlife*, 1999: *figs. 74, 75*
Je Sais Tout, 1926: *fig. 208*
J. P. Lauer: *fig. 13*
R. Lichtenberg (sources of the author's drawings): *fig. 69, fig. 96* A. J. Spencer, *Death in Ancient Egypt*, 1982; *fig. 140* F. Jonckheere, *Autour de l'autopsie d'une momie*, 1942; *fig. 214; fig. 230*

R. L. Moodie, 1931: *fig. 209*

G. Perrot and C. Chipiez, *Histoire de l'Art dans l'Antiquité*, vol. 1, *l'Égypte*, 1882: *figs. 10 A and B, 29, 16*

M. A. Ruffer, 1911: *fig. 207*

A. J. Spencer, 1982: *figs. 94, 149*

Univers des formes, l'Égypte du crépuscule: fig. 124

J. G. Wilkinson: *fig. 205*

C. Zivie-Coche, *Sphinx: History of a Monument*, 2002: *fig. 16*

Acknowledgments

Christiane Ziegler, chief curator of the Department of Egyptian Antiquities of the Louvre, authorized us to photograph the objects from the Louvre that illustrate this book. We thank her warmly, along with Marie-France Aubert, curator of the Department of Egyptian Antiquities in charge of Roman Egypt, and Catherine Bridonneau, who so ably assisted us in taking the photos. We also thank Alain Zivie, who permitted us to reproduce the photographs of the skeleton of Huy, along with the photos and X-rays of the cats from the Bubasteion (MAFB), and Patrice Josset, who authorized us to reproduce a CAT scan of the mummy in the Lyon Museum of Natural History that he studied along with J.-C. Goyon.

We are also indebted to the French Institute of Oriental Archaeology in Cairo for entrusting us, for ten years, with the exploration and study of the necropolis of Dush. Our experience in the field owed much to the friendly collaboration of several of its members, in particular, Nessim Henein, Alain Lecler, and Patrick Deleuze. And, of course, we must not forget our friend and colleague, Jean-Louis Heim, professor at the Paris Museum of Natural History, with whom we carried out this work.

The Egyptian Antiquities Organization, with its directors and inspectors, in particular Adel Hussein Mohammed and Ahmed Bahgat Ibrahim at el-Kharga Oasis, was always helpful to us. We are happy to express our gratitude to the organization, and also to the Egyptian workers who have worked, and continued to work, with us at the sites in the oasis.

From the very outset of our labors, V. Benderly, G. Quinson, and R. Guillet, along with the commercial engineers of the Société Kodak-Pathé, constantly aided us with their advice and by providing us with X-ray film and the chemicals to develop it. Here, we are happy to thank them all.

We also thank the Société Philips, which provided us with the Massiot-Philips-90/20 X-ray equipment with which most of the X-rays were made. Those from one campaign were made with a Microsécurix CGR machine provided by J. P. Lautman of the Compagnie Générale de Radiologie. He has our deepest thanks.

Index

Page numbers in italics refer to illustrations. Page numbers in bold italics refer to both text and illustration.

el-Deir, 78, 106, 141, 167; animal mummies at, 109, *110*, 185; Christian mummification at, 127; demographic findings at, 170–71, 174–75, 177. *See also* el-Kharga Oasis

Deir el-Bahari, 50, 61–62, 64, 133, 146, 209n16; discovery of mummies at, 39–41, 136, 148

Deir el-Medina, 51, *52*, 72, 88, 172, 179

de la Fontaine, Guy, 134

Delorenzi, E., 140

Dendara, 92

Dental pathology, 158, 164, 166, 172, *179, 180*; causes of, 151, 155–56, 163, 177–78

Derry, D. E., 137, 193

Description de l'Égypte, 134, *135*

Dessication. *See* Natron bath

Diocletian, 115, 123

Diodorus Siculus, 12, 81, 108–9, 112, 128

Direction des Fouilles, 134

Diseases, 149, 151, 152, 159, 165, 209n25; at el-Kharga Oasis, 74–75, 171, 175–77; methods of identifying, 137, 146, 156–57, 175–77. *See also* Anatomopathology; Paleopathology; Skeletal conditions

Dismemberment, 9, 15, 35, 54, 110, 203n32

Djedamuniufankh, tomb of, 68

Djedbastetiufankh, coffin of, *98–101*

Djedkare Izezi, 13

Djed-pillar, 63, 67, *99*

Djedptahiufankh, *59–60,* 198

Djedthothiufankh, coffin of, *66*

Djehutinakht (nomarch), 27

Djer, King, *10*

Djoser, pyramid of, 13, 16, 17, *18, 19,* 68

DNA studies, 142, 143, 146–47, 150, 165

Dogs, 109, *110,* 161, 162, 185–86

Donadoni, S., 166

Drovetti, B., 134

Duamutef, 28. *See also* Horus, Sons of

Dunand, F., 140, 141, 166

Dush, 82, 87, 106, 133, 183, 213n18; demography of, 170–71, 173; excavations at, 140–41, 166; health conditions at, 177, 178; mummification techniques at, 77–78, *125–26,* 179. *See also* el-Kharga Oasis

Dynasty 1, 9–10

Dynasty 2, 10

Dynasty 3, 16

Dynasty 4, 13, 15, 16, 21

Dynasty 5, 15, 16, 21, 22

Dynasty 6, 13, 15, 16

Dynasty 11, 26–28

Dynasty 12, 28–29, 34

Dynasty 13, 30

Dynasty 17, 37, 189–90

Dynasty 18, 46, 50, 104, 190–94, 198–200; identification of mummies from, 143, 146, 149–50, 209n16; tomb furnishings during, 49

Dynasty 19, 47–48, 194–95

Dynasty 20, 47–48, 50, 59, 178, 195–96

Dynasty 21, 49–50, 62–63, 80, 196–98; mummification techniques during, 59–61, 154, 178; tomb security during, 64–65, 133

Dynasty 22, 49–50, 61, 63, 80, 118, 198

Dynasty 23, 59

Dynasty 25, 65–66, 80

Dynasty 26, 59, 66–71, 113, 171

Dynasty 30, 115

Egyptian Mummies (Smith and Dawson), 148

Electron microscopy, 147, 157

Embalmers, shunning of, 12, 94–95

Embalming ritual, 78, 97, 158

"Embroiderer," the, 127–28, 160

Empereur, Jean-Yves, 85, 172

Endoscopy, 144

Excavation sites, study of mummies at, 140–41, 163. *See also specific sites*

Excerebration, 27, 45–46, 128, 154; and classes of mummification, 94, 95, 179, 181–82

Faiyum, the, 5, 108, 116

Faiyum portraits, 82–84

Fakhry, A., 68, 88

Falcons, 111, *121,* 161, 162, 185; symbolism of, 108, 120

False mummies, 75–76, 120, 150, 162

Field Museum (Chicago), 162

Figurines, 31–33, 48, 92, 103, 106–7. *See also Shawabtis*

Fingerprints, study of, 156

First Intermediate Period, 25–26, 33–34, 133

Fish, 110, *111,* 162

Fletcher, A. H., 156

Food offerings. *See* Offerings

Fouquet, M., 133

French Institute of Oriental Archaeology, 166, 172

Frogs, *110–11, 112,* 203n32

Funerals, 21–22, 101–6, 114

Funerary beds, *86, 100, 101*

Funerary beliefs, x–xi, 52–56, 187; Christian, 128–30; of First Intermediate Period, 25–26; Graeco-Roman, xi, 71, 90–93; Middle Kingdom, 33–36; and morality, 56–58, 71, 92–93; Old Kingdom, 21–24

Funerary masks, *28–29,* 44, 46, 61, *62,* 78; during Graeco-Roman Period, 82, *83, 84, 85*

Funerary wrappings, 10–11, 94, *100–101,* 158, 160–61; of Christian mummies, 126, *127–28;* during First Intermediate Period, 25; during Graeco-Roman Period, *78–80,* 83–84, *85,* 97–98; during Old Kingdom, *15*

Gabbari, 172

Gaillard, C., 137, 161, 186

Garner, P., 96

Gayet, A., 165–66

Gebel Adda, 139, 144, 163

Gebelein, 5, 7, *15,* 20

Nag Hammadi, 123
Nakhtankh, 156
Nakht (weaver), 139, 153
Napoleon Bonaparte, 134
Naqada Period, 5, 7, 9, 171–72
Natron bath, 13, 15, 94, 96, 113; and Christian mummies, 124–25; effect of, 26
Natural mummies, 1–2, *8–9*, 75
Nazlet Khatar, *5*
Nebamun, tomb of, *118*
Nebqed, *104*
Nebseni (priest), 45, *46*, 200
Nedjmet, Queen, 59, *60, 149, 196*
Nefer, 15
Neith, 47, 48, 110
Nekhbet, 120
Nephthys, 37, 46, 47, 48, 58, 80
Nesikhons, Queen, *61*, 149, 197–98
Nesperennub (priest), 140
Nestanebetisheru, 198
New Kingdom, 37–39, 52–56, 148–49, 178; body position during, 46, 77; coffins and sarcophagi of, 44–45, *46–48;* discovery of Deir el-Bahari mummies from, 39–41; discovery of Valley of the Kings mummies from, 41–45; funerals during, 54, 103, 104, 105; funerary masks during, 46, 78; moral beliefs of, 56–58; mummification techniques during, 45–46, 94; tomb architecture of, 50–52, 203n28; tomb furnishings during, *37–39,* 43–44, 48–50, 105, 106–7, 206n24. *See also specific dynasties and rulers*
Nicholson, P., 185
Nile, crossing of, 102–3
Niwinski, A., 32
Noble tombs, 10, 22–23, 31, 33–36. *See also* Mastabas; Social differentiation
Nofret, *23*
Notman, D. N. H., 161
Nut, 35, 46, 62, 63, *67;* Graeco-Roman representations of, 80, *81, 82*
Nutrition, 149, 171, 174–75, 177. *See also* Growth arrest lines

Observation, clinical, 143
Ocular prostheses, 28, 59, 97, 154
Offerings, 9, 36, 49, *70,* 92; animal, 108, 119, 161, 185–86, 207n3; by Christians, 129–30; and funeral ceremonies, 103, *104–6;* during Old Kingdom, 20, 22, 24
Old Kingdom, 98, 105; funerary beliefs during, 21–24; mummification techniques during, 13–16; tomb architecture during, 16–21. *See also specific rulers*
el-Omari, 5–7
Opening of the Mouth ritual, 21–22, 54, 66, 103–4, 114
Osirian position, 46, 76, 164, 183, 203nn18, 32
Osiris, 25, 46, *52–58,* 106, 110; deceased's identifi-

cation with, x–xi, 22, 34–35, 53, 58, 67; Graeco-Roman view of, xi, 80, *91, 92*
Osirwer, stela of, *106*

Pääbo, S., 142
Pachomius, 128, 130
Paintings, *7–8,* 18–19, 22–23, 105, *124;* Graeco-Roman, 82–84, *85, 88–90*
Pakhet, 118
Paleodemography, 173–75. *See also* Mortality rates; Population
Paleopathology, 150–51, 158, 166, 172, 175–78. *See also* Anatomopathology; Dental pathology; Diseases; Skeletal conditions
Paraschistes, 12
Parsche, F., 161
Pashed, tomb of, 51, 172
Passalacqua, J., 159
Paul, Saint, *124*
Pedubaste, tomb of, *89,* 103
Peftjauneith, coffin of, 67
Peiresc, F. de, 133
Pennsylvania University Museum, 140, 151–53
Pepiseneb, 25
Persian Period, 69, 213n18
Petesuchos, 116
Petosiris, tomb of, *69, 70–71, 89,* 93, 103, *105*
Petrie, W. M. F., 9, 13, 30–31, 32, 37, 66, 78, 83, 137
Pets, 111
Pettigrew, T., 134
Photography, 143–44
Pinudjem I, *65,* 196
Pinudjem II, 41, 42, *64,* 149, 197
Pinudjem (priest), 50
Pneferos, temple of, *117*
Pollios Soter, 80
Poor, burial of, 10–11, 16, 20–21, 33. *See also* Social differentiation
Population: during Graeco-Roman Period, 72, 164, 165; during prehistory, 5; study of, 173–75. *See also* Mortality rates
Portraits, 82–84, *85*
Predynastic Period, 7–9
Prehistoric Egypt, 5–7
Priests, 36, 50, 101–2, 103–4, 105; burial of, 61–62, 64–65
Private tombs, 20–21, 65, 68–69, 107; Graeco-Roman, 85–90; New Kingdom, 49–50, 51–52. *See also* Social differentiation
Processions, funeral, 101–3
Prominska, E., 124–25, 126
Psammetichus, Prince, stela of, 114
Psusennes I, 61, *62,* 97, *181,* 198
Psusennes II, 65
Ptah, 108, 112
Ptah-Sokar-Osiris, *106*
Ptolemaic Period. *See* Graeco-Roman Period

FRANKLIN SQUARE PUBLIC LIBRARY

3 3080 00233 0655

393.3093 Dunand, Francoise.
D
    Mummies and death in
    Egypt.

DATE			

FRANKLIN SQUARE PUBLIC LIBRARY
19 LINCOLN ROAD
FRANKLIN SQUARE, NY 11010
(516) 488-3444

JAN   2007

BAKER & TAYLOR